Religious Syncretism

SCM CORE TEXT

Religious Syncretism

Eric Maroney

scm press

© Eric Maroney 2006

British Library Cataloguing in Publication data

A catalogue record for this book is available
from the British Library

0 334 04018 3/9780 334 04018 7

First published in 2006 by SCM Press
9–17 St Alban's Place,
London N1 0NX

www.scm-canterburypress.co.uk

SCM Press is a division of
SCM-Canterbury Press Ltd

Typeset by Regent Typesetting
Printed and bound in Great Britain by
William Clowes Ltd, Beccles, Suffolk

Contents

For Kasia

Love is a church where all religions meet;
Islam, or Christ, or Tavern, it is one;
Thy face of every system is the sun –
O Sun that shines in the Beloved's street.
Where Love is there's no need of convent bell,
And holy living needs no holy frocks;
Time ticks not to your monastery clocks;
Where goodness is there God must be as well.

Shams-ud-din Muhammad Hafiz (*c*.1320–89), *Odes From the Divan of Hafiz,* trans. Richard Le Gallienne, Boston: L. C. Page & Company, 1905, from Ode 79, p. 49.

Preface

Several years ago I was listening to a radio programme about Islam in post-revolution Iran. A shepherd was being interviewed, and he said an astonishing thing: Islam had been healthier under the Shah. When the Shah was in power and someone prayed, the shepherd explained, you could be sure he did so from conviction. After the Islamic Revolution, when *everyone* had to pray, you could no longer be certain who prayed from conviction and who prayed from fear. This statement was extraordinarily perceptive. The Islamic revolution in Iran was meant to create an Islamic state and to form a more just and equitable society than the Iran of the Shahs. But there was an unintended result: enforcing religious practice condemned the authentic expression of religion. The very attempts to inculcate a sense of religious duty into an entire population all but doomed Islam in Iran to ignoble failure. In a state where everyone must practise a religion or be punished, there is the danger that the legitimate observance of that religion will be undermined or even destroyed. Indeed an Islamic state, which means to foster Islam, can often kill it. This paradox was the central motivation for writing this book.

The rise of fundamentalism in the three Abrahamic religions – Judaism, Christianity and Islam – has long been noted as one of the conspicuous features of the late twentieth and early twenty-first centuries. The Islamic revolution in Iran in 1979 is only one part of this overall trend, albeit an important one. Almost everywhere, fundamentalist versions of the Abrahamic religions have been on the rise. They are finding a place in debate about all sorts of matters: political, ethical, social, scientific and medical. The role of religion in the West seems to be taking on a new, vital importance.

What has been missing in this debate is a more nuanced view of Judaism, Christianity and Islam. The stunning variety of these faiths and the astonishing range of their expression are difficult to summarize or condense. Capturing some of this variety was a further motive for the writing of this book. I wanted bold examples, and could think of none bolder than those of religious syncretism in Judaism, Christianity and Islam. Syncretism, or the phenomenon of one religion borrowing elements from another religion, has long been recognized as a nearly universal phenomenon. But few works have tried to tackle the subject alone. For one, there are conceptual problems. Although many scholars of religion will concede that syncretism occurs in all religions, at all times and places, how to study this phenomenon proves daunting, both hopelessly wide and broad. Still, some areas of religious studies have long been accustomed to examining syncretism. Gnosticism, an ancient and varied religious movement, has been recognized as syncretistic in nature, drawing together traditions as diverse as Christianity, Zoroastrianism, Graeco-Roman philosophy, and mystery cults, among others. Similarly, a staple of the study in Graeco-Roman religions is the examination of their syncretistic nature. Ancient Greek and Roman religions went through radical transformations both during Alexander's expansion into Asia and also in Rome during the long period of its empire, when much was rapidly and effectively borrowed from Eastern religions to enliven old Graeco-Roman cults with incredible vitality.

But other, more mainstream areas of religious studies have hardly examined syncretism at all. Part of this may be political squeamishness. 'Fringe' and dead religious movements such as Gnosticism and Graeco-Roman religions can be examined as syncretistic far more safely than the alive, warm bodies of Judaism, Christianity and Islam. Calling a religion 'syncretistic' is often a way of saying that it is the sum of its parts, or of beginning to reduce or dissect it. Religions that are still practised are not often subjected to such scrutiny, either from habit, fear or reticence, despite the interesting and unusual fruit the examination would bear for the study of religions.

The SCM Core Text on Religious Syncretism is an investigation of just this area, and begins to examine some forms of Judaism, Christianity and Islam, and their relationship to syncretism. It does so with two goals. One is to illustrate that syncretism occurred in the Abrahamic religions and continues to occur today, as syncretism is a vital element in the formation of a religion, and continues to play a role in a religion's transformation through time. The second goal is to show that, while the three Abrahamic faiths have borrowed heavily from one another, they have also been quite affected by that wide and diverse group of religions that have been practised and are known as 'pagan'.

This is primarily a book of examples. It is not a book that sets out a systematic, theoretical model of how syncretism works and then attempts to show how this theory conforms to examples. I have set out to *show* what syncretism is, rather than lay out a lengthy theoretical discussion about its nature and dynamics. Of course, in the discussions of these examples some theoretical analyses are necessary. But I have endeavoured to make these as brief and few as possible, and to let the story of syncretism begin to unravel itself, to allow readers to make their own judgements.

The growth of so-called 'fundamentalism' has pushed religious debate into the forefront of popular culture and people are beginning to ask hard questions about the role of religion in the post-modern world. In ways this book will illustrate, syncretism is often the opposite of fundamentalism. So with the idea in mind that comparison is part of the process of forming judgements, each chapter of this book begins with an example of modern fundamentalism, followed by the main topic under discussion. At the conclusion of each chapter, the fundamentalist example of the religion and the syncretistic example are compared and contrasted. The connections between the 'fundamentalist' introductions to these chapters and the syncretistic chapter topics are not meant to be strictly related by cause and effect. Rather, they illustrate contrasting views on the nature of religion, in order to spur debate and examination of some of the varying ways that Christianity, Judaism and Islam have been practised and expressed. Most of all, they are meant to show the diversity of responses to changing circumstances that people have had in these three faiths, and how people have moulded the religions to suit the times in which they were living, the social and political circumstances by which they were surrounded, and cultural crises they were facing, and above all, the unique needs of their different communities of believers.

Finally, this book was written as a textbook, and as such, it is overwhelmingly didactic in its goals. It was written for a general audience and for undergraduates taking introductory courses in religion. The subject matter is intended as a primary text for classroom work, or to supplement the material handled in introductory religious courses. The topics under discussion complement the more mainstream studies of the Abrahamic religions, and provide unusual and even exotic versions of these faiths, which may have a direct bearing on how we study and define religious movements. Movements on the 'fringe' of mainstream religions often have a great deal to show us about these religions as a whole. *The SCM Core Text on Religious Syncretism* is structured as a learning tool, the main goal of which is to foster more interest in the study of syncretism. Each chapter ends with a series of questions designed to stimulate discussion and debate, and some suggestions for further reading. It is my hope that this work will contribute to ongoing debate about the nature of the three largest religions the West has produced, and invite an atmosphere of subtle and nuanced investigation among scholars, students and the general reading population.

1

The Exalted Cranes: the Question of Purity and Impurity

'What! Shall ye have male progeny and God female? This were indeed an unfair partition. These are mere names and your fathers named them such.' (Qur'an 21.3.)

The Buddhas of Bamian and religious exclusion

In March of 2001 the Taliban government of Afghanistan destroyed the colossal Buddhas of Bamian. The two statues were the largest of several Buddhas found in this area of Afghanistan, which from the second century until the time Islam entered the region in the ninth century was a thriving centre of Mahayana Buddhism. Bamian was situated along the Silk Road, and since Graeco-Roman times it has played an important role in the transfer of both ideas and goods between the East and the West. In fact, the statues themselves represented a style of standing Buddha called the Gandharan style that was deeply indebted to Greek art. The ruling group during the ninth century, called the Gui-Shang or Kushang, were wildly eclectic in their religious tastes. At an earlier time, they seem to have been fire worshippers in the Zoroastrian tradition, but it was eventually Buddhism that flourished in the kingdom, spurred by increased trade with China and Central Asia. Hellenism also retained its presence in Afghanistan, and excavations in the region have yielded thousands of examples of Ganharanan art exhibiting the hybrid Hellenic-Buddhist style. In and around the statues, small caves and niches were homes to early Buddhist monks. When the Chinese Buddhist pilgrim Xuanzang visited Bamiam in AD 630 he described the valley as a bustling Buddhist centre 'with more than ten monasteries and more than a thousand monks'. The town of Bamian was destroyed by the invading Mongol armies in AD 1221, but many of the statues, including the massive Buddhas, survived, even as Buddhism ceased to exist as a living religion in Afghanistan.[1]

With the arrival of Arab armies in AD 637, most of Afghanistan began to embrace Islam, but deep ethnic, cultural and linguistic fractures opened. The culture remained (and continues to be) primarily tribal and clan-based. Islam has had an overarching impact on the country, primarily when strong and popular leaders have used it as a rallying cry or

when external enemies have threatened the country. Although the importance of Islam in Afghan society cannot be overstressed, there are equally
important, and not as widely known, local 'feudal' practices, which are
often at odds with Islamic law. Vendettas, both individual and collective,
are common and many have been maintained for generations, often con-
tradicting the strictures of Islamic justice.[2]

The clan-based nature of Afghan culture often causes its groups to fall
outside the legal norms of strict Sunni Islam. In addition, Afghanistan
had, before the Taliban regime came to power, a small but significant
number of religious minorities who were not Muslims. A population of
Jews, Hindus and Sikhs resided in the country, mainly in the urban centres, and far older populations of non-Muslims existed well into modern
times. An intriguing group called the Nuris, or Nuristanis, currently live
in the north-east of the country. They were forcibly converted to Islam at
the beginning of the twentieth century, but before that time were known
as *kafir* (infidels) and practised a form of polytheism, carving wooden
figures to adorn the graves of their dead. Many Nuris have light skin and
eyes, red or blond hair, and claim ancestry from Greek settlers, but a
more probable theory holds that they are the aboriginal people of Afghanistan, forced into the remote highlands by later migrants.[3]

A strong tradition of Sufism exists in Afghanistan that is unlike the
staunch Wahhabi type of fundamentalism practised by the Taliban; several Sufi mystical orders, the most prominent being the Qadiriyya and
the Naqshbandiyya, with their veneration of *murshits* or *pirs* (spiritual
teachers) are strong in some areas of the country. Unlike the political
quietism of some branches of Sufism, Afghan Sufism had been closely
intertwined in politics and opposed to foreign influence. During the late
nineteenth and twentieth centuries, several Sufi *pirs* were involved in up-
risings against the British and at a local level, Sufism and *pir* veneration
are still extremely popular, as witnessed by the *ziarats* (tombs or shrines)
with fluttering flags that are a common site in the Afghan countryside.[4]

Despite this history of cultural and even religious diversity (and notably, even diversity within Islam in Afghanistan) the Taliban government
decided to destroy the statues and all pre-Islamic art in Afghanistan in
early 2001. Although the final explosion that brought down the Buddhas
was broadcast worldwide, it took nearly a month to destroy the statues
completely. The Taliban Information Minister Quadratullah Jamal explained that 'this work of destruction is not as easy as people may think.
You can't knock the statues by shelling as both are carved into a cliff;
they are firmly attached to the mountain.'

But despite the mechanical difficulty they were destroyed, after having
survived in the Bamian valley for nearly 1,500 years. The destruction of
the Buddhas was roundly condemned by UNESCO, Western nations and
most Muslim governments,[5] but the destruction, as bad as it was, was

only a harbinger. The destruction of the Buddhas was a herald: in early 2001 the world was alerted to the dangers of a phenomenon that been quickly growing since the close of the Cold War, but had not yet fully taken the world stage. Many scholars had noted the rise of fundamentalism in the Abrahamic faiths – Christianity, Islam and Judaism – as one of the most salient features of the post-Cold War era. But the public had yet to take note. For the rise of fundamentalism went against the grain of the expected trajectory of the post-modern world. Rather than conform to the growing trends of secularism, democracy and a liberal open society – the very values that seemed victorious after the struggle of the Cold War – fundamentalism veered in the very opposite direction. The kind of uncompromising stance of the Taliban regarding the Buddhas took the world by surprise. The menace of fundamentalism was not fully understood, so few knew how to even ask the question: Why were these people so enraged?

Eventually, of course, the West was forced to ask that question. The fact that other, more open versions of the three Abrahamic faiths have always existed and the idea that they eschew the dogmatics of exclusion that lie at the heart of fundamentalist agendas was lost in the debate about modern fundamentalism. The destruction of the Bamiam Buddhas became an early model for much of the West's thinking about Islam in the Age of Terrorism. The images of Islam as wholly exclusionary and militant were difficult to avoid. This view excluded the marvellous variety within Islam. In this paradigm, Islamic fundamentalism was the only version of Islam considered, and many people fully accepted it, never asking if Islam had ever practised accommodation with the faiths and cultures around it. The history of the type of religious practice explored in this book, called syncretism, gives ample evidence that such accommodation has occurred. The Taliban were unwilling to incorporate the elements of pre-Islamic Afghan culture and religion in their Islamic practices, but other groups in other places were not so rigid. In the next section, we will explore an example of religious inclusion that is closer to home.

The Green Man and religious accommodation

Looking up, one views leafy faces that are revealed and simultaneously concealed, and one cannot help but be struck by this polarity, for although Green Men are merely architectural adornments, they can be oddly, even electrically, alive. Green Men inhabit the nooks of Christian sacred spaces all over Europe, and their lack of centrality to the pageantry of Christian worship is actually an excellent marker of their importance. They could not be wholly discarded by the propagators of the Christian faith in the early years of its arrival in Northern Europe, yet they could not be too completely incorporated. A kind of compromise was worked out. Green Men would be ornaments; they would inhabit the cracks between Christianity's towering physical and theological structures; they would be reminders of what came before the entry of Christ into such places as Norwich, Exeter and Canterbury. In the space between pre-Christian religions and the arrival of the Church, the subtle reminders of the precursor – the native religion – comfortably dwell. Sometimes forgotten, sometimes remembered, they have never been wholly erased.

For such a simple symbol, there exists a bewildering array of variations on the Green Man theme. Most often, a face peers down from the top of a column or ledge, from behind a veil of leaves and branches. The most salient features of the human face remain: the eyes, mouth, and often, a nose. But the vegetation is the paramount image – and what makes the Green Man *green* – and it is what originally gave him a place of honour in some of Europe's sacred Christian spaces, both great and small. Sometimes the green of the Green Man is merely a mask. At other times, the green leaves and bowers grow from his open mouth and spread in a wild profusion, much like that other figure of disquieting vegetative fecundity sometimes found in old English and Irish churches, Sheela-Na-Gig, who opens her vagina with outstretched hands, releasing plumes of leaves and sprigs of flowers.[6] And like Sheela, there is a definite impression that the Green Man is in some fashion responsible for the fertility of the world, both of fauna and flora, and of humans and their earth.

The Green Man's presence becomes more explicable when we see the rites associated with him in pre-Christian times and the folk traditions still enacted after the coming of Christianity – some of which are still performed today. Sometimes called Green George, or Jack in the Green, or the Old Man in the Woods,[7] his cult was celebrated in the spring and associated with the rites of vegetative rebirth. Often, a Green Man substitute, usually a manikin, was thrown into a body of water and his literal and symbolic death brought about the renewed life of a nascent, budding spring. The Green Man cult was celebrated through morris dancing, a form of folk dance meant to wake up the slumbering earth through the stomping of feet and banging of sticks on the ground; often, the dancers wore wooden clogs to add to the tumult and sported elaborate floral costumes, top-heavy headdresses, and brightly coloured rags and streamers, as if to illustrate to nature, quite concretely, what she needed to do.

The Green Man was associated with death and renewal; his death was an individual sacrifice for the continuous well-being of the community. The devotees of his cult long understood that his worship was a symbol of a mighty cosmic truth: for life to continue there must be death. It becomes quite easy to see how the Green Man became a logical complement and accompaniment to churches where the newly arrived cult of the risen Christ preached a similar, if not almost identical message.

The survival of the Green Man image is really a splendid example of the psychology of religious conversion. Conversion involves shedding one set of beliefs and practices for another, but that transfer is never wholly complete; some notions, and often very important ones, pass over the bridge between worlds as others are left behind. The Green Man's survival, whether through conscious attempts to ease the burdens of conversion, or through the unconscious transference of like elements to like elements, speaks with a certain understated and bold dignity about the power of the common people to give themselves what they need. Ecclesiastical powers may want a converted people to accept their novel religion wholesale and undiluted. But repeatedly through history, the people – the *folk* – have mixed their creeds to suit their needs, and they have done this despite attempts by religious authorities to impose a foreign orthodoxy and conformity. The faith of the Green Man was a polytheistic, earthbound religion. It represented a plurality of moving forces in the world, and stood against the notion of a singular god looming above creation, a notion which belongs to the Judaeo-Christian heritage and the Abrahamic religions of Judaism, Christianity and Islam. Christianity carries a binding moral code that, while altered somewhat by the arrival of Christ, it brought from Judaism. The Green Man faith, while no less lofty and morally binding, was a faith of natural necessity. Things are born and die not because they are fulfilling a plan, but simply because things must die for other things to live. People in northern Europe brought along the Green Man when they embraced Christianity, despite the pressure to move from a polytheistic creed – with all its associations of impurity, chaotic worship, local practice and parochialism – to monotheism, which carried the badge of universality, and as such, the supposed imprint of a higher moral and ethical stature. Why did the converted people do this? Why bring the Green Man along? Why be 'impure' when one can be 'pure'?

This book is about notions of purity and impurity in religion – how the notions began, and what they mean to religiously inclined people. Why is there a drive for purity? Why is it important to some people, at some times, to have a singular religious unanimity, while at other times it seems of no importance whatsoever? Does the drive to purity say something essential about a people's origins? Does the ability to live with the contradiction of a mixed heritage state a human truth no less important? For the individual person, hiding one's origins is often of no real consequence. But organized religion at the beginning of the twenty-first century continues to illustrate the need for disclosure of its foundations in dramatic ways.

How can a mostly complacent West try to understand Islam now that the dramatic differences between Islam and the West are continually imperilling Western lives? How are we to explain or understand the motivations of *other* people who are so convinced they are right in their actions and thoughts, when we believe that they are fundamentally wrong? How can we convince the self-proclaimed *pure* to accept our 'impurities'? How do situations that allow for such violent disparity arise, historically, religiously, socially and cognitively? Were things always this way? Were there alternatives?

Syncretism defined

We will attempt to answer some of these questions. In a sense, our mission is simple, because our topic – borrowing – is simple. Borrowing is an easy concept to grasp. We borrow a ladder from our neighbour to clean our windows. When we return the ladder, if we have not broken it, it still belongs to our neighbour wholly and intact, just as our windows continue to belong to us wholly and intact. The exchange involves no admixture of our neighbour and us or his ladder and our windows. But we will examine syncretism, a type of borrowing that takes place in religions, an area of study that is rife with complexity and has strange dynamics. Syncretism, in the dictionary definition, is a reconciliation or fusion of differing systems of belief in religion, especially when the result is heterogeneous (incongruous or dissimilar). So unlike borrowing a ladder from a neighbour, syncretistic borrowing involves exchange and transformation. It is as if windows and ladders could merge into hybrid objects, both similar and dissimilar to their component parts.

Syncretism occurs when one religion adopts, absorbs or otherwise accepts elements of another religion. But this simple definition masks a great deal of complexity, which reveals itself most fully when we see some of the reactions that Islam, Judaism and Christianity have had to the practice. Syncretism has often been the sworn enemy of the three great Abrahamic monotheistic religions of the West. Whereas other religious traditions often openly adopt the practices, customs, styles of worship and even the deities of other religions, the Abrahamic faiths have infrequently acknowledged the debt they owe their predecessors and contemporaries. In the crucible that creates religious movements, a certain self-serving amnesia seems necessarily to accompany the creation of a new religion. Orthodox Jews, Muslims and Christians will seldom acknowledge *borrowing* from other traditions even though the Abrahamic religions show a marked preference for accepting from other people's credal formulae, sacred writings and practices. Syncretism is a suspect notion to fundamentalists even when it is obvious, to the eye unaffected by a religious agenda, that the categories we use to separate religions are not as fixed as they appear.

The Satanic Verses controversy and syncretism

The problem here involves our notions of what separates one religion from another, and who borrows what from whom. This problem may seem remote, but it continually rears its head and causes perplexing crises. In 1988, *The Satanic Verses,* by Salman Rushdie, became an unlikely conductor of syncretism. A novel about transformations, *The Satanic Verses* creates a fictional world where anything can transform into anything, and as such, this novel is necessarily the enemy in a religious system that requires stasis in heaven and earth.[8] The novel, among other things, acknowledges the hidden foundations of the faith of Islam, and Islam's deep indebtedness to the milieu of sixth-century cult practices in pre-Islamic Arabia. Much of the controversy surrounding the novel centres on the satirical treatment of a prophetic character who resembles Muhammad and his early followers, the first Muslims of the Islamic era. But much of the invective aimed against *The Satanic Verses* was surely directed against the title, and the historical weight of what the term 'Satanic Verses' means to religious Muslims. These verses, allegedly part of an early version of the Qur'an, were referenced in early Arab biographies of the Prophet (but not in current versions of the Qur'an), and were meant as a conciliatory gesture by Muhammad to the priests and devotees of the polytheistic cults of Mecca. They were meant as a compromise between the religion that existed in Mecca before the advent of Islam, and what Muhammad wanted to create: an all-Allah faith in Arabia. (It has long been known that Muhammad had predecessors in this regard: the *hanifs* of Arabia were reformers who preached an all-Allah, monotheistic creed which was gaining popularity with time and was further bolstered by the spread of Christianity and Judaism in Arabia.) But the tradition of the verses is clear: they were provided not by the angel Gabriel but by Satan, who in exercising his traditional role as an adversary, was trying to fool the Prophet into error. According to tradition, the verses were quickly retracted. The uncompromising stance of Muhammad and his early followers toward Arabic polytheism resumed, but the taint of the verses remained. The spectre of a less than holy alliance with a power (polytheism, or the belief in a plurality of divine beings) that Islam, as a pillar of the divine unity and singularity of God, would see as an utter anathema, lingered like an after-image: faint but still somewhat unsettling to view.

Sura 53 of the Qur'an (which is called 'The Star' because it deals with the astral worship of pre-Islamic Arabs) begins:

Have you thought upon al-Lat and ul-Uzza
And Manat, the third, the other?

The Satanic verses, which were excised from the canonical versions of the *Qur'an*, then followed:

> These are the exalted cranes
> Whose intercession is to be hoped for . . .

Birds are animals with a special place in spiritual narratives; they can fly to the heavens, and as such, can be intermediaries with God. Muhammad, however, calls al-Lat, ul-Uzza and Manat birds euphemistically to soften what he is saying and to hide what he is implying: that they are goddesses, consorts, daughters (or both) of Allah, the supreme God in the Arab pantheon. In Rushdie's novel, the ghost of the goddess returns. The exposure of a syncretistic compromise, initially made but then abandoned, reveals a human framework beneath a faith that claims to be of strictly divine origin. The Prophet faltered, blundered and recovered. Ultimately, it is not the recovery that matters – it is the fact that he could have blundered in the first place that is a matter of such importance.[9]

Even outside the pages of the Qur'an and its expurgated elements, one can see the deep indebtedness of Islam to its predecessors and contemporaries, in particular in the practice of the Hajj pilgrimage to Mecca. It has long been known that ceremonies practised at Mecca have a pre-Islamic origin. The *al-hajarul aswad* (the black stone at the Ka'ba), the casting of pebbles at the demons at *Mina* and the mountains outside of Mecca called *Jabalu r-Rahma* were all pre-Islamic pilgrimage sites and practices, which were subsequently incorporated into an Islamic framework. Even the most important image in the Islamic world, the crescent moon, points to a pre-Islamic origin: pre-Islamic Allah, who was head of a family of wives, daughters and sons, was associated with the moon, and may well have been a lunar god. Muhammad and his followers, as residents of Mecca, were no doubt very aware of this. It seems that the pagan practices of what would become the *hajj* were not the problem in themselves, so Islam simply absorbed them.[10]

This state of affairs seems to have been quite conscious. All aspects of Islam's pre-Islamic origins, and the syncretistic nature of this last of the Abrahamic revealed religions, are masked by a strategy of dominance. Islam certainly portrays itself as superior to the paganism that preceded it and also presents itself as the final answer to the corruptions and unanswered questions untidily left by Judaism and Christianity. Islam incorporated into the Qur'an stories from the Hebrew Bible and the Talmud, as well as from apocryphal Jewish sources, the Gospels and extra-canonical traditions about Jesus. These reiterations were viewed by Muslims as a sign of Islam's status as the final revealed religion – a complete wrapping up of the semi-fallacious and corrupt stories of its antecedent religions – but certainly not marks of syncretism.[11]

We have every right to call this type of syncretism one of domination, and concealed domination at that. Islam needed to hide the extra-Islamic origins of absorbed cultic practices, creeds and canonical works behind the façade of revelation. These were all to have come unaltered from God in heaven, the tradition states, unsullied by a compromising human hand.

By many, syncretism is viewed as a corruption of the original revelation of Moses or Jesus or Muhammad – a sullying, in human hands, of a wholly divine message through such diluting avenues as political and social compromise with one's neighbours or the ignorance or isolation of one's religious community. So syncretism, in the eyes of some religious authorities, is a form of deception. Every religion starts somewhere. Every peripheral place may be central to someone else's world. And syncretism, in its numerous forms, lies at the genesis of the Abrahamic faiths. But the politics of movement-building and the consolidation of religious traditions made it all but impossible for the early representatives of these religions to acknowledge their past debts.

Ultimately, one reason *The Satanic Verses* controversy produced a visceral reaction was because it struck at the heart of this conception of an 'immaculately revealed' religion. Even *debate* about issues of the formation of the monotheistic Abrahamic faiths carries a threat, since simple acknowledgement that there could have been non-divine factors at work in the making and compiling of a religion (and its sacred works, and its line of transmission through history) has great destructive potential.

Syncretism, folk religion and a summary of the topics

But even above and beyond this type of syncretism (the syncretism of religious origins), there is a more overt variety. This syncretism occurs once an established religion moves beyond the borders of its cradle and far from its traditional territorial bounds, and makes progress through areas that are founded on different cultural footings. As we shall see, the Muslim clerics who spread Islam through the recently captured Ottoman Turkish lands in the Balkans were schooled in more heterodox forms of mystical Islam known as Sufism. They were not interested in orthodox standards of purity, instead propagating a more easy-going brand of Islam – an Islam we could call folk Islam. They viewed this version of the faith of Muhammad as primarily akin to the folk Christianity practised by the peasants of the Balkans.[12] For the most part, these Sufi mystics saw the outward rites of organized religion as a veil – as a series of formal conventions meant to express in a starkly tangible form certain deeper, inner truths for people. The expression of faith, for these Ottoman mystics, was but the rind of the fruit; for them, Islam, Christianity and

Judaism were ultimately and merely the revealed patinas on the surface of Supreme Truth. We shall see how the Ottoman Turkish rulers, eager to have a cushion of converted (or even half-converted) people in their conquered Balkan holdings, did not ask uncomfortable questions about the orthodoxy or heterodoxy of its subjected people. In this environment, discussed in Chapter 3 and parts of Chapter 4, a distinctly native European variety of Islam took root and grew.

This sort of syncretism, where a lax political system creates a hybrid religion that blends elements of folk Islam and folk Christianity, can be contrasted with a form of syncretism created by the opposite political impulse: the drive to create a national and religious uniformity. This can be seen in the attempts, by the royal houses of Spain and Portugal in the late thirteenth century, to solidify political gains by uniting the peoples of the Iberian peninsula (who were a mix of indigenous Jews, Christians and Muslims) as Roman Catholics. Forced conversions of Jews and Muslims led not to the greater homogenization of people on the Iberian peninsula (at least not at first) but to creeping fear of crypto-converts: Marranism and Moriscoism.[13] This fear of crypto-ism, or the outward profession of Roman Catholicism and the secret, mostly domestic practice of Judaism or Islam, led to an atmosphere of distrust on the Iberian peninsula which only really disappeared in the nineteenth century; and for some areas of rural Portugal, that distrust continued well into the century we have just vacated. Attempts to root out this phenomenon failed because crypto-Judaism transformed into Marranism, a hybrid religion that is a syncretistic cocktail of Roman Catholicism and Judaism. Marrano practices were altered through the effects of time and the erosion of individual and collective Jewish memory, and more importantly, through the self-conscious alteration of Jewish rites in order to make them clandestine.

The discovery of Marranism in the town of Belmonte in Portugal at the beginning of the twentieth century, its rediscovery in the early 1990s and the attempts to bring Marranos back into the fold of normative Judaism illustrates this point.[14] Marranism is neither Judaism nor Christianity; it is both and neither. Attempts to re-Judaize Marranos en masse always failed, because the kernel of Judaism in Marrano life had long ago been transformed by external pressure and the isolation of communal life into something distinctly different from both Roman Catholicism and Judaism; once uprooted from the traditional soil of the heartland of Marranism (rural north-east Portugal), it all but dies.

Another form of syncretism, related to Marranism but different in key ways, occurs not from the purposeful laxness of rulers in converting subject peoples, or movements to create religious uniformity, but from isolation. Isolation, along with its cousin, ignorance, creates a decidedly rural, folk-based syncretism. We see this most often in the cults of saints. All three Abrahamic religions have or have had thriving cults for their saints, both officially and unofficially venerated. Saint worship is traditionally the great storehouse for folk-based, demotic expressions of religion, most often of a syncretistic variety. The Roman Catholic Church excised much of the corrosive influence of syncretistic elements in saint cults by incorporating and formalizing that worship through official channels, but the folk element is always visible through the haze of ecclesiastical officialdom. The brown Madonna of Guadalupe, worshipped as she is in a location that was once the centre of the veneration of the Aztec Goddess Tonantzin, on Mount Tepeyac, is a rather obvious nod by the church in Mexico to its aboriginal antecedents. Here the Virgin was said to have been sighted by an Indian, and the Madonna conveniently addressed him in his native tongue, the language of the gods and goddesses of the Aztecs.[15]

One of the other great events in Mary's career, the appearance of the Virgin at Lourdes, also occurred to a peasant. Bernadette's conversations with Mary in the local French vernacular, the Bigourdan dialect, commenced with: *'que soy era Immaculada Councepciou'* ('I am the Immaculate Conception.') This reference to a recently promulgated papal doctrine in a vernacular tongue is surely a turning point in the history of worship on a par with the appearance of the Virgin in Mexico. Purely local manifestations of the Virgin, expressed in vernacular tongues (one of a conquered people in Mexico, and the other of a rural people in France, near the border with Spain, whose language is viewed as debased and mongrel) are surely the syncretistic blending of elements of indigenous religions and cultures with that of their conquerors. In a very real sense, Lourdes and Guadalupe were acts of sabotage by converted peoples. If we must take your gods, these manifestations of Mary tell us, we will mould them to our liking.[16] The Roman Catholic Church, for the most part, had come to realize the necessity of flexibility, and rather than fight the propensity, it harnessed it for the greater good of the Roman version of Christ's Church on earth. When it failed, the Church suffered losses. One such failure involved the Rites Controversy in China, in which the Dominicans, convinced that Confucianism was a religion, refused to allow Chinese converts the right to practise the veneration of ancestors. At the same time, the Jesuits, convinced that Confucianism was only a social custom and secular philosophy, permitted it. The ensuing debate crippled the Church during what turned out to be the narrow window allowed to the Roman Catholic Church for its activities in China.[17]

So the shrines of Mary at Lourdes and Guadalupe started as parochial movements but became, through the force of their primitive usefulness, international shrines, fully sanctioned by national and ecclesiastical authorities.[18] This impulse to graft elements of an old religion onto a new one is even more evident in the host of minor and often unofficial saints found in the Roman Catholic world. In many cases, the hidden identity of the male or female saint as a previous god or goddess is concealed beneath the thinnest of membranes. This is a syncretism of the vestigial kind: the old divinities of the glades, forests, mountains, glens and pools are dressed in flimsy Christian costume. Far away from the centres of ecclesiastical power, or even in the cracks close to the locus of control, the old gods and goddesses of the subjected people performed much the same role they did in the old regime, but with a shifted emphasis. We will also see this in the final chapter, where we briefly examine the New World syncretistic religion Santeria.

For the Islamic world, saint veneration was most often expressed in Sufism, the mystical movement(s) in Islam. Varieties of this form of mysticism, the same kind that produced a hybrid Islam in the Balkans, also spread the faith in India, Pakistan and Indonesia. In the long and successful history of Islam on the Indian subcontinent, the common folk venerated Muslim saints, and quite often, Hindus and Muslims worshipped Muslim holy men and women in acts of public worship. In equal measure, some Muslims venerated Hindu saints, and to a great degree, elements of cultic practice from both faiths deeply penetrated each other. Where else but on the Indian subcontinent, with the Hindu faith as a model of vast, dizzying inclusion, where alien religions easily take root and throw on the guise of native Indianness, could this occur? That Islam, Judaism and Christianity, when rooted in India, could take on the foundational flavour of that country is a tribute to that land's long history of religious harmonization.[19] We will also examine saint veneration in Morocco among both Jews and Muslims. Looking at examples from this North African country, and also from India and the Balkans, we will quite clearly see the cross-cultural elements of saint veneration peering out through the changes of dress, climate, language and the procession of time.

We will also see how Akbar, the great Mogul ruler of seventeenth-century northern India, becomes a single representative of syncretism writ large in Indian life. As a man brought up in Orthodox Islam, and having taken upon himself the role of the secular guarantor of Islam's hegemony in India, his actions were wildly ironic. As we will see, Akbar's quest to create a religion that was a mixture of all the major religions of India, in a real and unimagined way, becomes the spiritual journey of both his time and ours. He had, in the bold ways we now also have, the power to impose his will on traditions that were malleable in his powerful hands. India, a land of many faiths, becomes a laboratory for living with religious complexity, and living with complexity is the central problem of our own time.

Finally we will examine a hero of syncretism from syncretism's Golden Age. We will survey the life, career and vast and fantastic migrations of Apollonius of Tyana, as written in Philostratus' *The Life of Apollonius of Tyana.* A demi-god of syncretism, his idealized (but by no means sani-tized) wanderings all over the map of Graeco-Roman antiquity will illus-trate for us how a pagan faith can be morally lofty while being culturally and religiously relativistic, how it can be monotheistic while embracing a divine plurality, and how it can reform but not seek to create religious innovations. Apollonius was the pagan answer to Christ in the first and second centuries, so much so that Eusebius, the famous church historian, wrote a small treatise against *The Life of Apollonius of Tyana.* We are lucky to have an original pagan document and the Christian and Ortho-dox reaction to it to compare, contrast and scrutinize.

Syncretism as a vital part of religious transformation

Inevitably, when we examine the problem of syncretism, we repeated-ly encounter the same set of problems, which goes something like this: a religion is *revealed* by God to a prophet. The revelations are written down (either by the prophet himself, or by his immediate followers), and the substance of these revelations differs so radically from its pre-decessors that it constitutes, either by design or by accidental conflu-ence, a wholly different religious movement from what came before. The prophet and his immediate followers set out to spread the faith, through warfare, through missionary endeavours, or both, and in the process of this engagement with a world already set in its ways, aspects of the new faith begin to transform. Former goddesses, through sleight of hand, become exalted cranes, and Jesus' mother (who has such a minor role in the Gospels), becomes a de facto goddess. Similarly, as we shall see, God is viewed as one essence in the most important doctrinal statement of orthodox Judaism, the *Shema,* but in the Kabbala, Judaism's mystical movement, God is broken apart into ten spheres or divine emanations (in Hebrew, the *sephiroth*). These pieces of God, in some of these Kabbal-istic traditions, behave very much like the cavorting gods and goddess of any pagan pantheon.[20] In all these cases, a process of accommodation begins to transform the movement, to a greater or a lesser degree, from the vision of its founder. Change, endemic to the universe, becomes in-grained even in our supposedly immutable religions.

After a time, reformers emerge whose mission it is to purge a faith of these erroneous foreign or extraneous elements. This impulse to get at the fundamental level of the prophet or law-giver's original faith can lead to wars, iconoclastic violence, regicide, sectarianism and schism. Fundamentalism cleaves to monotheistic religions because a historical-ly revealed faith *must* have a starting point. The Abrahamic religions, Islam, Christianity and Judaism, do not view time cyclically. To them, time is a traditional narrative: it has a beginning, middle and end. These religions tend to view time as a progressively corrosive force – especially with regard to human corruptibility. Each generation is more sinful than the last. Time corrodes the magic purity of the faith's genesis. There is an enchantment in Islam with the Prophet and his original followers and the first four 'rightly guided' Caliphs, in Christianity with Jesus and his early disciples, and in Judaism with Moses and Aaron (and the sages of the Mishnah and the Talmud). The fundamentalists of these religions act as if the laws that govern human life – the psychological, social and political fractiousness that invariably accompany history – did not exist during those fabulously enchanted early days of the faith. Things are worse now; things were better then.

This mania for purity is an interesting impulse. How do we explain it? This trend stands in stark opposition to syncretism, which is about evolution, accommodation and mutation. As we saw in the example of the Taliban's iconoclastic tendencies, we see fundamentalism strongly represented in Islam today; but ironically, Islam spread (in part) due to its adaptation to the cultures it found in the burned shell of the old Roman Empire. Islam became heir to the West's great flowering of classical culture not because the faith refused to incorporate outside influences, but because it accepted them greedily. One writer even stated that 'Islam [has a] dogmatic imperviousness to pagan achievements', and ignored centuries of Muslim eagerness to absorb elements of the Graeco-Roman world.[21] Various Islamic fundamentalist movements, like the Wahhabis of Saudi Arabia, and like puritanical strains in all religions, have tried to turn the clock back on this broad heritage, to lay bare the essential message of the Prophet in its primal simplicity and purity.

Similarly, Christianity spread like wildfire throughout Rome not merely because of Constantine's legalization of the cult, but because of the early movement's flexibility in adapting itself to local conditions. The Reformation began to peel back this trend. A strong component of evangelical Christianity (the Reformation's most stringent heir in the United States and elsewhere) is a rejection of 'pagan' elements that Christianity absorbed in its western Mediterranean cradle and carried abroad. In the same way, rabbinical Judaism is the heir to a Jewish tradition that was once far more pluralistic than it is today. Before the destruction of the Second Temple by Titus' armies, there were several Judaisms.[22] The compilers of the Oral Law tried to conceal this fact with some historical sleight of hand in one of the early tractates of the Mishnah, the *Pirkei Avot*, or the Chapters of the Fathers. Rabbinical Jews are the heirs of the Pharisees, who in the New Testament and other places were accused of creating laws that are not in the Torah.[23] The so-called Oral Law, the body of Pharisaic interpretations of the Torah, was put in writing in the early years of the growing strength of the Christian Church (and most likely, in part, in response to that growing power). In the famous first chapter of the *Pirkei*, we are given the line of transmission of the Oral Law from Moses down to the very men that compiled the Mishnah, and whose sayings are found within it. The message is clear: a divine stamp had been given to a venture that the Pharisees' enemies viewed as a purely human folly.[24] Eventually, Jewish groups cried out against the rabbis' laws, and one of Judaism's rare schisms was inaugurated. In the end, 'pure' origins were created, but not everyone completely accepted them.[25]

Purity and interpretation

This impulse toward purity, as we shall see, has many sides. As with the examples we have briefly mentioned, it almost always involves some sort of active subterfuge. Something new is portrayed as something old. But fundamentalism is a uniquely modern phenomenon. Fundamentalist groups often use the conceptual and political tools and concepts that they reject in secular modernity.[26] Part of the origin of the fundamentalist impulse is inherent in the design of a revealed religion that has a book or sacred scripture as its centrepiece. When a book becomes canonized and set, interpretation becomes the centrepiece of a faith – and there will always be differing views of what words mean, as there will always be readers who claim to know the original meaning of these words.[27] So fundamentalism is endemic to monotheistic and revealed religions.

This drive to purity is often politically motivated, and in the hands of certain rulers, it has been a tool for political consolidation. Additionally, and most interestingly, this impulse toward purity is psychological. Religious fundamentalists often seem to desire that life be completely explicable. They crave transparency to life and to history – a universe in a glass box revealed by God to a prophet and sent down in a book. They seek a blueprint that parses existence's multiplicity into a simple unity. Syncretism is their sworn enemy; it reeks of impurity and is unpredictable and often radically and frighteningly mutable. It bears the marks of human handiwork, and as a human creation, it seems to them a sullied article.

The structure

Syncretism is often ad hoc and this book will not attempt to present the ad hoc in a systematic way. We need to learn the language, tempo and rhythm of syncretism by examining examples. We are in danger, of course, of trying to use a language to learn an identical language – a circular pursuit that would surely end with dry conclusions. But looking at individual instances allows us to learn the language of syncretism.

Although our theme (religious borrowing) is rather simple, the questions surrounding it are complex. Can a strictly human pursuit be truly religious? Can faith operate even if overwhelmingly guided by human hands?

The examples in the following chapters are primarily from Europe and the Middle East. This is a stylistic choice, and in no way reflects a lack of examples from other regions of the world. In fact, syncretism is found in nearly every religion, at every time, and has a nearly universal and cross-cultural reach.[28] Each chapter will begin with an example of contemporary fundamentalism closely tied, religiously and culturally, to the topic of the chapter. This will illustrate some of the key differences between syncretistically oriented religious traditions and fundamentalist ones.

Chapter summary

Religious fundamentalism has been called one of the most pressing issues of our time.[29] One of the paramount reasons for its ascendance is the growth of a world culture, and with it the ease of communication and transportation. Quite suddenly, geographical areas that had been previously isolated from other cultures, and particularly from the West, were confronted by them. Where there once had been a single option for religious faith, there is now a bewildering multiplicity. Fundamentalism has been called a crisis about the 'awareness of differences'[30] and, in part, it is a rejection of modern plural culture and its crisis of freedom and choice.

The former Taliban regime turned its back on the vast historical heritage of Afghanistan in order to embrace a narrow and ideological definition of Islam, and in so doing ignored or suppressed native elements of Islamic expression which had existed in Afghanistan for centuries. The Taliban sought to eradicate Sufism in Afghanistan, rid the country of religious minorities, including Jews, Hindus and Sikhs, and finally, in a rigid interpretation of Islamic strictures against the display of images,[31] rid the country of its pre-Islamic heritage – the greatest expression being the destruction of the Buddhas at Bamian.

Other religious traditions, both Islamic and otherwise, have had a more expansive view of importing elements of other religions and cultural traditions. As we saw, so-called Celtic Christianity may have been an example of this. The form of Christianity practised by the Celts appeared to have a more lenient attitude toward pre-Christian, pagan practices and images and incorporated them. Syncretism is the vital component in this mechanism.

Syncretism stands opposite to fundamentalism. Rather than reject multiplicity, it embraces it. Where the three Abrahamic religions do not exercise the rites of exclusivity of their fundamentalist cousins, we can see interesting variations of Judaism, Christianity and Islam. We saw one example in this chapter: the early worshippers of Christianity in England in its Celtic and Anglo-Saxon forms, who adapted some of their traditional and pagan symbols to their new faith. A form of syncretism was at work here,[32] which stands in stark contrast to the Taliban's violent iconoclasm, where a break with Afghanistan's past was self-consciously pursued, and a radical form of fundamentalism was practised which sought rigid lines of demarcation from elements of other religions.

Draw your own conclusions

How are fundamentalism and syncretism both reactions to cultural change and stress?

Why do groups like the Taliban destroy or suppress elements of previous religious traditions?

Why do other groups, like the early Celtic Christians, incorporate elements of previous religious traditions?

Is religious innovation possible? Or are ideas and practices always borrowed?

Is it possible to get at the 'original meaning' of the New Testament, the Hebrew Bible, or the Qur'an?

Is fundamentalism inevitable in revealed religions like the Abrahamic faiths?

Further reading

For a wide look into the relationships between three Abrahamic faiths:
John Corrigan, Frederick M. Denny, Martin Jaffee and Carlos M. N. Eire (1998), *Jews, Christians and Muslims: A Comparative Introduction to the Monotheistic Faiths*, Upper Saddle River, NJ: Prentice Hall.

For more on fundamentalism in the Abrahamic faiths:
Malise Ruthven (2004), *Fundamentalism: A Search for Meaning*, Oxford: Oxford University Press.
Karen Armstrong (2000), *The Battle for God*, New York: Alfred A. Knopf.

For the numerous aspects of *The Satanic Verses* controversy:
Daniel Pipes (1990), *The Rushdie Affair*, New York: Birch Lane Press.

For a short history of the rise of Islam, see the early chapters of:
Albert Hourani (1991), *The History of Arab Peoples*, Cambridge, MA: The Belknap Press of Harvard.

For a short work on the subject of Celtic Christianity and its relationship to nature, see:

Ian Bradley (1999), *Celtic Christianity: Making Myths and Chasing Dreams*, Edinburgh: Edinburgh University Press.

Notes

1 Martin Ewens (2002), *Afghanistan: A Short History of Its People and Politics,* New York: HarperCollins, p. 15.

2 Ewens, *Afghanistan,* pp. 5–6.

3 Ewens, *Afghanistan*, p. 8.

4 Ewens, *Afghanistan*, p. 7.

5 W. L. Rathje (2001), 'Why the Taliban are Destroying the Buddhas', in *USA Today* (22 March). Available online at www.usatoday.com/news/science/archae-ology/2001-03-22-afghan-buddhas.htm.

6 Perhaps the best-known example of Celtic syncretism is the Irish saint Brigit. Many scholars consider her cult a continuation of a Celtic fire goddess. The site of her worship has been identified by archaeologists as Kildare, and her feast on 1 February coincides with the pre-Christian spring festival of *Imbolc*. See Richard Fletcher (1997), *The Barbarian Conversion*, New York: Henry Holt and Company, p. 241.

7 Sir James George Fraser (1993), *The Golden Bough: A Study in Magic and Religion,* New York: Wordsworth Reference. Fraser writes of the Green Man in Chapter X, 'Relics of Tree Worship in Modern Europe' p. 129, as part of an overall discussion of tree veneration and, regarding the Green Man, spring rites. Here we read that:

> In England the best-known example of these leaf-clad mummers is the Jack-in-the-Green, a chimney-sweeper who walks encased in a pyramidal frame-work of wickerwork, which is covered with holly and ivy, and surmounted by a crown of flowers and ribbons. Thus arrayed he dances on May Day at the head of a troop of chimney-sweeps, who collect pence. In Fricktal a similar frame of basketwork is called the Whitsuntide Basket. As soon as the trees begin to bud, a spot is chosen in the wood, and here the village lads make the frame with all secrecy, lest others should forestall them. Leafy branches are twined round two hoops, one of which rests on the shoulders of the wearer, the other encircles his claves; holes are made for his eyes and mouth; and a large nosegay crowns the whole. In this guise he appears suddenly in the village at the hour of vespers, preceded by three boys blowing on horns made of willow bark. The great object of his supporters is to set up the Whitsuntide Basket on the village well, and to keep it and him there, despite the efforts of the lads from neighbouring villages, who seek to carry off the Whitsuntide Basket and set it up on their own well.

8 Salman Rushdie (2000), *The Satanic Verses*, New York: Picador Press.

9 Daniel Pipes (1990), *The Rushdie Affair*, New York: Birch Lane Press. Most of the material here about both the Satanic Verses in Islamic tradition and the novel *The Satanic Verses* comes from Daniel Pipes' masterful book about this subject. There Pipes delineates the historical, religious, social, artistic and political impact of Rushdie's novel, pp. 56–9.

10 John Corrigan et al., *Jews, Christians and Muslims*. For a discussion of the origins of the *hajj* pilgrimage, see p. 265. For the normative explanation of the symbol of Allah, the crescent moon, (the *Hilal*), see the same, pp. 263–7.

11 Hourani, *The History of Arab Peoples,* p. 21.

12 The costly war in Yugoslavia, and then in Bosnia and Hercegovina, and later the attempts by Milosevic to ethnically purge Albanian Muslims, were unfortunate reminders for most Westerners that there is a native Islam in Europe. Work on Islam in the Balkans was gleaned from Peter F. Sugar's (1997) *South-eastern Europe Under Ottoman Rule, 1354–1804*, Seattle and London: University of Washington Press, and an article by S. Vryonis Jr in *Aspects of the Balkans,* whose notes are detailed in the bibliography for Chapter 3.

13 The Moriscos, the crypto-Muslims of Spain, will not be a topic of this book, because this community suffered different vicissitudes than the Jews of Spain. The *Columbia Encyclopaedia* (available online at www.bartleby.com/65/mo/Moriscos.html) explains:

> Moriscos [Span.,=Moorish], Moors converted to Christianity after the Christian reconquest (11th–15th cent.) of Spain. The Moors who had become subjects of Christian kings as the reconquest progressed to the 15th cent. were called Mudéjares. They remained Muslim, and their religion and customs were generally respected. After the fall of Granada (1492), Cardinal Jiménez converted many Moors by peaceful means. However, the rigorous treatment of those who refused conversion or apostatized from the new faith led to an uprising (1500–1502) in Granada. This was soon suppressed. Faced with choosing between conversion or banishment, the majority accepted conversion, but many continued secretly to practise Islam. The Moriscos at times provided the Ottoman Turks with information facilitating Turkish raids on the Spanish coast. Persecuted by the Spanish Inquisition and subjected to restrictive legislation (1526, 1527), the Moriscos rose in a bloody rebellion (1568–71), which Philip II put down with the help of John of Austria. The Moriscos prospered in spite of persecutions and furthered Spanish agriculture, trade, and industries. However, in 1609 Philip III, influenced by Lerma, decreed their expulsion for both religious and political reasons. Bibliography: See H. C. Lea, The Moriscos of Spain (1901, repr. 1969).

14 Frederic Brenner and Stan Neuman, Directors, (1997), *Les Derniers Marranes: The Last Marranos* / Les films d'Ici, Canaan Production. *The Last Marranos*, an important documentary about Belmonte's cypto-Jews, was filmed in the late 1980s and early 1990s, in Belmonte and the towns that surround it, which formed a kind of last vestige of authentic Marranism in Portugal. Among the many interesting elements in this film is the conflict between the new religion (the reintroduction of normative Judaism to Belmonte) and the old one (Marranism, practised in Belmonte for nearly 500 years). Crypto-Jewish practices were, by their very clandestine nature, domestic routines, and the lore of Marranism was transmitted almost exclusively by women. The baking of Passover matzoth and the lighting of Sabbath candles are Jewish rites that are house-bound, and as such, in the domain of women. The reintroduction of normative Judaism in Belmonte was a male initiative. The tension of this curious mixture of the old and the new (many of the film's subjects even confuse themselves by speaking of

Judaism as the 'new' religion, and Marranism as the 'old' one) and the impossibility of their peaceful coexistence, form one of the poignant elements of the film.

15 C. Ebertshäuser, H. Haag, J. H. Kirchberger and D. Sölle (1998), *Mary: Art, Culture and Religion through the Ages,* New York: A Crossroad Herder Book, p. 206.

16 Ebertshäuser et al., *Mary: Art, Culture and Religion through the Ages,* p. 207.

17 Michael Pollack (1980), *Jews, Mandarins and Missionaries,* Philadelphia: Jewish Publication Society, pp. 15–38. This book about the Jews of the Chinese city of Kaifeng explores, among other topics, the Western reactions to the discovery of this unique Jewish community. Pollack also examines the inner life of this community. Interestingly enough, he explores how Chinese customs gradually became mixed with Jewish rites, including a Hall of the Ancestors adjacent to the synagogue, where figures from Jewish history, like Abraham, Isaac, Jacob and Moses were venerated in a Confucian style.

18 George H. Tavard (1996), *Mary of a Thousand Faces,* Collegeville, MN: Liturgical Press, pp. 171–87.

19 Islam and Sufism on the Indian subcontinent will be taken up later. Suffice it to say here that the same eclecticism that marked Hinduism also left a deep mark on Indian Islam.

20 Rafael Patai (1990), *The Hebrew Goddess,* Detroit, MI: Wayne State University Press, 'The Kaballistic Tetrad', pp. 113–30.

21 For a general discussion of Islamic learning, see Hourani, *The History of Arab Peoples,* pp. 75–8. See in particular in this section about the great age of translation (the eighth to the tenth centuries) when Muslim intellectuals translated into Arabic works of Indian, Iranian and Greek science, art, mathematics and medicine. The quote here is from William McNeil (1963), *The Rise of the West: A History of the Human Community,* New York: New American Library, p. 521.

22 The first-century Jewish historian Josephus provides us with glimpses of the different sects of First Temple Judaism mainly in his works *The Jewish War* and the *Antiquities.* See Corrigan, *Jews, Christians and Muslims,* p. 17.

23 In *NJB* Mark 7. 8–10, p. 1153, Jesus says that the Pharisee's 'laws' are human creations, not divine.

24 R. Abraham, J. Elrich and A. Tomaschorf (trans.) *Pirkei Avot,* A Kaplan Kusick Foundation Project. *Pirkei Avot,* often translated as the Chapters of the Fathers, is considered the oldest of the Mishnah, preserving the early sayings of late Pharisee and early Rabbinical leaders.

25 The Karaites rejected Jewish oral law, spawning what was in effect a fundamentalist movement within Judaism:

> During the ninth century, a number of sects arose that denied the existence of oral torah. These sects came to be known as Karaites (literally, People of the Scripture), and they were distinguished from the Rabbanites or rabbinical Judaism.
>
> The Karaites believed in strict interpretation of the literal text of the scripture, without rabbinical interpretation. They believed that rabbinical law was not part of an oral tradition that had been handed down from God,

nor was it inspired by God, but was an original work of the sages. As such, rabbinical teachings are subject to the flaws of any document written by mere mortals.

The difference between Rabbanites and Karaites that is most commonly noted is in regard to the Sabbath: the Karaites noted that the Bible specifically prohibits lighting a flame on the Sabbath, so they kept their houses dark on the sabbath. The Rabbanites, on the other hand, relied upon rabbinical interpretation that allowed us to leave burning a flame that was ignited before the sabbath. Karaites also prohibited sexual intercourse on the sabbath, while Rabbanites considered the sabbath to be the best time for sexual intercourse. The Karaites also follow a slightly different calendar than the Rabbanites.

According to the Karaites, this movement at one time attracted as much as 40 per cent of the Jewish people. Today, Karaites are a very small minority, and most Rabbinical Jews do not even know that they exist. (From http://www.jewishvirtuallibrary.org/jsource/Judaism/Karaites.html – the Jewish Virtual Library.)

26 Armstrong, *The Battle for God*. See Armstrong for modern fundamentalism's deep debt to the modernity it seeks to eradicate, especially Chapter 9, 'The Offensive (1974–79)', and Chapter 10, 'Defeat? (1979–99)', pp. 278–371.

27 For the formation of the canon, see Bard Ehrman (2003), *Lost Christianities: The Battles for Scripture and the Faiths We Never Knew*, Oxford: Oxford University Press, pp. 203–27. Also consult this book for an overview of the variety within Christianity in its first three centuries. Additionally, see Elaine Pagels (2003), *Beyond Belief: The Secret Gospel of Thomas*, New York: Random House, pp. 114–42. This small work provides some details about the dynamics of the formation of the Christian canon, and the role of interpretation in that dynamic.

28 Kurt Rudolph (1987), *Gnosis: The Nature and History of Gnosticism*, San Francisco: Harper. In an aside in his masterful overview of Gnosticism, Kurt Rudolph says 'every religion is strictly a syncretistic product, pure religions only existing as theoretical constructions by scholars', p. 286.

29 Ruthven, *Fundamentalism*, for a fuller treatment of these issues.

30 Ruthven, *Fundamentalism*, p. 48.

31 It seems the iconoclastic stance of the Taliban did not extend to their leadership. After the American invasion of the country in late 2001, the Taliban leader Mullah Omar's home was discovered outside Kandahar. The spacious and well-furnished home, luxurious beyond compare for Afghanistan, was adorned with paintings. See Justin Huggler, 'Mullah Omar, The Ascetic With Golden Chandeliers', *The Independent* (UK), 13 December 2001.

32 Ian Bradley (2003), *The Celtic Way*, London: Darton, Longman & Todd. Celtic Christianity is held out as an exemplar of an egalitarian, pluralistic, nature-respecting, form of Christianity. Ideas such as this are explored in *The Celtic Way*, by Ian Bradley, especially Chapters 2 and 3. Also, the syncretism of Christianity with its pagan predecessor in the British Isles and Ireland is discussed on pp. 93–4. Many scholars debate the existence of a 'Celtic' Christianity. Richard Fletcher has this to say of it: 'For example, the notion widely entertained today, especially by dewy-eyed ecologists, that the spirit of the so-called Celtic

church was a pollen-strewn blend of love and nature and Irish mythology is one of the silliest misconceptions which the mushy credulity of our age has devised.' Fletcher, *The Barbarian Conversion*, p. 520. Also, p. 92, for brief comments. For a fuller treatment, see Donald Meek (2000), *The Quest for Celtic Christianity*, Edinburgh: Handsel Press.

2

Family Resemblances: the Crypto-Jews of Spain and Portugal Become the Syncretistic Marranos

'I come here to visit neither wood nor stone, I come only to worship you, Highest Adonai, who is that governs us.' (Marrano prayer on entering a church)

Islam returns to Spain

In early 2005, Spanish Muslims opened the first mosque in Granada since their expulsion from southern Spain in 1492. For the Muslims of Spain, the location was propitious. The mosque was built in the old Moorish village of Albaicin, a gentrified neighbourhood of red-tiled and whitewashed villas with narrow, winding lanes which are reminiscent of North African or Middle Eastern villages. There are tea shops, a butcher and a bakery selling baklava and kenafa, a type of soft cheese. In October, signs can be read proclaiming 'Feliz Ramadan', and at the nearby University of Granada, it is not uncommon to see women wearing the hijab, the Muslim headscarf. In the pharmacology school there, nearly 40 per cent of the 2,100 students are from Arab or Muslim countries.

The discomfort created by having a large number of Muslims newly residing in Spain is difficult for non-Spaniards to understand. Spain, like Sicily and the Balkans, was controlled by Muslim polities for a significant period of time. Parts of Spain were ruled by Muslim states for over 700 years, from AD 711 to 1492. For Roman Catholic Spaniards, Muslims residing in Spain, especially when they build mosques in old Muslim strongholds like Granada, conjure up strong historical associations. The Madrid train bombings orchestrated by Al-Qaeda in 2004 add to the nation's tensions and ambivalence about Spanish Islam, especially because Osama bin Laden has mentioned in at least one address that the reconquest of Al-Andalus (the Arabic name for Spain and Portugal) is a goal of his organization.

The increasing cultural diversity of modern Spain caused by immigrants from Muslim countries has forced the formerly monolithic religious and ethnic culture to re-examine its relationship to Islam, and the relationship of Islam to Christianity, Judaism, and modern European secularism. In Spain, where the Roman Catholic Church wields considerable power, the government has reversed plans to make the Catholic curriculum mandatory in public schools. It has also set up a fund to help subsidize Spain's minority religions, which include Judaism, Islam and Protestant groups. The presence of large numbers of Muslims in Spain seems to have contributed to the country's re-examination of its past, and its search for the common relationships between the Abrahamic religions. This chapter will examine those relationships, and use a bit of Spanish history to suggest that a spurious dividing line exists between Judaism, Christianity and Islam.[1]

The loss of a Golden Age: Al-Andalus in its prime

The Jews of Spain were forced to convert to Roman Catholicism in 1492 or face expulsion from the country. Many left, but many others chose conversion rather than exile, for most Spanish Jews had lived in Spain for centuries, and considered the country an earthly paradise. The poems of the Andalusian Jew Judah Ha-Levi (1075–1144) pulse with the vibrations of a rich and textured life, and a culture that was viewed by its members as vastly superior to anything that had come before. Ha-Levi wrote more than 1100 poems: his range included *piyutim*, or poetry meant to be recited in the synagogue, to love songs to young women, tomb inscriptions, laments about ageing, speculations on the soul, personal enquiries to God, martial Zionist odes and rhymes on the vicissitudes of travel. His masterpieces of Hebrew poetry explored the fullness of the human experience. A short poem called 'The Cruel Lover' laments a lover's helplessness in the hands of his beloved, where the narrator pleads 'my fate is in your hands'.[2] The fanciful little poem called 'The Laundress' is about the poet's love of a simple washing woman, who washes her clothes with the narrator's tears. She does not need spring water because 'she has my two eyes'.[3] His love poems are bawdy. They seldom acknowledge Judaism, unless as a counterpose to his theme, such as in a poem entitled 'The Sensitive Doe'. Here the maiden's eyes 'violates the laws of God', and her nipples drink the narrator's blood without compunction.[4]

Incredibly, a poet capable of such vivid erotic images also crafted long religious-historical poems like 'The Murder of Zechariah', or the lament for the land of Israel called 'Ode to Zion', where the narrator is 'like a jackal when I weep for your [Zion's] affliction'. His most famous poem, 'My Heart is in the East', is a lament about Jewish exile: he explains 'It would be quite easy' for him to leave behind the wonders of Spain and see dust of the ruined shrine.[5] But there is a disingenuous note to that last line, since Ha-Levi had great difficulty disentangling himself from the allures of the Arab world. As a Jew in a Muslim land, he was an enormous success. He was a physician and travelled widely in Andalusia's Muslim and Christian states. After the invasion of Spain by fundamentalist Berbers from Morocco, Iberia became increasingly inhospitable for Jews. Ha-Levi then travelled widely, visiting the Holy Land and eventually settling in Egypt. He wrote with nostalgia of Spain: its opulent cities, its rich religious and intellectual life and the beauty of its inhabitants. For Ha-Levi and many Spanish Jews, Spain was a second Holy Land.

His peregrinations mirrored those of Moses Maimonides (1135–1204), the great Andalusian physician and theologian. Maimonides was forced to leave Spain as a young man after another invasion by fundamentalist Berbers from North Africa. He was a man of immense talents and energy. He was a physician, like many talented Jews of his time, and served the Muslim court in Cairo. He was also the leader of the Jewish community in Egypt. He had one of the greatest minds in the Muslim West, and his pen never rested. He wrote a voluminous correspondence to Jews all over the world. He compiled the *Mishneh Torah*, meant to complement or even replace the Talmud as a reference for Jewish law. He composed the *Guide of the Perplexed*, a treatise on the connection between philosophy and Judaism. And as it was for Ha-Levi, Spain was always a bright beacon of nostalgia for him during his years of exile. Although Maimonides lived most of his life in Egypt, in the introduction to his *Mishneh Torah* he identified himself as *Moshe ben Maimon ha-Safardi*, Moses the son of Maimon, the Spaniard. The *Mishneh Torah* was written in Mishnaic Hebrew and was meant for dissemination to Jews all over the world. Maimonides wanted to stress his Spanish pedigree and share the varied and vibrant culture that nurtured and developed him.[6]

It is against this immense backdrop of cultural vitality that we must understand the conversion of the Spanish Jews in 1492. For many of them, Spain was the new Holy Land, and cities like Cordoba and Grenada were like New Jerusalems. Leaving was a horrifying prospect. Spanish Jews, or 'the Sephardim' in Hebrew, always considered themselves the aristocrats in the Jewish world. Until the coming of the courts of Hasidic rabbis in Central and Eastern Europe, rabbinical Judaism had few dynasties and was extremely egalitarian, but the Sephardim were different: they had ancient lineages of scholars, statesmen, noted scientists and philosophers. Many had great wealth and access to international resources in both the arts and in finance. For many of these proud Sephardim, exile was the only option after the decree of 1492 and later, in Portugal, in 1498.[7]

For those who chose conversion rather than departure, there were two options: become fully fledged Roman Catholics and forget Judaism, or find a way to compromise. Those who compromised practised Judaism in secret while professing Catholicism in public. So began a singular adventure in religious history – that of crypto-Judaism. Crypto-Jews, or secret Jews, were called New Christians by Spaniards who looked favourably or neutrally upon this group, and Marranos (a word that probably means swine) by the rest. They were always a suspect population, as their devotion to Roman Catholicism (and since Roman Catholicism and Spanish national identity were merging, to Spain itself) was always in question. Eventually, their closet Judaism mutated into something entirely different from crypto-Jewish practice and they formed a sort of true Marrano culture. They embraced the negative nomenclature of their detractors and transformed themselves into something alien to both Judaism and Roman Catholicism, a hybrid that has resemblances to both but also great dissimilarities. The movement from Jews to crypto-Jews to Marranos was long and before we examine this, some general issues must be confronted. We must see how the practice of a crypto-religion is possible in some religions while not in others.

Some relationships between the Abrahamic religions to better understand crypto-Judaism

We often hear that Christianity and Islam are offspring of Judaism. It is said just as frequently that Islam is part of the Judaeo-Christian tradition. These simple assumptions mask a great deal of complexity. It would be more accurate to say that Christianity (in its various forms) and rabbinical Judaism evolved simultaneously in the years following the destruction of the Temple in Jerusalem in AD 70.[8] They are sister faiths, butted against each other as they formed, often coalescing in reaction to the other, and they took, by turns, strategic advances and retreats in the first three centuries of the common era.[9]

We can see from sections of Acts of the Apostles that not all members of the early Church were clear about the role *Jewishness* should play in their movement.[10] Not every member of the early Church was certain whether something truly new was occurring, or if the Jesus movement was just one of the numerous petals in the sectarian flower of Second Temple Judaism.[11] Indeed the Jewish oral law, which defines the parameters of rabbinical Judaism, was set into writing just at the time period when Christianity was becoming the state religion of Rome. Jewish leaders were eager to delineate Judaism from the followers of Jesus, who also used the Hebrew scriptures as part of their liturgy and also claimed as *their* heritage Israel's divine history.

So rather than Christianity evolving from a static, changeless Judaism, which has become the popular view, a more accurate picture is of two sisters both claiming an ancestral birthright. This birthright was the mantle of ancient Israel's *election* as God's chosen people. Both religions actually have a great deal in common. Rabbinical Judaism and Christianity survived the turbulent time following the destruction of the Second Temple in part because they both transformed the concept of the Messiah to change him from a military leader into a supernatural saviour. A survivor's guilt clings to both faiths to this day, for it seems probable that Christianity and rabbinical Judaism weathered the destruction of the Second Temple merely because of their conciliatory attitude toward Rome. When the dust of revolt settled in AD 70, these two faiths, because of their mythological transformation of the Messiah from a political concept with spiritual overtones into a spiritual one with political overtones, were allowed to exist (eventually) relatively unmolested in the cosmopolitan mix of the Roman Empire. The concept of the Messiah in Judaism never went beyond the spiritual, and the ingathering of Jews in rabbinical Judaism was always visualized on a mythological plane: the Messiah would come at a future date, and usher in the Messianic age. In some predictions of this future age, the natural laws of the universe will be suspended. In others, the Messianic age is a time of prosperity and political independence for Judaism in the land of Israel. For Christianity, the second coming of Christ was always associated with a mythical age in the future. In the early Church, that time was viewed as imminent, but with the passing of time, the end of the world that we know became a more and more remote event.

Islam, as a relative latecomer to the Judaeo-Christian heritage, had a less challenging task in taking up the mantle of divine authority. The Christian sacred books, the Gospels, Acts of the Apostles, the apostolic letters and Revelation, are literally appended to the Hebrew sacred books. Readers can *read* from Genesis to Revelation to peruse the entire length of sacred history, from God's creation of the world and human beings until the final reckoning in the reign of a returned and triumphant Christ. The very genius of creating a seamless and (once translated from the Hebrew and Greek into a uniform Latin or vernacular tongue) monolingual sacred book does a great deal of the difficult work of religious translation for Christianity. The Hebrew Bible, once it is separated and translated from the layered and deeply equivocal world of Hebrew etymology and semantics, can be bent or shaped into a Christian mould.[12] This can work in the other direction as well, for as we shall see below, the translated Hebrew Bible, prefixed to the New Testament as the Old Testament, provided the Marranos with invaluable knowledge of Judaism's historical and liturgical past.

For Islam, the Qur'an is a written revelation unto itself, which is physically separated from the Jewish holy books and the Gospels, but according to its own claims is so complementary to them that it supersedes them. The Qur'an is not a literal, physical appendix to the Hebrew and Christian revelations. And while there have been some Muslim theologians and commentators who read the books of Moses and Jesus and utilized them for their work,[13] that practice has been, unlike the Christian tradition, more the exception than the rule. In general, the Muslim world looks with a traditional wariness on attempts to read the Bible or the Gospels, as if doing so denigrates the Qur'an's position as the ultimate and final revelation that began with Moses, rose to a penultimate notch with Jesus, and ascended the final rung of the prophetic ladder with Muhammad.

On the other side, the Qur'an itself is hardly read by Westerners. There is a long tradition of Qur'anic translation and scholarship in the West, but only by specialists and the occasional Orientalist dilettante. Most investigations of Islam were instigated by Christian missionaries seeking knowledge of the faith in order to disprove it and, of course, show Muslims that Jesus actually fulfils the promise of Muhammad better than Muhammad himself.

The Qur'an's physical isolation from the Old and New Testaments does much of the heavy work of replacing its predecessors. Without an Arabic translation of the Jewish and Christian scriptures, the rank and file in the Islamic world will not have access to the books of Moses and Jesus. And the Qur'an itself tells and retells the stories of its grandfather and father faiths: Adam, Noah, Abraham, Isaac, Jacob, Joseph, Jesus, Mary and John the Baptist all enter and exit the Qur'an according to the idiosyncratic scheme of its compilation, and are recast in a distinctly Qur'anic mould. In many cases, the stories are only told to support Muslim claims to historical hegemony. The most famous example is Abraham's sacrifice of his son. The Christian and Jewish traditions assert that the son is Isaac. The Islamic tradition has always asserted that he is Ishmael. According to the Hebrew Bible, Ishmael is Abraham's first son through his wife Sarah's servant, the Egyptian Hagar. Isaac is the son that Abraham receives from Sarah during their old age. Isaac is the progenitor of Israel, while Ishmael was viewed as the ancestor of the Arab peoples. So the binding of Abraham's son is an important bone of contention between the two faiths. The two versions of the story reflect the two related peoples' notions of election and primogeniture. God asks Abraham to sacrifice his favourite son. The Muslims, as ancestors of Ishmael, think this was Ishmael, while the Jews, as the descendants of Isaac, think it was Isaac. We can give chronological support to the Hebrew Bible's version of the story of the binding of Abraham's son, but we cannot discount the import of the story in the Qur'an. According to most Muslim interpretation, the revelations in the Qur'an are the truth, while the stories told in the Hebrew Bible and Gospels have been corrupted or falsified. At the conclusion of the Qur'an's story of Abraham's sacrifice of his son, the book says as much 'We blessed him [Ishmael] and Isaac: but of their progeny are (some) that do right, and (some) that obviously do wrong, to themselves' (Qur'an 37.113). It is questionable for

Muslims to trust Jewish interpretation of biblical stories. So it is not just redundant for Muslims to read the stories in the Bible, it is a grave error.

Islam's enemies have long noted the extra-biblical and (for most Christians of a missionary bent) profane origins of many of the tales told in the Qur'an. But with the exception of Islamic scholars and the occasional Arabophile, that has been the extent of Westerners' attention paid to the Qur'an. A very unflattering treatise of the very mundane origins of the stories of the Qur'an (now available online)[14] was written by the Reverend W. Goldsak of the Christian Literature Society of London, Madras and Colombo in 1907. One section of this book explores the stories of Christian, Jewish and pagan origin in the Qur'an. His multi-barbed thesis explores how Muhammad pilfered his contemporaries' 'sacred books', at times seemingly randomly, for ideas and tales; and for the most part, Muhammad made non-canonical, and hence bad, choices. Rather than using the divinely sanctioned books of Judaism and Christianity, Muhammad borrowed from the apocryphal writings of Christian groups and from stories found in the Talmud (which Goldsak believed was merely a chronicle of bold-faced lies). He pointed to the famous story of Jesus fashioning birds from clay in his infancy, which was, we are told, pilfered from the spurious Gospel of the Infancy. Goldsak's spiteful book about Islam illustrates one of the great problems with forming a new religion. Compared to Christianity and Judaism, Islam was formed relatively recently; people can check its sources. Many of the Qur'an's sources point overwhelmingly to the syncretistic nature of Islam and its debt to the Jews and Christians of the Prophet's time.[15] A possible reason for the non-canonical stories found in the Qur'an is that the Jewish and Christian communities in Arabia did not yet have orthodox standards for their literature. Arabia was an area of the world that fell between the great world cultures of antiquity, and as such it became home to diverse people with heterodox thinking about the two monotheistic faiths of the West. The so-called Wild Jews of Arabia led semi-nomadic and nomadic lives with almost full political autonomy. Whether they recognized rabbinical authority in matters of scripture or not is unknown, but they were certainly powerful enough to offer significant military problems to the early followers of Muhammad. Arabia was also home to unorthodox Christian groups escaping from the control of the Church in Roman lands.

For the followers of Islam, the non-canonicity of the Qur'anic stories is not a marker of pilfering, but a special badge of distinction. Islam says that it tells stories about Jesus and the prophets of Israel unknown to their own traditions because Jews and Christians have corrupted those faiths and their works. Islam's history of interpretation has long held that portions of the Jewish and Christian bibles have been physically corrupted, which they say has mirrored, in a real sense, the corruption of the followers of their faiths. There was also a widespread belief in

Catholic circles, particularly in the seventeenth century, that the Hebrew bible had been altered and corrupted by rabbinical Jews in order to strike references to Jesus from the divine record.[16] Part of Islam's mission to prove itself correct rests on the assumption that Christians and Jews have corrupted the vessels of the original, pure, Abrahamic faith that Islam claims to represent and resurrect. For Muslims, the Islamic method of reading wins out and since there are no easily available translations of its predecessors, there is little opportunity to compare and contrast the stories it tells. The conclusion is rather clear: Islam is all that is needed and the Qur'an is all that needs to be read.

Judaism, Christianity and Islam, the Abrahamic religions, are related to each other, and have dense layers of overlap. But like with most families, conflicts have compounded through history and have been exasperated by poor communication, so there is no easy way to quickly untangle the areas of connection from those of disjuncture. Judaism rejects the divine claims of both Jesus and Muhammad. Christianity accepts the authenticity of the Jewish scriptures (and actually depends on the history of Israel), but not as an independent entity; only vis-à-vis their role as the sacred foundation for the coming of Jesus Christ through his kingship of Israel, and his function as the universal Messiah. Christians toss aside the whole array of Old Testament laws concerning ritual purity, sanctioned and forbidden foods, as a yoke that the coming of Jesus removed from the necks of Jews and Gentiles alike. Islam accepts the veracity of Judaism and Christianity as monotheistic movements and accords them certain rights under Islamic law, but only with a whole series of qualifications.[17] Jesus' divine sonship, and the whole apparatus of the Trinity, is anathema to Islam. It is idolatry at its worst, for it takes Jesus, whom traditional Islamic theology views as a great Jewish prophet in a line of prophets, and makes him a demi-god. Islam's rejection of Christianity even includes a denial of the physical facts of Jesus' crucifixion.[18] When crypto-Judaism developed in Spain and Portugal, these distinctions became highly relevant, as they allowed the Marrano faith to be created in a Christian milieu. A parallel event in the Muslim community, Moriscoism found more rocky soil, and crypto-Judaism hardly occurred at all in Muslim lands.[19]

Spanish identity and Roman Catholicism: the Cid and the purity of blood laws

History often seems to revolve around an axis of irony when historic actions have the opposite of their intended effect. The phenomenon of the Marranos of Iberia is an excellent example of this axiom. While we do not need a detailed history of the 'Reconquest' of Spain, we need to briefly address the historical backdrop of the creation of the Marranos.[20] For a very long time, the Christian Reconquest was viewed as a holy war to rid the peninsula of foreign North Africans, in order to re-establish the pure Roman Catholic Church in Spain, along with the Latin mass and all its accoutrements.[21] The story of the Reconquest was officially viewed through the lens of modern Spanish Nationalism, but the picture is more complicated than the pleasing stories that scholars and writers have told and retold about the Christian military encounter with Islam in Iberia.

We know that the picture of the Reconquest is considerably muddled. The impulses that led to the ousting of the Muslims of Spain and the subsequent unification of the peninsula under the combined house of Aragon and Castille had little do to with drives toward religious and racial purity,[22] which is a gloss that came from latter-day historians. We can see this no more clearly than in the cycle of tales told of the Cid, the legendary hero of the Spanish Reconquest. We seem to be presented with two Cids. The first is the Cid of the epic tales of romance and chivalry, and especially the Cid of the *The Poem of the Cid*, which shows us a man brimming with Christian piety. He is in and out of churches, genuflecting and praying. He is framed by his enemies and fights the Moors when exiled by the king of Castile. He selflessly helps to consolidate the holdings of the royal house that expelled him for the greater glory of the Crown and Church. But we also have the second Cid of the historical record: the mercenary prince who sold his services to the highest bidder, Muslim and Christian alike, and who at the end of his long and successful martial career apparently grew weary of enriching other people's coffers with his services and installed himself as a prince in the port city of Valencia.[23] His real name was Rodrigo Diáz de Vivar (*c.*1040–1099) and he was a minor nobleman from Castile. His *nom de guerre* reflects his mixed status: he was called *El Cid Campeador.* Cid is a Spanishized version of the Arabic title *Al Sayyid*, or the Lord, and *Campeador* is from the Spanish word for champion. His divided nickname seems to illustrate his dual loyalties.

The two versions of the Cid parallel two competing ways to read the Reconquest: one interpretation is a sacred tale, and the other is guided by more profane impulses. The rulers of Spain, both Muslim and Christian, were far more interested in advancing their own power in the shell of the once glorious Al-Andalus, than in any overarching pan-Christian or pan-Islamic sentiments. Later historians propagated the myth of the religiously motivated Reconquest. What really motivated the Christian counter-offensive in Muslim Spain was a host of power interests, often at odds with one another, and the religious purity of the peninsula was somewhere near the bottom of the list of motivations.

What is important for us is simply the *idea* of religious purity in Spain. And though it was not the paramount concern of the players in the

Reconquest, it took on vital importance in the years that followed. In this period immediately following the Muslim expulsion, considered Catholic Spain's Golden Age, we see in the very flowering of Spain's zenith, the kernel of decay. When the famous Ferdinand and Isabella died after 1514, the reign of the Habsburgs in Spain began. The Habsburg rulers, zestful players in European affairs, tossed Spain into the ring of international politics with mixed results. They went to war with France and England and in 1588 the famous Spanish Armada was sunk, sounding the first note in Spain's long descent into a politically and culturally challenged country.

In this time of growing national contraction, Spain suffered from an identity crisis that brought the Jewish problem to the forefront. The defeats Spain suffered, after such a promising start following the expulsion of Muslims and Jews during the Reconquest, led to a search for the causes of the national calamities. The obvious and unresolved problem of crypto-Jews, or Jews who had converted to Christianity in order to remain in Spain, but who practised Jewish rites in private, began to gain unprecedented importance in Spanish national self-consciousness. Suddenly, Spain became obsessed with cryptoism in all its manifestations. Undermining crypto-Judaism became central to the Spanish quest to root out the underlying cause of their national woes. One document that became central to this pursuit was a much older edict known as the *Estatutes de Limpieza de Sangre*, or 'The Statutes of the Purity of Blood'.[24] The statutes were written in 1449, but not used until the sixteenth century, and under the auspices of the Inquisition. The laws tried to prevent 'New Christians', the term used for converted Jews (many of whom were not recently converted at all, but in some cases the appellation 'New' remained with the descendants of the converts for centuries) from holding important positions in the clergy, in government and in education. The *Estatutes* were religious documents used for the secular purposes of stamping out crypto-Jewish religious practices in Spain, and later Portugal, by barring such people from important positions in the government and Church.

This had not always been the case. The forced conversion of Jews had largely been a formality. Officials were little concerned with the actual practices of the new converts and titular Catholics seemed satisfactory. Jews could leave Spain, and thousands did. But thousands did not and some, no doubt, embraced Christianity and forgot their Jewish roots. But many simply lived dual lives. For a time, a collective lie seemed satisfactory. Few officials asked uncomfortable questions, so eventually, the Christian quest for religious purity actually led to the very opposite result: a further muddling of religious identity. Spain developed a mania for secrecy, and we get the impression from the literature and accounts of travellers of the time, that the Spanish nation was controlled by a few clandestine cabals whose nefarious designs somehow manipulated every facet of the nation. The very pressure Spain put on its New Christians actually created the phenomenon it sought to avoid: Marranos, rather than disappearing from the pressure exerted on them, merely retreated further into the cracks while, in some instances through strategically offered bribes, they strengthened their hold on Spanish life. In the end, a second expulsion was deemed necessary, and Marranos travelled away from Spain to America, England, Holland and the lands of the Ottoman Empire, creating singularly unique slivers of Jewish life and sometimes going back to the fold of Judaism after a lapse of two centuries or more.[25]

It seems that many historical accounts of crypto-Jewish survival in Spain and Portugal in modern times may be inflated, motivated on the part of some researchers to prove nationalistic truths about Judaism. The Golden Age of Marranism on the Iberian peninsula was over by 1540. In Gittitz's exhaustive study of Inquisition documents related to crypto-Judaism, we can see that time did not strengthen Marranism, but weakened it. The loss of the collective memory about Jewish practice, coupled with the methodical patience of the Inquisition, led to the virtual eradication of most crypto-Jewish practices. But the fact is that some crypto-Jewish practices in Spain and Portugal survived, and in some cases well into the twentieth century, and there must have been some dynamic in place that helped preserve them. The Inquisition in Spain did not officially conclude its work until the early nineteenth century, but even the cessation of official inquisitional activity failed to eradicate the perceived stench of crypto-Judaism in the Spanish air, particularly in the countryside where archaic practices tended to continue with little friction. Something must have nourished these practices, and if Jewish memory is not the overriding factor, nor the pressure of the Inquisition, then what can it be?

Crypto-Judaism stopped being a true phenomenon in Spanish life by the eighteenth century, and certainly lost most of its vitality by the nineteenth century. But there seem always to have been people in Spanish lore who lit candles on Friday nights, very often placing them in a cupboard, sometimes without realizing that they were practising a Jewish rite with a distinctly Marrano flourish. So Marranism in its heyday offers us a golden example of syncretism with all of the characteristic elements in place – and a few unique to Marranism.

Marrano syncretism was not one of the organic types that came from the long acculturation of one religion exposed to an alien culture, nor was it the syncretism of one religion that had been forcibly annexed. Crypto-Judaism was, at first, an imposed syncretism. This is an important difference. The Jesus movement flirted with Greek culture over a long period of time, just as Islam accrued elements from its subject peoples over a period of 500 years or more. But the syncretism of the Marranos was abrupt. It happened almost overnight. After the practice of Judaism was outlawed in Spain, and shortly thereafter in Portugal, if formerly Jewish people wished to continue practising the faith of their ancestors, the only option was secret worship. But a dual allegiance to Judaism and Roman Catholicism quickly led, within the span of a few generations, to the development of a hybrid faith, born of oppressive circumstances, but quickly assuming a normative character.[26] For the crypto-Jew, Roman Catholicism was a false religion; the unsavoury circumstances of conversion led to its outward adoption, while Judaism was performed in secret at home. For the Marrano, that dualism became normative to such an extent that the paranoia of the crypto-Jew survives in the practice of Marranism, even when the forces that created the phenomenon were long gone, and despite the fact that after a certain point no one cared who was a Jew and who was not. As we shall see, an echo of the paranoia of the Marrano continued well into modern times, and the fear of discovery was incorporated into the body of Marranism even when the Marrano did not know what he or she was supposed to fear.

The crypto-Jews of Spain become the syncretistic Marranos

Rumours of crypto-Jewish holdovers circulated in Spain, Portugal and elsewhere well into the twentieth century.[27] The romantic idea of Jewish holdovers kept the rumours in currency, and the kernel of Marrano practices that did survive fed that need. In an important sense, these secret cabals of crypto-Jews became one of the abiding legends of Spanish life. The impact of Judaism and Islam on Spain was deep and the forces that uprooted it were violent and severe. Once the roots of Islam and Judaism had been excised from Spanish soil, the pain of extraction lingered on for generations. And for those outside the Iberian peninsula, ideas about the immutability of the Jewish nation fed the desire to find crypto-Jewish survivals.

At the beginning of the last century parts of rural Portugal near its northern border with Spain were as remote as any place on this globe. Very little in the way of change had arrived in the Bera Baiza region, where the towns of Belmonte, Fundao and Coriha can be found.[28] These sleepy, backwater villages proved to be the final enclaves of Marranism on the Iberian peninsula – at least in the forms that had existed in premodern times. These communities were 'discovered' in 1917 by Samuel Swartz, an itinerant mining engineer from Poland,[29] though it was actually locally well known that this area housed pockets of people who still associated themselves with Judaism, even as they professed an outward Catholic faith. The office of the Inquisition in Portugal certainly knew of their existence. These Portuguese Marranos were probably Spanish Jews who fled to Portugal to escape either conversion to Catholicism or expulsion from Iberia in 1492, only to be forced to convert by an order of the Portuguese Monarch (under pressure from Spain) in 1497.

This group of crypto-Jews was converted forcibly, in a single day. So, unlike in Spain, where at least exile was offered as an alternative to conversion (and where most Spanish Jews who converted presumably either had only a tenuous link to their faith to begin with, or decided that other factors – like keeping their possessions and remaining in their homes – were more important than remaining Jewish) the Portuguese Jews were the most nominal Catholics of all. Crypto-Judaism was thus robust in the New Christian community of Portugal.[30]

So Portugal started the same odyssey of chimeral purity as Spain, and set in motion the drives that created Marranism and preserved it, if in a somewhat fossilized form, until our time. It is noteworthy to mention that the last alleged Marrano burned at the stake by the Inquisition in Portugal was in 1760, a full 243 years after the mass conversions. The Inquisition was officially abolished in 1821.[31]

The Marranos discovered by Swartz were soon forgotten. They were 'rediscovered' in the 1930s by a Portuguese of New Christian blood named Barrios Basta, who made their cause his own and attempted to bring the Marranos of Portugal and Spain back into the fold of normative Judaism. After some initial successes, he ultimately failed.[32] The Marranos were forgotten again. The Marranos of Belmonte were then discovered once more in the 1990s, and once again we saw a popular groundswell of sympathy for their plight, and the desire to bring this long-isolated pocket of neglected Judaism back into the mainstream of Jewish life.

For the most part, the attempts to bring Marranos back to Judaism were dismal failures. Basta's victories, although seemingly successfully at first, proved to be hollow. Eventually, the Marranos of this remote region just resumed their old ways. The revival of Judaism in Belmonte in the last decade is therefore a bit disconcerting as past attempts to bring Marranos back into the Jewish fold have usually led to their abandoning both Marranism and Judaism. Much of that failure can be attributed to well-intentioned people confusing crypto-Judaism with Marranism, when they are two distinct phenomena. Crypto-Judaism existed by conscious fraud and deceit, but Marranism was mostly unconscious impulse, even though its shared similar fraudulent and deceitful strategies as crypto-Judaism. Marranism was a syncretistic creed, and one that needed secrecy in order to thrive. Bringing it out of doors killed it. The exposure of Marranism by well-intentioned outsiders actually accomplished what the Inquisition, with all its mechanisms, including its campaign of intimidation and its command of an organized structure of violence, could not fully do: root out what little crypto-Jewish practice remained in these isolated areas. Missionary Jews failed to see that Marranism was an evolution from their faith, and not a debased form of Judaism. Crypto-Judaism is kept hidden but also kept pure, as much as possible, behind the veil of secrecy. But Marranism is a real melding of Jewish practice with the Roman Catholic faith. It was a syncretistic faith, and was very different from either of its parents.

Some aspects of Marrano syncretism

The psychology of crypto-Judaism, and its offspring, Marranism, is rather easy to conceive: people were forced to observe a religion that was imposed upon them, and practise in secrecy the faith they preferred, or at the very least were attached to by familiarity and custom. The need to maintain secrecy was the abiding factor, and what led the crypto-Jews to mould their communal and individual life. Any or all outward, visible signs of Jewishness had to disappear from the outset.[33] Eventually a form of collective schizophrenia developed.

Almost from the beginning circumcision was discontinued, as it was too easy for the agents of the Inquisition to discover if a male child had a foreskin. The communal apparatus of Jewish life, like the procuring of ritually pure food and the avoidance of ritually impure food, became a problem that grew more and more difficult for crypto-Jews to solve. At first, it is most likely that many groups slaughtered animals in secrecy, but during the heyday of the Inquisition, this had to stop. What replaced it was a kind of ad hoc solution: crypto-Jews would not eat pork, for instance, on the Sabbath or important holy days. Fasting, always a component of Jewish worship, took on added importance for the Marranos. In order to avoid polluting themselves on festival days, they took to adding fast days to avoid possible contamination. Eventually, even the disclosure to Marrano children of their true identity became problematic, as children were more inclined to reveal secrets to outsiders than adults, so a custom developed where children were only told of their true identity as crypto-Jews on their thirteenth birthday. An ironic disclosure, the event shadowed a bar mitzvah: at the age when normative Jews are ushered into full membership of the Jewish ranks, the Marrano youth was simply told that he or she was a Jew.[34]

As the sixteenth century progressed, two generations of crypto-Jews were born with no first-hand knowledge of their religion. Here some of the classic hallmarks of staunch Marranism formed. As the normative, communal elements of Judaism faded, women, as the keepers of the hearth in pre-modern Spain and Portugal, became the bearers of Marrano culture. The documentary *The Last Marranos* demonstrates this quite clearly when a struggle ensues between the women of Belmonte,

who are the bearers of Marrano lore, and the men, who attempt to introduce (or reintroduce) Judaism. Women became the holders of collective
knowledge of the Marranos simply because Marranism, as a secret, domestic cult, fell within the confines of women. As we witness in *The Last
Marranos*, any and all questions about liturgy, the dates of festivals and
holidays, or dietary requirements and restrictions, are brought to two or
three older women who, in turn, learned this lore from their mothers.

This leads to an interesting aspect of Marranism: Judaism is highly
literate and as such bound to sacred books, written in Hebrew with commentaries in Hebrew and Aramaic. Crypto-Judaism, and then Marranism, soon had to dispense with written materials, both because having
Hebrew books or books about Jewish themes in Spanish or Portuguese
was a signal to the Inquisition of one's Jewish status; and also because, as
time progressed, fewer and fewer people had a knowledge of the ancient
tongues of Jewish learning and liturgy. So Marrano knowledge became,
with few exceptions, almost entirely oral. Eventually, Marrano knowledge of Hebrew was confined to a single word: *Adonai*, or 'My Lord'. In
later periods, as the influence of Catholicism fully permeated Marrano
religious life, this word became a fixture in Marrano prayers and was
often one of the few Jewish elements to be found in Marrano liturgical
expression. Historically, Jewish literacy has often been one of the most
important elements that has kept Jewish groups separate from their Gentile neighbours. The Talmud, in particular, is the lens through which
rabbinical Judaism views the world; it is a Jewish world in microcosm,
part sacred lore and part biblical commentary, and it provides the Jew
with a blueprint for the continuance of communal life. Without it, the
Marranos were left with the only book they had access to: the Hebrew
Bible, translated as the Old Testament in Latin, Spanish or Portuguese.
For a time, vernacular religious books were banned in Spain and possession of books in the Spanish or Portuguese tongues was viewed as a sign
of Marranism. This was an ironic enough situation for Jews whose very
conversion was designed to make them Catholic and hence more Spanish
or Portuguese.[35]

As we mentioned in the beginning of this chapter, the physical act of
placing the Hebrew Bible before the Gospels had the effect of grafting
Israel's sacred history on to Christianity's. But in the case of the Marranos, this grafting had a curious side-effect: it gave Marrano groups
access to their people's history, and while this glimpse was not viewed
through a rabbinical lens, it is still amazing how much resistance the
Marranos exhibited toward Roman Catholic presumptions of biblical
interpretation.

In the early first century and a half of Marrano existence in Iberia,
Marrano groups ransacked the Old Testament for their knowledge of
Jewish customs, but in many cases, the rules they found had ceased to

be practised by rabbinical Jews. For example, many Marranos refused to touch animal fat, in a zealous interpretation of the Levitical ordinance.[36] So they were forced to use vegetable oil in cooking, and because of this, oil-based foods have always been associated with distinctly Jewish cuisine in Iberia. Such foods as aubergines were associated, in the Spanish mind, with Jews and Muslims, so the Inquisition focused on foods like aubergines, and the special consumption of Jewish ritual foods in their enquiries into crypto-Jewish practice.[37]

There have always been enemies of Judaism who viewed the religion through the lens of Christianity. Some have envisioned Jewish practice as a cruel parody of Christianity: mock Masses, desecration of the host, and ritual slaughter of Christian children in a sacrilege of the passion of Jesus.[38] Eventually, as crypto-Jews took a turn to Marranism, they too began to view *Jewishness* through a christological lens. One common move was the conflation of Christian notions of the doctrine of individual salvation (through belief in Jesus Christ) with a belief in the Law of Moses. In other words, the Law no longer needed to be followed, but only believed in as an article of faith.[39]

An even more important christological distortion was the Marrano emphasis on Esther, the heroine of the biblical story in the book of the same name.[40] Purim, the Jewish holiday that celebrates the exploits of Esther, is a relatively unimportant festival in the normative Jewish calendar. But for the Marranos, Esther assumed the status of the most exalted cult figure, even evolving, in the later years of the Marrano experience, the name St Esther and even Queen Esther, who became a rival to Mary the Queen of Heaven.[41]

Purim is consciously crafted to be humorous. The well-known rabbinical injunction is that celebrants of Purim must get so drunk they cannot distinguish the phrases that curse Haman, the villain of the Esther story, from the blessings of Mordecai, the male hero. We find no such injunction in Marrano custom. Quite the contrary, the celebration of Queen Esther was one of the most solemn festivals in the Marrano calendar, eventually even rivalling Yom Kippur, the Day of Atonement. The reason this relatively unimportant holiday was elevated to such importance is simple: Just as Western Jews place a great deal of importance on the minor holiday of Hanukkah because of its proximity to the important Christian holiday of Christmas, so the Marranos elevated Esther because she bore the imprint of their distinctive communal and individual needs. Esther, forced to marry the king of Persia and hide her identity as a Jew, was the first Marrano. She was compelled to pray to the false gods of Persia, but maintained her devotion to the Jewish people and the Jewish God. At first, Esther's worship as a renegade Marrano acted as an effective compromise with Catholic practice. Worshipped in saintly garb, but from a distinctively Jewish angle, Esther, before becoming Saint Esther or Queen Esther, was a pathetic and poignant reminder of several elements that the converted Jews of Iberia had lost and never truly regained, including an independent Jewish communal life and an individual religious self-determination. It was as if, from the shattered orb of Jewish life, this half-Catholic and half-Jewish soul sprang up to fill the breach. She is, by necessity, an entity that fulfils many roles. She is the avatar of Jewish national aspiration, survival and victory in the face of the external pressures of destruction. But we find that she is a vestigial Jewish expression of the increasingly Catholic world-view of the Marranos. As more and more of the Jewish religion became a dim memory, Roman Catholic ideas, which were the only formal religious force in the lives of most Marranos after the first two or three generations in Iberia, became the only benchmark for religiosity. Even the expressions of revolt, like the worship of Saint or Queen Esther, took on a Catholic flair, and as this Jewish national hero transformed, she became, in essence, a Marrano version of the Virgin Mary. Her cult developed marked similarities to Marian worship; Marrano religion, as a religion of the oppressed, inevitably absorbed the values of the oppressor, even as they used the oppressor's values as an instrument of revolt.

Other rites were associated with Marranism. Washing hands was commonly associated with crypto-Judaism,[42] as well as a proclivity to face east, towards Jerusalem, during prayer. Refraining from eating pork became a kind of Marrano act of defiance par excellence in the classical ages of persecution.[43] Ironically, eating too much pork in public view (to throw people off the trail) was often viewed as a marker of crypto-Judaism. As we mentioned, fasting was a Marrano practice brought about to prevent eating banned food on holy days. As the cycle of the Jewish calendar became more confused and uncertain in the decades after the forced conversions, fasting became more and more prevalent. Fasting, though not unknown in the Roman Catholic liturgical cycle, became a suspect activity, and excessive fasting soon became a hallmark of crypto-Jewish practice. Sabbath worship and the refusal to worship images were two of the early fixations of the Inquisition.[44] The reason the Inquisition focused on these was that they are particularly stubborn forms of crypto-Judaism. The quote at the beginning of this chapter is a notorious invocation made by Marranos before entering a church: 'I come here to visit neither wood nor stone, I come only to worship you, Highest Adonai, who is that governs us.' Once that was said, the Marrano would then worship in the church like any other Catholic. Oddly, these practices, when conspicuously *not* practised, led to a kind of counterbalancing suspicion; it was as if the conspicuous consumption of pork, overindulgence in the worship of images and the marked preference for public work performed on the Sabbath were suspect activities that were meant to conceal Marranism.

In this context of pressure, secrecy and compensating poses, eventually both Marranism and the attempt to root it out became ironic gestures that accomplished very little. Marranos would practise crypto-Jewish rites that were increasingly divorced from normative Jewish practice. The Inquisition, in turn, would attempt to root out the vestiges of Jewish rites that remained! The Marranos would try to fool the Inquisition by making Jewish practice exclusively into domestic rituals run by women, or, in rural areas, by holding communal services outdoors and away from prying eyes. To further throw the authorities off their trail, Marranos would often celebrate the few holidays they still practised two or three days after the normal celebration day. And the Marrano religious calendar, which had become confused due to the devolution of knowledge about the intricacies of the Hebrew calendar, became even more of a muddle.

Eventually, the only holidays to survive (with the exception of some Sabbath worship and the holiday of Purim transformed into the Feast of Saint Esther) were Passover and Yom Kippur. Two of the most important festival days in the Jewish calendar, they are also days with an important domestic and individual component.[45] The preparation of Passover bread, a female rite done in secrecy in the home, took on added importance in Marrano communities. Yom Kippur became the *Dia Pura* in Portugal and Spain, as fasting can be done in relative privacy, and through certain precautions, detection can be avoided. In the early days of crypto-Judaism, when a great deal of Jewish identity was maintained but Jewish learning had deteriorated, Marranos gleaned their information about Passover rites from the Old Testament. They cooked whole lambs and held staffs in their hands, practices mentioned in the Bible but no longer performed by rabbinical Jews. As in the case of the worship of Saint Esther, Christianity's window on its common roots with Judaism helped to nourish Marranism even as it diluted Judaism. A form of primitive Judaism practised by the ancestors of modern, rabbinical Jews was both a reflecting and refracting element in the life of worshipping Marranos as it made them Jews and took their Jewishness away in one gesture.

We saw that the practices of crypto-Islam and Moriscoism in Iberia never developed as they did for the Jews.[46] One reason is that Muslims were tied to the reins of power in Spain, and hence they left in large numbers once they lost territory, returning to North Africa. Also different rules applied to the Muslim community that remained in Spain than did to the Jews. But, most importantly, Moriscos could not learn about their heritage from Christian books, so practising a secret existence, always difficult even under the best of circumstances, was nearly impossible for Spanish Muslims and their descendants who chose conversion over the option of leaving their ancestral home. Islam's status as the late revelation, and the physical isolation of the Qur'an from the Hebrew and Christian Bible, hurt the Moriscos' survival.

The phenomenon of Marranism has a kind of inevitable poetic logic and beauty. Marranism's genesis and continued existence in the isolated and sparse pockets of modern Portugal illustrate a lesson about religion, and the people who practise it, that is well worth recognizing: seemingly irreconcilable elements can always be reconciled by someone, somewhere. Dissimilar parents can raise a child they never anticipated. And something that is *impure* is often pure in someone else's eyes. It is telling to realize that most Marranos who lived in isolation (until the birth of mass media) believed themselves to be the last Jews alive on the earth. There is a fitting justice to this apocalyptic vision: to be unique is to be alone. There were few lonelier people than the crypto-Jews and their progeny, the Marranos. Marranism *became* a cult whose very secrecy inbred a sense of isolation; and isolation, in turn, bred a sense of secrecy. It became a stark circle of loneliness, only mitigated by the sense of community that we found expressed among Marranos. Marranos knew who they were; they knew each other and they had the distinctly Jewish preoccupation with unfolding history, the inevitability of suffering that often accompanies it, and the communal sense of mission that can elevate suffering to a vision of the sublime.

For many Jewish writers, crypto-Judaism and Marranism became symbolic of Jewish resistance in the face of persecution, and this took on additional emphasis following the Holocaust. But Marrano survival is only partially a monument to the persistence of Jewish memory; it is also a keynote to the human universality of the inevitability of change and transformation. The Marranos were not merely a religious and cultural hangover from a time of great stress and turmoil. Islam and Judaism were wrenched free of the Iberian soil, a drastic event for the region that was much like losing a limb. For the Spanish and Portuguese, attempts to purify the land had only accomplished the opposite effect: a sense of semi-permanent pollution. Defeats in the world only seemed to confirm this sense of contamination. There followed purges, burnings, accusations, secrecy . . . and from this brew Marranism emerged, and its vitality in the face of opposition was truly impressive. But its existence and continued survival were not a monument to an amputation. Quite the contrary, Marranism was about transformation and regeneration – it was about syncretism in its boldest sense.

Syncretism and transformation: Marranism as a syncretistic blend of Judaism and Roman Catholicism

This important conclusion leads to the question: what is the nature of Marranism? We need to look at the attempts to bring the Marranos back into the fold of normative Judaism to understand this general question.

The great Marrano revival of Barros, in the early part of the twentieth century, failed. After some initial success at the beginning, Marranos went back to their old ways, or simply abandoned Marranism altogether. Judaism, a religion that is more preoccupied with communal salvation than with individual redemption, brought the Marranos into the public sphere, but Marranism had incorporated secrecy, duplicity and stealth into the very fabric of its existence, while normative Judaism had not. Once secrecy was taken out of the Marrano equation, impulses to become a Jew withered away. People can learn to incorporate fear into a practice until it becomes, in a certain sense, comfortably mundane. The Marranos were no longer Roman Catholic and no longer Jews: they were a third phenomenon that was a syncretistic blend of the two. As we see in the case of the Marranos, syncretism can take on astonishing forms; all manner of practices that seem contradictory can exist harmoniously. We see this when Marranism works, and we see it fall apart when Marranism is brought to light. The Marrano is no longer a Jew or a Roman Catholic. She must remain what she is or die.

We are far from the vision of men like Judah Ha-Levi and Maimonides, who seem to have little in common with Marranos slinking about in back rooms, secretly making matzoth in an atmosphere of tension and haste. The masters of the Sephardic world were Jews whose work has a universal appeal. They did not live secret lives. Marranos seem to be the last in line of Spanish Jews – a mere shrunken remnant. In terms of visibility and influence they stand at the opposite pole to the great Jews of Spain's history, public figures of great eminence like Samuel Ha-Nagid (933–1055), who deserves a place with Maimonides and Judah Ha-Levi. Ha-Nagid was the court vizier to the Muslim king of Granada, a poet, linguist (both in Hebrew and Arabic), a classical scholar and a soldier. Supposedly, he led the King of Granada's troops into battle and is credited with being the first Jew to lead an army since the Bar Kochba rebellion in AD 135. He scandalized pious Muslims for this and lesser 'offences' like riding a horse and carrying a sword, activities which were illegal for Jews in a Muslim state. His high profile and visibility as a Jew in the public arena was the very opposite of a Marrano. We can see this in the great range of his poetry, considered some of the finest verse ever penned in Hebrew. There are very public records of his feats in war leading Muslim troops, and he celebrated some in poems like 'The Battle of Alfuente', where he describes with vividness the chaos of battle, where 'every face turned red or black'.[47] Ha-Nagid also wrote a poem to his absent brother called 'Lament for His Brother', a paean to the brevity of existence in 'The Prison', and odes to wine in 'Winter Wine Song' and simply 'Wine'.[48] There is a love poem to a young man, entitled 'The Beautiful Boy', and a long, bitter lament about the inevitability of death called, appropriately, 'The Fear of

Death'. Samuel Ha-Nagid was a man who lived his life in full view. His pen recorded his experiences, making his life and career the very opposite of the Marranos', his unlikely descendants. If Samuel Ha-Nagid was a hero of normative Judaism, then what was the Marrano?

Even if the Marranos had little to offer normative Judaism, they have much to add to the study of syncretism. The Marrano teaches us that the standard lines of demarcation between the Abrahamic religions are specious. Jews can become Christians and still believe they are Jews. Jewish notions can take on Christian dress, and become a third thing, related to its parents but curiously different. Most members of a 'pure faith' dislike hybrid religions because they illustrate that barriers created between two 'pure' religious expressions are artificial and not inevitable. They can easily dismiss the Marranos as a fringe case existing on the borderline of religious experience. But often the 'borderline' can teach much about the 'core'. Where else can ideas be tested than against a point of contact with dissimilar ideas? We will see this repeatedly when examining other examples of syncretism: in the Balkans, where Islam and Christianity clashed and a tremendous amount of creative religious energy was released; in Akbar's India, where rival religions warred and coalesced into new creations; and in the Kabbala, where age-old notions of polytheism returned to Judaism, colliding with the world of monotheism to unleash a marvellous world of mythology not seen in Judaism since the early days of the religion. The clash of colliding opposites can release energy of an astonishing magnitude and it gives us our first promising look at syncretism's wide range, variety and regenerative properties.

Chapter summary

Islamic Spanish culture from AD 711 to 1492 was a time of great contrast. Christians, Jews and Muslims lived in close proximity to each other, sometimes in peace, sometimes at war, sometimes working closely together, and at other times segregated. In general, the Islamic polities in Spain were tolerant towards Christians and Jews, allowing them to work in government, often at high levels, and participate in the artistic and cultural life of the distinctive Andalusi culture that soon developed on the Iberian peninsula. Muslim rulers in Spain tended to be pragmatists, searching for the most talented men for government posts regardless of religious affiliation. Although the stresses and strains of pre-Reconquest Spain and Portugal should not be downplayed, there was an element of inclusiveness in the Muslim societies in Iberia that was severely curtailed once Spain was united in 1492 under Christian monarchs. Recently, the return of Muslims to Spain, especially in such old Muslim strongholds like Granada, has exposed these tensions. Spanish culture has been forced to confront religious and ethnic pluralism for the first time in nearly 500 years, and the growing pains have been considerable.

The expulsion and conversion of Jews in Spain in 1492, and later in Portugal in 1497, was one of early Spain's answers to the vexing problem of religious diversity. These conversions, rather than fostering unity, led to the problem of crypto-Judaism, in which people practised a secret, mostly domestic Judaism, while publicly performing the rites of Roman Catholicism. Eventually, this religious schizophrenia in Spain and Portugal produced the Marranos, groups of people who practised a syncretistic religion that incorporated elements of Jewish rite with Roman Catholicism. Many fascinating inversions and ironic productions were created by individual Marranos and Marrano communities; one startling example involves Saint Esther, the heroine of the Book of Esther, who is celebrated yearly during the celebration of Purim. This joyous holiday in normative Judaism became, for the Marranos, a day of fasting and sorrow. Esther transformed to Saint Esther, and finally Queen Esther, taking on many of the attributes of the Virgin Mary.

The Marranos moulded their saints with a strident tone of defiance. Marrano identity was forged by coercion and deception, and was highly irregular and idiosyncratic, making many of their customs and practices prime examples of the porous nature of the boundaries between the Abrahamic religions.

Draw your own conclusions

Is the relationship between the Abrahamic religions strictly hierarchical?

Due to the order in which they were created, does Judaism inform Christianity, and is Islam, in turn, informed by Judaism and Christianity?

Using the Marranos as our standard, how can we best define the complex set of relationships between the Abrahamic religions?

Again, using the Marranos as our benchmark, what role does borrowing and syncretism take in those relationships?

Is Marrano syncretism aberrant or abnormal? What does normality mean in religious life and organization?

What does Marrano syncretism tell us about the lines of demarcation between Judaism and Christianity?

Is syncretism between Judaism and Christianity more likely than between Judaism with Islam or Islam with Christianity?

Further reading

For a sample of Andalusi Jewish poetry:
T. Carmi (trans. and ed.) (1981), *The Penguin Book of Hebrew Verse*, Hebrew and English Edition, New York: Penguin.

For a scholarly overview of the challenges of reading the Qur'an:
Neal Robinson (1996), *Discovering the Qur'an: A Contemporary Approach to a Veiled Text*, London: SCM Press.

For a brief history of Iberia from the fall of the Visigoth kings to the consolidation of Spain by the House of Castile and Aragon:
Richard Fletcher (1990), *The Quest for the Cid*, New York: Alfred Knopf.
Maria Rose Menocal (2002), *The Ornament of the World: How Jews, Muslims and Christians Created a Culture of Tolerance in Medieval Spain*, Boston: Little, Brown & Co.

For more detailed accounts of Marrano history and practice:
David M. Gitlitz (1996), *Secrecy and Deceit: The Religion of the Crypto-Jews*, Philadelphia and Jerusalem: The Jewish Publication Society.
Joachim Prinz (1973), *The Secret Jews*, New York: Random House.
Cecil Roth (1947), *A History of the Marranos*, Philadelphia: The Jewish Publication Society.

Notes

1 Tracey Wilkinson, 'Islam's Claim on Spain', *The Los Angeles Times*, 18 January 2005.

2 Carmi, *The Penguin Book of Hebrew Verse*, p. 344.

3 Carmi, *Hebrew Verse*, p. 343.

4 Carmi, *Hebrew Verse*, p. 342.

5 Carmi, *Hebrew Verse*, p. 347.

6 Moses Maimonides (1989), *Mishneh Torah, Hilchot Yesodei Hatorah (Laws of the Foundation of the Torah)*, Rabbi Eliyahu Touger (trans.), Jerusalem and New York: Moznaim Publishing, p. 32.

7 Menocal, *The Ornament of the World*, pp. 248–51.

8 Hyam Maccoby (1981), *Revolution in Judea: Jesus and the Jewish Resistance*, New York: Taplinger, for a general discussion of the politics surrounding the first Jewish Revolt and the role of Jesus and his followers in that revolt.

9 George W. E. Nickelsburg (2003), *Ancient Judaism and Christian Origins: Diversity, Continuity and Transformations*, Minneapolis: Fortress Press, for a rigorous view of the complex relationship between first-century Judaism(s) and the early Christian movement.

10 Acts of the Apostles, 11.1, 15.1–40, 16.1–4, *NJB*.

11 Pierre-Antoine Bernheim (1996), *James, Brother of Jesus*, John Bowden (trans.), Paris: Noesis. I am thinking specifically of the so-called Council of Jerusalem in Acts of the Apostles 15.1–22, and Paul's letter to the Galatians, 2.1–10; here the early Church debated the issue of circumcision of Gentile converts and

the wider issue of adherence to the Jewish Law in general. Both in Acts and Paul's letters we can see that there was a strong Judaizing element in the early Church and an equally vocal element that wanted to relax or even do away with Jewish Law. See Bernheim's book for more on this topic.

12 Francine Klagsburn (1996), *Jewish Days*, illustrated by Mark Podwol, New York: Farrar, Straus & Giroux, pp. 74–5. The Greek translation of the Hebrew Bible by the Greek-speaking Jews of Alexandria into Greek was a seminal moment in the history of Christianity. The miracle of its translation was a feast day for the Jews of Alexandria, but for later rabbinical Jews it was viewed as a calamity and they observed it with a fast.

13 Andrew Rippin (1993), 'Interpreting the Bible through the Qur'an', in G. R. Hawting and Abdul Kader A. Shareet (eds), *Approaches to the Qur'an*, London: Routlege. According to Rippin, few Muslim scholars actually read the Hebrew or Christian bible until contemporary times. There was a mediating body of literature, compiled by Muslims and written in Arabic, that interpreted Bible stories through a Qur'anic lens, pp. 249–59.

14 http://www.answering-islam.org/Books/Goldsack/Sources/index.htm

15 The nineteenth-century French Orientalist Ernest Renan said Islam was born and grew 'in the full light of history'. For a more complex view, see Fletcher, *The Quest for the Cid*, Chapter 2, 'Al-Andalus', pp. 10–27. For a more orthodox delineation of Islam's formation, see Hourani, *The History of Arab Peoples*, Chapter 1, 'A New Power in the World' pp. 7–21.

16 Michael Pollack (1980), *Jews, Mandarins and Missionaries*, Philadelphia: Jewish Publication Society, pp. 15–38.

17 So called Dhimmi status (from the Arabic root 'dh-m-m', where 'dhimma' means 'being in the care of') conferred rights and restrictions on Peoples of the Book – mainly Christians and Jews, but often other groups as well. The most salient are the following.

Rights:
· protection of life, wealth and honour by the Muslim state (even against other co-religionist states)
· right to reside in Muslim lands
· right of worship according to their own religion
· right to work and trade.

Exemptions:
· exemption from paying *zakah* 'alms to the poor'
· exemption from being drafted in military service
· exemptions from religious duties specific to Muslims
· exemptions from personal Muslim laws (e.g. marriage, divorce).

Obligations:
· paying *jizya* (Poll tax)
· paying land tax.

For more, see http://en.wikipedia.org/wiki/Dhimmi

18 Hourani, *The History of Arab Peoples*, p. 28.

19 Dan Ross (1984), *Acts of Faith: A Journey to the Fringes of Jewish Identity*, New York: Schocken Books. There are examples of crypto-Jews in Muslim cultures. See above pp. 62–82 for a brief treatment of crypto-Jews in Iran; for crypto-Jews in Turkey, pp. 83–98.

20 Menocal, *The Ornament of the World* is an excellent popular treatment of this topic as well as others relating to Islamic Spain.

21 Menocal, *The Ornament of The World*, pp. 67–78.

22 Gitlitz, *Secrecy and Deceit*, pp. 15–18.

23 For the Cid of romance, see Rita Hamilton and Janet Perry (trans.) (1984), *The Poem of the Cid*, London: Penguin Classics. For a full treatment of the Cid of romance, history and myth, see Fletcher, *The Quest for the Cid*. Here, the phenomenon of Rodrigo Diaz is treated against the entire backdrop of post-Roman Empire Iberia, including a look at the resurgence of the Cid in the twentieth century in the hands of Spanish nationalists.

24 Prinz, *The Secret Jews*, pp. 60–4.

25 For more on the Marrano Diaspora, see Jonathan Irvine Israel (2002), *Diasporas Within a Diaspora: Jews, Crypto-Jews, and the World of Maritime Empires 1540–1740*, Leiden, The Netherlands: Brill.

26 Gitlitz, *Secrecy and Deceit*, p. 81.

27 This is also the case in other Spanish-speaking areas of the New World, including the American South West and California.

28 Ross, *Acts of Faith*, p. 18.

29 Ross, *Acts of Faith*, p. 27.

30 Gitlitz, *Secrecy and Deceit*, p. 50.

31 Ross, *Acts of Faith*, p. 30.

32 For more information on Basta and the Portugese Marranos, see Ross, *Acts of Faith*, pp. 26–51.

33 Roth, *A History of the Marranos*. Most of the information in this section is from Chapter 7, 'The Religion of the Marranos'.

34 Roth, *The History of the Marranos*, p. 174.

35 Gitlitz, *Secrecy and Deceit*, p. 428.

36 Roth, *A History of the Marranos*, p. 179.

37 David Gitlitz and Linda Kay Davidson (1999), *A Drizzle of Honey: The Lives and Recipes of Spain's Secret Jews*, New York: St Martin's Press, for an interesting reconstruction of crypto-Jewish cuisine, p. xiv, and pp. 46–8 where aubergines and crypto-Jews are discussed.

38 Gitlitz, *Secrecy and Deceit*, p. 24.

39 Gitlitz, *Secrecy and Deceit*, p. 89. Apparently, this was common in the Morisco community as well. James T. Monroe (1974), *Hispano-Arabic Poetry: A Student Anthology*, Berkeley, CA: University of California Press. Read Monroe's extensive survey of Arabic poetry in Al-Andalus (Spain and Portugal) for how this impulse expressed itself among crypto-Muslims, pp. 70–1.

40 A late book in the canon, one of Esther's major claims to fame is that it does not contain a single reference to God (a distinction it shares with The Song of Songs).

41 Ross, *Acts of Faith*, p. 159.

42 Roth, *The History of the Marranos*, p. 178.

43 Roth, *The History of the Marranos*, p. 179.

44 Roth, *The History of the Marranos*, p. 180.

45 Interestingly, American Judaism underwent a similar transformation. As American Jews adopted American culture, Jewish expression became increasingly domestic. See Joselit Weissman (1994), *The Wonders of America: Reinventing*

Jewish Culture 1880–1950, New York: Hill and Wang.

46 See note 39 about the Moriscos.
47 Carmi, *Hebrew Verse*, p. 286.
48 Carmi, *Hebrew Verse*, p. 297.

3

The House of War: Islam for the Shady Grove

A secret turning in us
makes the universe turn.
Head unaware of feet,
and feet head. Neither cares.
They keep turning. (Rumi)

Redecorating Balkan mosques

The Balkans have long been a hotbed of religious and ethnic tensions, and to such a degree that the term 'Balkanization', as it has entered the English language, usually means to divide (a region or territory) into small, often hostile units. With the fall of Yugoslavia in 1991 many such small, hostile units quickly set about destroying each other. A curious by-product of the Balkan War was a reminder that a native form of Islam exists in the south-eastern corner of the continent. In 1992 Bosnia and Hercegovina declared independence from the crumbling Yugoslav state. The most ethnically diverse of the former Yugoslav republics, Bosnia was 44 per cent Muslim, 31 per cent Serbian, and 17 per cent Croatian.[1] Tensions between these three groups soon reached boiling point, and by 1995, when the Bosnian War was over, thousands were dead, millions were displaced, and many of the physical structures in the region were damaged or destroyed.

Centuries'-old ethnic and religious tensions ignited the conflict. Bosnian Muslim civilians were singled out for rape and ethnic cleansing by Serbs and Croatian Christian militias. The physical inheritance of Muslims in the region was nearly destroyed: mosques, libraries and madrassas were looted and burned. The 500-year-old cultural and religious inheritance of the Bosnian Muslims was nearly wiped out in 4 years of conflict.

In the aftermath of the war, Bosnian Muslims have rebuilt many of their most important architectural symbols. The Stari Most, the Old Bridge spanning the Neretva River in Mostar, Bosnia, which was designed by the great Ottoman Architect Hayudrin in 1556, was destroyed by Croatian gunners in November 1993. Under the auspices of UNESCO and other groups, the bridge was rebuilt according to its original plans in 2004. But other rebuilding projects have not been as benign. During the war the exterior and façade of Sarajevo's greatest mosque, the Gazi Husrevbeg, were damaged, while its ornate and rich interior, which is one of the finest examples of Islamic sacred buildings in south-eastern Europe, survived more or less intact. Recently, Saudi Arabian and Gulf State aid groups have begun to 'reconstruct' Balkan mosques damaged during the war, but often, as was the case with the Gazi Husreveg, this reconstruction has a political agenda. The work done to the Gazi Husreveg went beyond repairs to the damaged exterior when the aid groups effectively stripped the interior of its ornateness, leaving what has been described as a 'white-washed box'.[2] Its interior now more closely conforms to Saudi-style Wahhabi fundamentalist notions of the proper interior decor of a mosque, and is illustrative of a certain trend: the spread of Wahhabi fundamentalist Islam to areas it did not traditionally reach. (We will examine Wahhabism in more detail in the next chapter.) The Wahhabi renovators' intentions are clear: they seek to eradicate the eclectic and syncretistic form of Islam practised in the Balkans for nearly 500 years. By making mosques in the Balkans conform to Saudi and Gulf State standards, they clearly hope to influence the doctrines expounded in those mosques, and spread Wahhabism abroad. This modern fundamentalist action brings us to a discussion of the particular form of Islam the Wahhabists are trying to eradicate. But in order to understand the startlingly diverse forms of Islam practised in the Balkans, we must begin with a look at the history of the region in some detail.

The syncretistic Turkomans and a shamanist version of Islam

In many ways we still live with the ghost of the Ottoman Turkish Empire. It is not one of those unobtrusive ghouls that strolls down the hall and disappears through a wall. This ghost makes a house nearly uninhabitable. The suppressed political, religious and social energies of Muslim peoples, kept at bay and controlled by the Ottoman Empire, were released when the Ottoman state collapsed.[3] The Ottoman Turks were the last Muslim government that could deal with the West as an equal on the stage of war and diplomacy. The problems we see today, of Muslim peoples subject to the West in various ways, did not exist in the same manner from the rise of the Ottoman state until the defeat of the Ottoman sultanate in 1918; Muslim peoples always had the option of looking to the Turks as an Islamic power that could deal effectively with the Europeans. The Turks had numerous military successes against Europe; at a time when Islam was retreating from Spain and Portugal in the west of Europe, the Ottomans were on the rise in the east, knocking on Europe's eastern door. Eventually, the Turks would drive deep into Central Europe, even threatening Vienna in 1683 before being repelled. They controlled a sizeable portion of the Balkans until the twentieth century, and continue to inhabit a chunk of Europe across the Bosporus to this day. The Turks destroyed the final vestiges of the Roman Empire in the East when they captured Constantinople in 1452, thereby crowning their military and political achievements with a unique brand of cultural infusion that combined their Turkish tribal past with Islam, blending this with the vestiges of the Byzantine Empire (the Eastern Roman Empire), which they had subdued and supplanted.

Importantly, the Turks, so firmly associated with Turkey, were not originally from the area that bears their name. We often forget that before modern transportation entire populations often moved, and often great distances; we live in a time when individuals can travel from one side of the globe to another with ease, and we tend to forgot that *whole peoples* often migrated from one area to another, no matter what difficulties were encountered. The Turks were a nomadic people that lived in the hinterlands of Asia, on the plains of southern Siberia and the expanse between the Caspian Sea and the Altaic Range.[4] They began to travel into the Muslim lands to the west some time in the tenth century, when a confederation of Ghuz and Oghuz tribes established themselves in the area of the Aral Sea. Following their conversion to Islam, they became known as Turkomans, and they began a gradual but steady ascent to power in the Abbasid state in Baghdad. The twists and turns of this don't concern us here, but the general picture does: the nomadic Turks were a restless people, and they organized themselves around strong men, their loyalty to whom made and broke confederations. Often, subordinates to these strong men revolted, or a strong man felt that his reign was threatened by a rising star, and this set in motion the movement of more Turks, who migrated to new territories in search of sanctuaries or new power bases. The natural migration pattern of the Turkoman peoples was west, away from established Muslim regimes and more settled Turks in the east, and toward the fringes of the Islamic world – at this time the border with the crumbling Byzantine Empire. Once Turks had established themselves as the rulers *pro tempore* in Baghdad in 1055, this movement intensified, since there were too many Turkomans to be usefully employed in the capital city of Islamic power.

The ghazi–akritoi wars: the base for Balkan Islam's syncretism

Interestingly enough, an area where perpetual warfare occurs is often a congenial location for a people prone to an unsettled lifestyle. This creates a curious situation where common enemies, fighting a continual war, end up having a great deal in common. They form a culture that can be quite different from the respective home fronts they are supposedly fighting for; in essence, long, protracted conflict between two fixed enemies creates a standard of measurement unique to both sides and not transferable to those on the outside.

From this welter, one particular Turkish group, who were descendants of the tribal chieftain Seljuq, and who were banned from Baghdad for political intrigue, established a power centre in Asia Minor, in Anatolia, the location of present-day Turkey. Starting in 1071 in this rough-and-tumble frontier zone, there developed a new class of warrior called the *gazi*. They organized themselves on multiple levels, and were a replenishable mercenary class. They set up shrines for their saints and holy men, and whenever possible moved into new areas, where they actively proselytized in new neighbourhoods. On the opposite side of the border, on the Byzantine Greek front, lived the *akritoi*, the Christian counterpoint to the *gazis*. This society of holy warriors, including both the Islamic and Christian sides, developed a code of behaviour and chivalry that was acceptable to both parties, and from this martial synchrony was laid the groundwork for the eclectic variety of Islam that would develop in Turkey and the Balkans. On the Byzantine–Turkic border there was a tendency on both the side of Muhammad and the side of Christ to ignore abstruse matters of theology and concentrate on more practical matters – like lost or gained territory, or rules of warfare. In fact, the *gazi* and *akritoi*, as defenders of the faith, fell far short of the orthodox standards of their day. Men on both sides of the religious gulf came from areas far away from the centres of Islamic or Christian power; in many instances, they were newly minted Christians or Muslims, still bearing the marks of the home-grown paganism they had supposedly so recently shed. A Christian–Muslim fusion religion gradually began to take shape. It was a mixture of superstition, mysticism, local traditions and pagan beliefs,[5] and the line between the faiths became blurred. Religion became more a matter of which direction the prevailing political wind blew than a matter of specifics about dogma and creed. In this area of the world, religion became more about local inclination than overarching policy.

The period of the *gazi–akritoi* fusion had a profound impact on this corner of Europe and Asia Minor, and also became a high water mark for syncretism in Europe, particularly in the east. This chapter will easily lead us into the next, about the worship of saints and their cults, since the *gazi–akritoi*, with their tradition of strong men/holy warriors, became hopelessly entangled with the inclination of the people of the Balkans to venerate holy sages. Often, in the history of syncretism, a movement that was peripheral, existing on the margins of an established world order, becomes central. Originally a struggle between two opposing systems, it became, by the very dynamism of people mixing and colliding at the margins, something wholly different and central. Some of the most colourful, long-lasting and strongest examples of syncretism were created in this welter. So on the border between Asia and Europe occurred a curious mix of forced and voluntary conversion to both Islam and Christianity and a colonization of Muslim Turks in the European Balkans. This proved to be the ripest possible ground for syncretism to flourish, and examples abound at the highest and lowest levels of Ottoman society. We are interested for the most part in the peasantry, but a quick glance at the upper reaches of Ottoman political culture is revealing as well.

Just like the Christian Reconquest of Spain, the Ottoman advance into Anatolia and south-western Europe was accomplished by military victories and strategic alliances. Byzantium had already crumbled into three smaller states by the time of the Turkish arrival in the area in the thirteenth century;[6] the Turks made some of these countries client states or vassals, solidifying their hold by well-arranged marriages between the Christian royal rulers and their own ruling families.

Within a generation, offspring of these unions appeared in Ottoman royal circles, and men who were literally half Christian and half Muslim eventually gained the reins of Muslim power. These men were primed for a religious eclecticism that went hand-in-glove with their political pragmatism. As products of two worlds, they felt naturally justified to claim power in each.

One example involves an Ottoman ruler named Bayezid I (1360–1403). He had four sons who after his death waged a protracted war against each other for the succession to their father's throne. Their names are an indication of the internationalism that existed in Ottoman ruling circles at this time: the oldest was named Suleyman, the Arabic equivalent to Solomon. Another was named Musa, the Arabic version of Moses. Next was Isa, the Turkish equivalent to the name Jesus, and finally Mehmed, the Turkish version of the name of the Prophet. All these children were the result of mixed marriages, and their subsequent political struggles were further complicated by their competing senses of loyalty. As with the struggle for control of Iberia, in the earlier stages of the fight for Turkey and the Balkans, there was no theological rule of thumb for political alliances. A crass (but honest) realpolitik ruled the scene.[7]

When rulers have this eclectic self-vision, we can expect it to trickle down to other parts of society, both in Turkey and in the Balkans. In this corner of Europe, syncretism became an instrument of rapid political conquest. Unlike the syncretism that was practised by the Marranos, it was not secretive. A religious uniformity, even though it was specious and superficial, was the rallying cry of Spain, a country that told stories to itself to justify bitter defeat. In the Balkans, a mixed faith was an open phenomenon; 'normative' Islam was not the norm at all during those days, nor was an Orthodox Christianity. Of course there were individuals who preached the Sunni and Orthodox hard line. But these voices of a *pure* creed were drowned by an even stronger chorus of voices: those of a new folk pragmatism.

The religious diversity of the Balkan peoples: the persistence of pagan practices

Often, 'simple' agrarian people give themselves what they need with startling sophistication. They do this despite cries from the outside that what they do is corrupt, and even while their extreme honesty appears crass and rude to outside eyes. No better example is found than in the variety of Islam practised in the Balkans from the time of the Ottoman invasions in the fifteenth century until, in some areas, well into the twentieth century and even today.

In order to understand this vibrant and eclectic Islam as it was practised – an Islam that is adorned, in so many ways, with the peculiar aroma of a particular people in a particular time and in a unique place – we need to backtrack just a bit.

In scholarship, *paganism* is usually a catch-all phrase for the religious and philosophical movements and trends that existed before the advent of monotheism, and its specific expression in the Abrahamic religions. This is, of course, a presumption that there is a clear line of demarcation between 'paganism' and the thing that superseded it, called 'monotheism'. The clearest supposed borderline between the two is the notion of one god versus a plurality of gods. Paganism is the realm of a plurality of gods, while monotheism is the arena of one god. However, many archetypal 'pagan' thinkers have often spoken as if there was one god (here Plato and Aristotle spring to mind, and a host of Hellenistic religions and philosophies that conceive of the divine in the singular[8]), while most monotheistic religions, including the Abrahamic religions, have a host of lesser deities that inhabit the divine realm and function as de facto gods and goddesses. In religions less squeamish about pluralism, they would be called such. The word 'pagan' is itself a telling artefact: the word comes from the Latin *paganus*, a country-dweller, which is derived from the word *pagus,* a country or rural district. In the Anglo-Saxon tradition this parallels the origin of the word *heathen*: one who lives in the country, heath or woods.[9]

These words capture in our language, like fossils, a moment in the evolution of Christianized peoples. Christianity originally took root in the urban centres of Rome and its provinces and only later did it reach the *pagus*. The idea of a pagan being a country-dweller is actually a misnomer, since it appears that paganism continued to exist as an urban phenomenon in all places and at late times, even in the dusk of Roman paganism.[10]

The suppression of paganism was an irregular and spotty affair, successful in some areas and a formal failure in others. But by the fifth century, the Roman Empire was officially a Christian state. Under the law code of the Emperor Justinian, every child born in the Empire had to be baptized. This made everyone born in the Empire (with the exception of the Jews) at least a nominal Christian, but enforcing actual orthodoxy was problematic. Despite repeated measures to eradicate paganism, it continued to be observed in the late Roman Empire, and even where Christian uniformity was successful, pagan practices still abounded. By AD 1000, Christianity had spread beyond the confines of the collapsed Roman Empire. The conversion of the Germanic peoples outside Rome's traditional borders was facilitated by the conversion of Germanic leaders, who then compelled their peoples, at least nominally, to convert. The Germans, in turn, waged holy crusades against their neighbours, the pagan Slavs, during the 1100s, who were collected as booty and converted to the conquerors' faith.[11] Entire Slavic countries were converted to Christianity either by way of their leaders' defections or through forced conversion through conquest (including Bulgaria in AD 865, Poland in AD 966, and Russia in AD 988).[12]

In the Balkans, there is no evidence of large blocks of *overt* pagans at the time of the Turkish invasions in the fourteenth and fifteenth centuries.[13] Quite the contrary, both rural and urban south-eastern Europe had been converted to both Latin and Orthodox Christianity in a first wave in the fourth to sixth centuries, and then in a second wave beginning in the ninth century. When the Turks invaded, then, they came across an area that had been at least *nominally* Christian for 500 years. Certainly the Balkans had had their share of difficulties with heresy; the Orthodox patriarchy was intricately bound up with the governing structures of the Byzantine Empire – so much so that when the Empire began to crumble, the Bulgars and Serbs went so far as to acquire their own patriarchates.[14] But despite this splintering, the Christian Orthodox dogma, which had evolved from seven ecumenical councils, was more or less uniformly accepted throughout the area.

A stated uniformity can be deceptive, however. The Orthodox Church had planted roots in the Balkans, but its victory over the religion of the *pagus* was pyrrhic. We see from the form of Christianity practised in the Balkans, especially before modern times and particularly in the countryside, that in order to survive and prosper Christianity had to make concessions to the native forms of paganism. This was true in the history of the spread of the Abrahamic religions. Often, the compromises were self-conscious gestures on the part of proselytizers, but more often, it seems they were just natural products of human nature: transitions from one state to another are never completely clean, and old habits are eradicated only painfully.

Byzantine church leaders were well aware of the survival of pagan practices and generally were unhappy about it. But the practices appear to have
been so widespread that they were powerless to do anything lasting about
them. A tenth-century scholiast (a commentator who annotated classical
authors), who annotated Sophocles' *Antigone*, referred to a section that
deals with the μύρδος (*murdos*) or the red hot iron held when swearing
an oath in antiquity, and explained: 'the Rhomaioi [this word means
Romans in Greek] still practice this today, erring in the Hellenic fashion
as in most everything else'.[15] John Canabutzes (fifteenth century), in his
commentary on Dionysius of Halicarnassus, tells us that 'The Christians
continue to reek and stink of Hellenic (pagan) obscenity.'[16]

What exactly was this stink that Canabutzes found so unappealing?
It was a belief in a world of nature crowded with spirits of a less than
orthodox demeanour. Popular belief in the Balkans centred on the *lamia*,
or weather spirits, who resided in the clouds and had clashes for supremacy that caused, among other disturbances, hail to fall from the heavens.
There is a Slavo-Christianized story that tells of the prophet Elijah pursu-
ing the *lamia* across the vault of the heavens in his celestial chariot.[17] The
Balkan peoples also believed that the forests, mountains and waters were
cluttered with female spirits or nymphs, known in the classical Greek
world as *dryads*, *oreads* and *nereids*. Additionally, the house snake was
the protector of the hearth in nearly every rural Balkan home; its predecessors came from the cult of Zeus Ktesios, who as the protector of
the hearth in Greek antiquity often assumed the form of a serpent. The
worship of trees, a practice that has a nearly global reach, found expression in the Balkans in the Serbian *zapis* or 'holy tree': annually, at the
time of the ripening of crops, the priest led a procession to the tree where
a lamb was sacrificed under its bowers and the blood was spilled on its
bark.[18]

The instantiation of meteorological events and the veneration of water
and trees were logical religious strategies for a people that was largely
agrarian and dependent on weather and water for crops. But there also
remained a concern with the human life cycle that had deep roots in the
pagan past, and continued to exercise an influence in Balkan life after the
advent of Christianity. In the eastern and southern Balkans, there existed
a belief that three *moirai*, or fates, presided over a newborn child. Marriage, an ecclesiastical event, also still maintained its pagan character for
Balkan peoples, particularly the use of crowns during wedding ceremonies. And Balkan peoples continued to observe old customs for death and
burial, including the use of professional female mourners, the placing of
money in graves for the dead (Charon's *obol* of ancient Greek myth), and
the preparation of a funeral meal made of raisins, sugar, almonds and
pomegranate (meant to represent the *panspermia*, or world seed, the cosmic principle of fecundity and rebirth). The Christian notions of heaven

and hell were also deeply affected by the Greek ideas of Charon-Hades and by the Slavic preoccupation of the returning dead, the *vrykolakas*, as Greek vampiric creatures.

Another interesting snapshot of Balkan pagan holdovers is the celebration of holidays, both Christian and nominally Christian. The Greek peasants of Thrace celebrated the feast day of Constantine and St Helen (the Roman emperor who converted to Christianity, and his mother, a much-venerated woman in the Greek Orthodox tradition), with the *Anastenarides* and *Kalogeros-Kukeri Mones*, an eight-day celebration which featured animal sacrifice, dance-induced ecstasy, fire walking (or *pyrobasia*), and nocturnal wandering in the mountains (or *oreibasia*). The *Kalogeros* or *Kukeri* mimes performed on 'Cheese Monday' to ensure the fertility of the fields. The hero of the drama was the *Kalogeros*, who probably descended from Dionysus, for like him, *Kalogeros* was born, ritually killed and reborn again. This drama was accompanied by ceremonial or ritual ploughing and sowing, with an abundance of phallic paraphernalia, such as *panspermia*, or cosmic seed, and a *liknis*, a sieve that was originally a cultic object in the worship of Dionysus, containing a medley of fruits and objects shaped like phalluses. In fact, all manner of quasi-sexual objects were employed in this festival, in the hope that simulated sex could ensure the real-time fertility of the earth. In a related way, the maintenance of one's health was a concern of the peasant and the city-dweller alike; for Christians in the Orthodox tradition, it is still not uncommon to dedicate silver or gold likenesses (literally, pieces of one's body moulded in precious metals) called *tamata*. This is not a Christian innovation, of course – the practice of offering moulded body parts goes back to the cult of Asclepius.

Christmas, most realize, is a holiday that preserves many pagan elements in all the Christian denominations.[19] The *duodecameron*, the Twelve Days of Christmas, begins with Christ's birth on 25 December and ends with his baptism on 6 January. Christ's birthday was not celebrated on 25 December until the fourth century; before that, the occasion was celebrated during the grand pagan holiday *Dies Natalis Solis Invicti*, during which rites of a bacchanalian type were performed. During this holiday season, the dervish *Kalikantzari* roamed the streets and, like Santa Claus, tried to enter homes by way of the chimneys. Also during this season *kollyva*, or *panspermia*, the cosmic seed, was offered to the dead and the water spirits. This practice led to an early Christian tradition: usually, at the conclusion of the Twelve Days of Christmas, a priest tossed a cross into a river, creek or stream whose waters were then cathartically used to cleanse tools, icons and important household items.

Saint veneration will be treated more fully later, but we must say a few things about it here, since the Orthodox Church has a myriad of saints' feast days, whose origins, in most cases, are only superficially Christian.

On 4 December, the feast day of Saint Barbara, the Orthodox Christian offers up *kollyva,* or *kollyvozomon,* a rich dish meant to simulate the world seed, to the saint to ensure good crops in the following year. This closely parallels the ancient *panspermia* that was offered up to the gods Dionysus and his antecedents, fertility deities who also controlled the souls of the dead. This one example among a literal thousand shows the marked propensity of Balkan peoples toward hagiolatry, the worship of saints and their icons and relics. As we will see later, saint worship is a great repository of syncretism in Judaism, Islam and Christianity. Saints are usually local figures, so they tend to preserve regionalisms, and as such are natural magnets for pre-monotheistic elements. Saints, and the keeping of their relics in a particular locale, usually end up fulfilling a particular (and usually curative) niche in the psychological life of a religion. Also saint cults, in pre-modern times and even today, served an important economic function: saint centres brought pilgrims to an area, and pilgrims require basic services. Often, these saint shrines were pre-Christian, pagan centres of worship that stubbornly remained holy sites through the exchange of one religion for another. We see this nowhere better than in the Balkans, which went through at least four distinct stages of religious dominance: Indo-European paganism, Graeco-Roman paganism, Byzantine Christianity and, in some places, eventual Ottoman Islamization. We shall see that the coming of Islam to the Balkans was not so much the replacement of Christianity by Islam, but the Islamization of the mix that was Balkan folk culture, a culture that was, for all the transformations it was forced to withstand, surprisingly conservative and resilient.

Turkish Islam in the Balkans: the 'conversion' of Christian groups in the Balkans

Turkified Islam confronted this hotchpotch, and as we saw at the beginning of this chapter, Turkic peoples, as recent converts to Islam, carried with them a storehouse of syncretistic practices that made their brand of Islam idiosyncratic and allowed it to find a wide range of expression. The official version of Islam for the Ottoman state was the Sunni variety, which is still the version practised by the majority of Muslims, and which is distinct from the Shi'ite brand. In essence, the Turkish state was orthodox Sunni, but away from the essence and ideas of purity, it had many of the 'imperfections' that we find in the supposed orthodoxy of the Church in the Balkans. One of the many great ironies in the history of Islam is that a faith many believe was spread by religious war or struggle has gleaned many, if not most, of its converts through trade and missionary activity. This occurs often in religious movements: the dominant myth of the religion's appeal is quite different from the factors that lead to its spread. We see this in the stories Christianity tells about its own nativity: Christianity was spread because of its appeal to the dispossessed poor in the Roman world at a time when the old paganism that had sustained Rome for nearly 2,000 years was nearing a state of absolute exhaustion, both morally and spiritually. We are told that Christ's message spread because of his new tonic of redemption, and not because the Emperor Constantine adopted Christianity in AD 312 and later legalized its practice in the Edict of Milan in AD 313, and then showered money down on the Church – a conjunction of Christ and Rome that would ensure the success of the Church against all rivals. Islam was spread through the relatively peaceful enterprises of trade and missionary work, and these led many peoples, particularly outside the Arab orbit, to adopt Islam.

This was certainly also the case with Islam in the Balkans. The kind of freewheeling religious attitude we saw with the warrior-syncretistic cults of the *gazi–akritoi* in Anatolia found a similar, though less martial expression, in the Sufi-dervish mystical orders that became popular features of Ottoman Islamic religious expression. We will handle Sufism, a general term for the varied mystical movements in Islam, in more depth in the next chapter on saints, since Sufi mysticism and saint veneration often travel hand-in-hand. The dervish orders that flourished in Turkish Anatolia in the fifteenth century preached a version of Islam that was a mix of mystical doctrines, which stressed the individual union of God with the worshipper, with popular superstitions, folk beliefs and religious philosophies that dervishes adapted from their wanderings in Persia, Iraq, India and Syria.[20] Why was this heterodox form of Islam allowed to flourish in the Ottoman state? Because it had powerful friends. The dervish order of the *Bektashis* was connected to the famous Janissary corps, the House of Ottoman's mercenary corps, and the order of the *Mevlevis* with the court ceremony of the sultans. It seems the Ottoman rulers felt there was little to fear from Sufism, which could often be politically neutral and passive. They believed that an alliance of the state and Sufism was an adequate bulwark against the more politically insurgent Shi'ite movement that was gaining power just to the east of Ottoman holdings. Heterodox Sufism and the Ottoman state are not unlikely bedfellows when we remember the spotty nature of the Islamization of the Turkic tribes that settled Anatolia and later the Balkans. The Sufi cult of personality, where a given order was centred around a mystic and his circle of devotees (or after his death, around his teachings and or grave/cultic shrine), meshed well with the old tribal Turkic concept of the leader/shaman whose powers ensured the abundance of pasture land and the fertility of herds, and whose military virtues maintained security. In all, the Sufi *baba*, usually in dervish form, was often a thinly Islamized shaman who communicated with the world of spirits to elicit favour on behalf of individuals and groups. Some Turkic tribesmen did not even alter their nomadic practices with Islamization or settlement in Anatolia. Christian writers talk of Turkish warrior cults that still practised human sacrifice and cults of the dead that included mummification and the belief that souls after death can shape-change into the forms of animals, birds or insects.[21]

Many elements of popular Turkic worship filtered down to the Turkish people in Anatolia when they became sedentary. If we add to this equation the scores of Anatolian Greeks, Armenians, Georgians and Syrians that were converted to Islam between the eleventh and fifteenth centuries, we see a great deal of crossover and filtration between the various cultures and religions of Ottoman society. The Turks mixed with these converts, further complicating the ethno-religious stew that their wandering Turkic ancestors had already begun, and added even more flavour to Islamization of the Christian Slavs across the Bosporus. Amazingly, in many cases the Turkic peoples who settled Anatolia had converted to Islam later than the Christians they were supplanting had adopted Christianity.

The activities of Muslim missionaries led to conversions in the Balkans. This, as well as active colonization of Turkish Muslims in the Balkans, is the only lasting, autochthonous segment of Islam found in Europe. Islam's forays into Spain, Sicily and Sardinia were eventually peeled back. Muslims in those lands eventually left or were converted to Christianity.[22] Only in the Balkans do we find ethnic European, mainly Slavic, Muslims. Unfortunately, how these communities developed is largely unknown, because the historical record is incomplete.[23] It seems likely that most Muslims in Europe were converts to the faith, while a core element in cities were colonists from Turkish Anatolia.

Islam also offered incentives for conversion. The tax load of Muslims in Ottoman society was significantly less onerous than for Christians and Jews.[24] A change of religion, at least for the upper classes, also meant greater social mobility, unfettered access to the corridors of power and unrestricted alliances with other wealthy families. Intermarriage also led to a great deal of conversionary activity. Muslim men could marry Christian women and the offspring of such unions were Muslims, at least legally and nominally.[25] Islamization was also fostered by the dynamics between groups in the Balkans – fear, a great universal motivator in human life, led to a great many conversions. Balkan peoples who had embraced Islam even nominally could rely on the state powers for protection against their traditional enemies – and in the cauldron of ethnic tension in the Balkans, this was not an unimportant factor. Combined with the soft and pliant brand of Islam that the itinerant Sufi-dervish preachers peddled, it actually seems surprising that more European peoples under Ottoman control did not convert. All the incentives were certainly there. But unlike in Spain and Portugal, where forced conversion became a powerful tool for state-sponsored hegemony, the Ottomans never truly used so drastic a weapon. Forced conversion of Jews and Christians is forbidden in the Qur'an, and was financially undesirable for the Ottoman ruling house. Some forced conversions of Christians to Islam occurred in Anatolia, where the Islamization of the local population was already very near complete, but it appears never to have been a significant factor in the spread of Islam in south-eastern Europe. For one, the revenues the Ottoman state collected from its re-ligious minority subjects was not marginal; if they forced them to con-vert, the tax base that the state relied upon would have been significantly reduced.

So, Islamization in the Balkans was a spotty affair; it moved in fits and starts, gaining momentum in some areas and never truly sparking and catching fire in others. The Ottoman state took censuses of its people, and one of the questions the state asked involved the religious composi-tion of homes. From these censuses, we can see the process of Islamiz-ation gathering a head of steam, from relatively few in the century before the 1520–30 census, to increasingly significant numbers in the three fol-lowing centuries. By far the most drastic case was Albania, which was almost completely Christian on all levels of society in 1430. The census reports that with the coming of the fifteenth century, Islamization had gained momentum in the north and eventually the south as well.[26] Today, nearly 70 per cent of the country is Muslim[27] – by far the highest popula-tion of Muslims in Europe by overall percentage. Around the fifteenth century, Islamization was also occurring in the north-east of Bulgaria, on the borders of Thrace and Macedonia. Other waves of Islamization took place there from 1666 to 1670 and from 1686 to 1690. Compared to the gradual infiltration of Islam in the previous waves, this spate of conversions was on a wider scale and of a different character. Entire vil-lages were converted; in fact, some 74 towns and villages were converted to Islam in Rhodope in south-eastern Bulgaria, and other regions in the vicinity as well. Among Greeks, the Islamization of the Vallahades in south-western Macedonia and of Cretans took place in the seventeenth and eighteenth centuries. The Greeks in the Vallahades were converted largely by the work of the dervishes, while those on Crete were converted primarily through the tensions that were produced by the Russo-Turkish wars.

One of the most interesting cases of Islamization in the Balkans was in Bosnia, not only because the plight of Bosnia and Hercegovina and the fate of its native European Muslims was so much in the news in the 1990s, but because in many ways the process of Islamization in Bosnia mirrored the spread of Islam in other areas. A quarter of a century after the Turkish conquest of Bosnia in 1489, there were about 25,000 Christ-ian 'hearths' in Bosnia, and around 4,500 Muslim 'hearths'.[28] Christians were 81.6 per cent of the population, while Muslims were 18.4 per cent – Christians outnumbered Muslims by nearly five times. However, by the census of 1520–30, Muslim hearths numbered 16,935 and Christian 19,619; the number of Muslim hearths in Bosnia tripled and the number of Christian dropped notably. It seems from these numbers that the process of conversion to Islam was at its peak in the 30 or so years between the censuses.

But statistics of Islamization in the Balkans give a one-dimensional picture, for when we say that Bosnia was dramatically transforming from Christian to Muslim from 1489 to 1530, we tend to presume there was a drastic break in the lives of the converted peoples, and that there was an appreciable gap between Balkan Christians and those who transformed themselves into Balkan Muslims. Of course, the situation was far from a vision of pure transformation. Several writers have noted that what gave Balkan Islam its distinctive characteristics were hagiolatry (the worship or veneration of saints) and the dervish brotherhoods, which made up the branch of Sufi mysticism that was so widespread in Turkey. In truth, Islam never really divorced the population of the Balkans, particularly in the country, from the 'seasonal religio-magical' calendar that was concerned with health and fertility. Popular Islam in the Balkans was syncretistic from the beginning because it needed to appeal to the rooted concerns of an agricultural, pastoral people. When coupled with the tendency of Islam in the Balkans, at certain times and in certain places, to convert whole villages and regions, this left many remaining Christian and pre-Christian elements. Mass conversions occurred in this way among the Albanians, Bosnians, Bulgar Pomaks and Greeks. An individual convert to Islam would perhaps carry former beliefs with him or her, but with death, those beliefs would perish. On the other hand, large groups of converts tended to preserve pre-Islamic customs which were passed to new generations. The Sufi-dervish orders, many of them manned by people who were either inadequately Islamicized themselves, tended to ignore the messy consequences of adherence to strict Sunni Islam. They brought a vital folk culture that was at odds with the strict orthodox Islam of many of their co-religionists to the east and had few qualms about mixing it with the folk Christianity they found in southeastern Europe. Added to this, the importance Christians continued to play in Ottoman society in vital areas like agriculture, maritime trade and commercial life makes this kind of benevolent Islam seem not only logical, but like sound political policy.

Balkan Islam took certain fundamental Christian practices and changed – even twisted – them to fit its own needs. The most important are baptism, animal sacrifice and hagiolatry. It seems that Anatolian Muslims who settled in Turkey before the widespread invasion of the area by Turkic tribes practised baptism. Baptism by Anatolian Muslims, and later by their Balkan counterparts, was performed not to satisfy any sacramental necessity, but from the popular folk belief that immersion in Christian holy water armed infants against disease and protected them from mental illness.[29] The common Christian practice of animal sacrifice, the so-called *thysia* or *kurban*, was also taken over by Muslims in this region, and it evidently had quite an old lineage in the folk practices of Greek, Armenian and Balkan Slavs.[30] Even the practice of the *dermatikon*, the 'priest's share', which is described in Greek inscriptions from antiquity in both in Greece and Asia Minor, was present in this folk custom. And just to add to the syncretistic brew, Balkan Muslims would often perform their sacrifices in the courtyards of churches.[31]

The power of saints, although much maligned in some Muslim quarters, has always been recognized in popular Islam, and it certainly found much effective expression in Islam as practised in the Balkans. There was already a rich and diverse local topography of saints and their shrines, along with Sufi-dervish Islam in this area. The Balkans were already prone to this sort of spiritual investiture and ran amok with the tendency to worship saints, often taking saints who had been only marginally Christianized from their pagan roots, and in turn, marginally Islamicizing them.

The Pomacks of Bulgaria practised a particularly lovely and egregious form of syncretistic Islam where many, if not all, of the old Bulgaro-Christian patterns that had developed for a millennium continued to be practised without anyone missing a step. The Pomacks continued to rely on the old magical practices that ensured the fertility of the land (which we saw in the *Kukeri* dances and mimes). They believed that taking Easter eggs from Christians assured one of good health and they believed that bringing sick children to church on Good Friday would guarantee a cure. They sought out the blessings of priests on feast days, and they took holy water from the same priests for the benefit of family members and even livestock. The Pomacks also continued to make offerings to Orthodox Church icons; they often even covertly kept church books and icons in their homes. Converts in Bosnia, Serbia and Macedonia followed suit. They dyed Easter eggs; celebrated Orthodox feasts days like those of Saints George, John and Peter; and on St Barbara's Day, they boiled *varica*, a wheat akin to the ancient *panspermia*, or cosmic seed, which was believed to be so important to universal fecundity. Like the Pomacks, they continued the old Slavic custom of animal sacrifice and families often remembered the days of their patron saints and continued to celebrate them privately,[32] much like the secret, domestic ceremonies of the crypto-Jews and Marranos.

Balkan Islam's relationship to 'orthodox' Islam

This complex of diverse practices is quite a lineage, and I can hear, in my
ear, the rages from the purist. This was not Islam, but a grave example
of the impurity to which religious practice can sink when left untutored
by the higher intellectual or moral trends of faith. Fundamentalists will
say that simple people, if left to their own devices, will create religious
abominations in the form of lumbering folk faiths – religions that de-
generate into superstition divorced from reason, riddled with practices
like necromancy, soothsaying, demotic prophecy, reliance on amulets
and spells. But over and over again, in the history of Christianity, Islam
and Judaism, we see authorities fighting these trends with little success.
The waves of orthodox revision that periodically sweep the Abrahamic
religions can never completely eradicate folk faith, because it is the very
process of assimilation, accommodation and synthesis that allows the
religions to continue forming and spreading to new areas. Often, this is
a source of uneasy embarrassment. Balkan Muslims exchanging Easter
eggs can be viewed by fundamentalist eyes as at best, an anomaly worthy
of correction, or at worst, a sign of the utter degeneracy of a particular
people in a particular place, practising a particular brand of Islam that
bears only a glancing resemblance to the faith of the Prophet.

As we mentioned above, Islam has the self-generated vision of the
jihad, the holy struggle for the propagation of the faith. While this version of the history of Islam's spread cannot be ignored or downplayed,
there remains a compelling counter-force that has existed in Islam from
its very early history: that of the Sufi brotherhood, or *turuq*. Islam's mystical branch, the Sufi (*tasawwuf*), with its numerous functions as a religious, social, military, and economic force, was paramount in the spread
of the faith out of its cradle in Arabia and the Mediterranean, to West
and Central Africa, the Sudan, the horn of Africa and the East African
Coast, to India and all of South-East Asia and the Balkans. The mystical
orders were the main channels for the conversion of non-Arab peoples to
Islam. The mystical dervish orders that brought Islam into south-eastern
Europe were accused by many orthodox circles of a lax religious sensibil-
ity and practice, and a marked tendency to assimilate local practices and
beliefs into their own mystical creed. The orders that spread the faith in
non-Arab cultures were also accused of lax conformity to the principles
of Islamic law.[33]

Folk-based Islam had a significant level of success in all these lands.
The easy explanation for its success is, of course, that the people who
converted had to do little active work to change to the new faith. Folkways were still in place or existed and were discreetly divorced from their
original contexts. In recent times, these tendencies have been peeled back
as their adherents, many of them exposed for the first time to Arabian

Islam (ironically, through Western advances in travel and communication) have attempted to learn the rigours of the old faith, which is, for
them, decidedly *new*.

The irony is obvious and deep: in order to 'return' to a faith that is
essentially foreign, they must repudiate one that acclimatized itself to the
culture. The trouble is that even something that is reputed to be older has
been formed by and has always had elements that are new. The myth of
antiquity in religious faith often has a disingenuous element of deception.
The human animal in its religious guise is always adapting the creed,
always inventing, always transforming the elements of a faith, which is
supposedly stooped with age, and pressing it into new moulds.

Chapter summary

Islam in the Balkans developed along very unique lines and syncretism
played a key role in its development from a very early stage. The Balkans
was a crossroads between the Slavic north, the Greek-speaking south and
Turkish Islam to the east, and this geographical centrality facilitated the
process of syncretization, as the various cultural and religious layers that
overlapped in the region left their vital imprint. Islam practised in the
Balkans was influenced by an eclectic form of Sufism brought with the
roaming Turks, who themselves were relatively recent converts to Islam.
They were shamanistic people, venerating the natural world, which they
believed was populated by spirits that were personified in nature. They
absorbed influences from Zoroastrianism and Shi'a Islam, and venerated
shamanistic tribal leaders as focal points of divine energy on the earth.
When this Turkish form of Islam entered the Balkans, and Slavs converted
to the faith, Greek Orthodox and Roman Catholic practices entered the
mix. But most importantly, a vibrant, pagan folk culture remained and
was practised by the Balkan peoples even when Orthodox or Catholic
Christianity continued to be practised in an Islamic milieu. This strong
folk culture remained surprisingly stable even when the peoples of the
Balkans converted from one Abrahamic religion to another. This made
Islam in the Balkans uniquely broad and syncretistic, and ideally suited
to this corner of south-eastern Europe. Most fundamentalist groups, like
the Wahhabis in Saudi Arabia, find this type of Islam inherently corrupt,
because Balkan Islam is a threat to groups like the Wahhabis. But like
the Marrano religion in the previous chapter, Balkan Islam illustrates the
permeability of the Abrahamic faiths, and also serves as an example of
how they are enriched by contact with paganism and local folk custom.

Draw your own conclusions

How 'orthodox' is Islam as practised in the Balkans? Have the core elements of Islam, or the so-called 'five pillars', been altered by Balkan Islam?

Does the prevalence of syncretism in the Balkans (as practised among Christians and Muslims) add to or subtract from the political and social harmony (or disharmony) in the region?

How important is the role played by 'paganism' in Balkan Islam?

Further reading

For a detailed history of the rise of the Turks:
Stanford Shaw (1976), *History of the Ottoman Empire and Modern Turkey: Volume 1: Empire of the Gazis: The Rise and Decline of the Ottoman Empire, 1280-1808*, Cambridge: Cambridge University Press.

For an examination of late forms of Hellenistic paganism:
G. W. Bowersock (1990), *Hellenism in Late Antiquity*, Ann Arbor, MI: University of Michigan Press.

For a diplomatic history of the disintegration of the Ottoman Empire:
David Fromkin (1989), *A Peace to End All Peace*, New York: Avon Books.

For more on Balkan Islam's religious practices:
Henrik Birnbaum and Speros Vyronis Jr (eds) (1972), *Aspects of the Balkans: Continuity and Change*, The Hague and Paris: Mountain Press.
Peter Sugar (1977), *South-eastern Europe under Ottoman Rule, 1354–1804*, Seattle and London: University of Washington Press.

For a general overview of the Balkans:
Dame Rebecca West (1994), *Black Lamb and Gray Falcon: A Journey Through Yugoslavia*, New York: Penguin Books.

Notes

1 Sabrina Petra Ramet (1992), *Balkan Babel: Politics, Culture and Religion in Yugoslavia*, Boulder, CO: Westview Press, p. 166.
2 'Erasing Culture: Wahhabism, Buddhism, Balkan Mosques,' Michael A. Sells, from http://www.haverford.edu/relg/sells/reports/wahhabismbuddhasbegova.htm. Apparently, a new reconstruction is under way to restore the mosque to an appearance closer to its original. See the website above for an update.
3 David Fromkin (1989), *A Peace to End All Peace*, New York: Avon Books,

is a diplomatic history of the events leading up to the break up of the Ottoman Empire and its aftermath.

4 Peter F. Sugar (1977), *South-eastern Europe Under Ottoman Rule, 1354–1804*, Seattle and London: University of Washington Press, p. 8.

5 Sugar, *South-eastern Europe*, p. 11.

6 Sugar, *South-eastern Europe*, pp. 9–10.

7 Sugar, *South-eastern Europe*, p. 25.

8 The question of whether the Greeks believed in one God or many is a complex one, and we don't have the room to examine it here. For some of the major Greek philosophers, at least, there appears to be one God who finds expression in a multiplicity of ways. If we examine a philosopher such as the Stoic Epictetus, for instance, we see numerous examples in his *Discourses* where he appears to endorse the idea of a single god, albeit a god that is distinctly Stoic in his dimensions (i.e. pantheistic, diffuse, disembodied, but unitary, at least from the standpoint of one god versus many). We can safely say that Hellenism was religiously polytheistic but monotheistic in philosophy. See John Corrigan et al. (1997), *Jews, Christians and Muslims*, Upper Saddle River, NJ: Prentice Hall, p. 83. For a more detailed look at the complex question of Graeco-Roman pagan polytheism and early Christian monotheism, see Robert L. Wilken (1984), *The Christians as the Romans Saw Them*, New Haven, CT: Yale University Press, particularly pp. 68–93 and pp. 126–63.

9 William Morris (ed.) (1994), *Webster's New World Dictionary*, Boston: Houghton Mifflin, 'pagan,' p. 942; 'heathen,' p. 608. For a brief discussion of the origins of the word pagan, see Corrigan, *Jews, Christians and Muslims*, p. 178.

10 G. W. Bowersock (1990), *Hellenism in Late Antiquity*, Ann Arbor, MI: University of Michigan Press. These lucid essays provide numerous examples of a late, thriving, often urban paganism in the later Roman Empire, even in the centuries when Christian Rome was flexing its muscles.

11 James Charles Roy (1999), *The Vanished Kingdom: Travels through the History of Prussia*, Boulder, CO: Westview Press, details the history of the Prussian Kingdom, including its expansion in the Middle Ages into Slavic lands to the East. The slave trade in pagan Slavs is explored, see pp. 43–64, pp. 65–85. Also see Richard Fletcher, *The Barbarian Conversion*, New York: Henry Holt, pp. 417–507 for a more detailed history of the spread of Christianity among the pagan Slavs.

12 Corrigan, *Jews, Christians and Muslims*, p. 447. For a more detailed treatment of the conversion of Northern Europe to Christianity, see Fletcher, *The Barbarian Conversion*, pp. 1–129.

13 S. Vryonis (1972), 'Religious Changes and Patterns in the Balkans, 14th–16th Centuries', in Birnbaum and Vryonis, *Aspects of the Balkans*, p. 152.

14 Vryonis, *Aspects of the Balkans*, p. 153.

15 Vryonis, *Aspects of the Balkans*, p. 155.

16 Vryonis, *Aspects of the Balkans*, p. 155.

17 Vryonis, *Aspects of the Balkans*, p. 155.

18 Vryonis, *Aspects of the Balkans*, p. 155.

19 Vryonis, *Aspects of the Balkans*, p. 158.

20 Vryonis, *Aspects of the Balkans*, pp. 160–1.

21 Vryonis, *Aspects of the Balkans*, p. 161.

22 Alex Metcalfe (2003), *Muslims and Christians in Norman Sicily: Arabic Speakers and the End of Islam*, London and New York: Routledge Curzon. See this study for the linguistic evidence of the progressive Latinization and Christianization of Sicily, transforming it from a primarily Muslim- and Arabic-speaking island before 1060 to a Romance and Latin-speaking island by 1250.

23 Vryonis, *Aspects of the Balkans*, p. 164.

24 Hourani, *The History of Arab Peoples*, p. 35, for a discussion of the *jizya* or poll tax for non-Muslims.

25 Vryonis, *Aspects of the Balkans*, p. 167.

26 Vryonis, *Aspects of the Balkans*, p. 168.

27 Robert Elsie (2001), *A Dictionary of Albanian Religion, Mythology and Folk Culture*, New York: New York University Press, pp. 51–2, for information on Islam in Albania see pp. 121–7.

28 Vryonis, *Aspects of the Balkans*, p. 169.

29 Vryonis, *Aspects of the Balkans*, pp. 173–4.

30 West, *Black Lamb and Gray Falcon*. West's monumental travel log (at nearly 500,000 words) written in the late 1920s and early 1930s, visits the syncretistic nature of Balkan religion as the narrator witnesses a sacrificial ceremony involving a large stone and numerous fowl. Otherwise painted in a bad light (the ceremony becomes, for West, a harbinger of the bloodshed that will occur in the Balkans during World War Two), her descriptions of the earthy nature of Balkan folk religion are compelling and indispensable for any understanding of Balkan politics, society and, to a lesser degree, religion. See especially 'St George's Eve II', in the Macedonia section, pp. 820–31.

31 A location deemed particularly efficacious.

32 Vryonis, *Aspects of the Balkans*, pp. 175–6.

33 Michael Gilsenan (1973), *Saint and Sufi in Egypt: An Essay in the Sociology of Religion*, Oxford: Clarendon Press, p. 2.

4

Mysticism and Saints' Cults in the Abrahamic Religions

> It is those who believe and do not adulterate their faith [in Allah's One-ness] with zulm [wrongdoing, i.e. associating other gods with God], for them [only] is there safety and they are rightly-guided. (Qur'an 6.82)

Sufism versus Wahhabism in the north Caucasus: the native and the fundamental

From the seventh to the seventeenth century, Sunni Islam began to pene-trate the Caucasus region, but the variety of Islam practised in the north Caucasus region has always been a faith with some admixture of pre-Islamic elements. During the eighth century, Arabs from the south began actively to convert the peoples of the Caucasus to Sunni Islam. When their activities were blocked by the rise of the Turks, they turned to the north-ern mountains and spread their religion to the ancestors of the Chechens and the Avars, who were centred in the mountains of Dagestan. Despite the success of Islam in the region, the religion as practised since its arrival has been described as 'Islamic-animist'.[1]

With the rise of Russian power to the north, and the spread of Rus-sian imperial power to the south, Islam in the Caucasus was forced to the defensive. So what was originally a clan-based religion, with little or no overarching sense of unity or organization, became, under the weight of Russian aggression and under the influence of charismatic Caucasian leaders in the eighteenth and nineteenth centuries, something resembling a unified front. Such men as Sheikh Mansur waged war against Russia while simultaneously tightening the hold of Islam in the Caucasus. In 1794 he proclaimed himself sheikh of the newly arrived Naqshbandi order of Sufis. In his sermons, he called for a return to an ascetic and purified form of Islam and vilified the use of alcohol and tobacco. He criticized certain pagan practices, like the cult of the dead and the reli-ance on the customary law of the area, the *adat*, which often practised a violent form of vendetta, in favour of Islamic law or the *shari'a*.[2] He was ultimately defeated by the Russians, but his legacy was lasting: he helped establish Sufism in the Caucasus and Islam in the mountainous areas of the north-west Caucasus.

Mansur set the stage for other great leaders in the nineteenth century. Imam Shamil set about to convert the Chechens from half-paganism to stricter Islam (under the banner of Sufism) while resisting Russian imperial aggression. He too helped spread Islam into the animist areas of upper Chechnya.[3] Ultimately, men like Mansur and Shamil lost to the overwhelming might of Russia's military, and for Chechens, the losses were devastating. Islam, having once been only a background to the primarily tribal pulse of the region, was increasingly turned to by Chechens for identity, for unity, and for a buffering element against their more powerful aggressor to the north.

Following the fall of the Soviet Union in 1991, Islam saw a resurgence in the north Caucasus region. For nearly a century, Islam in this area had been on the defensive. The atheistic government of the Soviet Union had practised a systematic policy of undermining Muslim identity, redistributing land, deporting entire peoples and shattering age-old patterns of life and religious organization.

The traditional Sufi Islam practised in the north Caucasus lived on despite Soviet pressure (and Muslim reformists' zeal), and Muslims in the Caucasus practised Sufi traditions we find the world over: they recited the Qur'an in cemeteries for the souls of their dead saints and heroes, wore charms to ward off evil spirits and, most importantly, made pilgrimages to the graves of their holy saints. Like Sufism practised in much of the Muslim world, Sufism in the Caucasus stressed a deep, personal relationship of the worshipper with God, whose presence was seen as so immanent in the world that many Sufis flirted with the idea of pantheism, or the belief that God and the world are identical. And like many Sufis, Sufis in the Caucasus were more concerned with their individual connection with God than with a strict observance of Islamic law, the *shari'a*.

With the fall of communism, the appearance of more permeable borders, and the influence of more fundamentalist versions of Islam from Afghanistan and Iran, the hegemony of Sufism in the Caucasus began to be challenged. Wahhabi missionaries appeared in the region and preached their more austere form of Islam, which eschews, among other things, saint veneration, which Wahhabis consider little more than gross idolatry. In many communities in Dagestan and Chechnya, Muslims have become divided between Wahhabists who reject Sufism, and traditionalists who continue to practise Islam as it has been practised in this area for several hundred years. In some cases, sectarian violence has erupted between the Sufis and Wahhabis. Why are fundamentalist groups like the Wahhabis so opposed to saint veneration? By looking at three examples of saint cults, one from each of the Abrahamic religions, this chapter will begin to illustrate one reason the practice of saint veneration is so threatening to fundamentalists: the veneration of saints is one of the prime arteries whereby syncretism flows into the Abrahamic religions.[4]

The rise of Wahhabism and its spread to Sufi lands

On the Arabian peninsula in the eighteenth century, a religious reformer named Muhammad ibn Abd al-Wahhab (1703–92) set about to *purify* Islam.[5] It seems that many of the folkways of Balkan Islam were even found in Arabia, the birthplace of Islam: a pervasive animism (or the belief that objects in the world have souls and are in some way alive) and soothsaying (or attempting to divine the future through certain mechanical means) were commonplace. In fact, all manner of magical practices were performed – and were anathema to al-Wahhab and his followers.[6] They believed that Sufism and shrine worship, which were in fact expressions of popular and folk Islam, were idolatrous distortions that should be rooted out, particularly in Arabia, the home of Islam's most sacred sites, and therefore a land of special sanctity. Eventually, under the influence of Wahhabism's special brand of purifying exclusivity, and the movement's collusion with the royal House of Saud,[7] all non-Muslims were banned from Arabia, a land deemed too holy for non-believers to sully. The particularly austere brand of Islam that followed attempted to return to the roots of the religion, and to have as its centrepiece only the Qur'an, the canonical biographies of the Prophet and the so-called authoritative sayings of Muhammad, which had been written down since his death.

But Wahhabism, originally a purely Arabian phenomenon, later found a more widespread appeal. The fruits of its religious philosophy, a kind of unequivocal interpretation of Islam and its social and political role in the world, have generated a widespread sympathy, particularly since the Western colonization of Arab states in the nineteenth and early twentieth centuries. It has been invested with a new rigor since the conclusion of World War Two and the spread of an Americanized version of modernity which was equally (if not more) bewildering than its predecessors.

Wahhabism's appeal is complex. Foremost, its principles may be easily warped into an anti-Western agenda. Its uncompromising stance can be moulded into a position of anti-modernity and anti-Americanism, since its cornerstone is a self-proclaimed hardline conservatism. Wahhabism, in some of its forms, views itself as the only true version of Islam and denies the validity of other forms of the faith. But like all fundamentalist movements, Wahhabism (especially as practised by the social and political elite in Saudi Arabia), is fraught with compromise and diluted when deemed necessary or expedient. All modern fundamentalist movements are moulded by the modernity they seek to escape or exclude.[8] Non-Muslims are allowed into Saudi Arabia when exemptions to the policy are helpful to the Saudi state. For example, people with skills that the Saudis view as socially valuable, such as host workers who perform domestic labour which native Saudis do not wish to perform, oil company specialists and, until recently, US troops, live in the kingdom as its special guests.

Wahhabism takes aim at other forms of Islam but it offers especially stiff resistance to the more heterodox forms of the faith practised around the world. Certainly, it does not favour even the most religiously conservative of the Sufi orders. V. S. Naipaul, in his travel book *Among the Believers*, and its sequel, *Beyond Belief*, depicts with marvellous subjective clarity how Islam spread in non-Arab countries like Pakistan, Indonesia, Malaysia and Iran. For Indonesia and Malaysia, Islam arrived not by military conquest but primarily through Sufi missionary activity. And Naipaul depicts how in contemporary times many conservative forms of Islam have arrived from the Middle East. Oddly, some of this movement was facilitated by the colonization of East Asia. The opening of steamer lines by the Dutch, French and English allowed Muslim peoples that had been more or less isolated from their co-religionists to have easier access to Arabia and Egypt, among other places, where they dipped into the well of Wahhabism and carried it back to their native lands. In some areas, radical Islam became coupled with rising movements of nationalism and, with the coming of independence, became intricately bound up with the trends that attempted to create a new national and social self-image for formerly subject peoples.

The folk Islam and Sufism that had always been practised with a distinctly syncretistic flavour in places like Indonesia began to be altered by this influx of religious ideas from Arab lands. In Indonesia, the largest Muslim country in the world, most of the folk culture is based on the heritage left from the Buddhist–Hindu empires that ruled the region prior to the coming of Islam in the early fourteenth century. This can be seen, among other places, in the *wayan* puppet shows and shadow plays,[9] which are often thinly disguised tales taken from traditional Hindu epics. These folk paths are being erased by orthodox Islam-educated Indonesians.[10]

Saint veneration and syncretism

Saint worship is not only a problem for Islam, for at various times Christianity and Judaism have struggled with these identical tendencies. One of the issues of the Reformation in its more radical form was the rejection of the Roman Church's cult of saints,[11] and various Jewish authorities have at different times also taken aim against this tendency and the host of practices that accompany it.[12] What is it exactly about the veneration of saints and their cults that is so troublesome to some sectors of Islam, and indeed to the three Abrahamic religions?

The simple answer is that saint veneration, and worship along with their cults and cultic practices, are the great storehouse for religious syncretism. A strong and nearly universal cross-cultural element exists in saint veneration. For Islam, the problem primarily resides in its various mystical branches, the Sufi movements, where saint veneration is most often found. For Judaism, the problem resides especially in the practical application of the Kabbala, Judaism's mystical movement, along with saint veneration, which often go hand in glove. Suspect practices seem to cleave to saint veneration like metal shavings to a magnet, but unlike wispy bits of iron, they require more than a swipe of the hand to eradicate.

For Islam, this influence has been particularly pernicious when it has come into conflict with cultures whose values drastically opposed its own. In India, this has occurred at celebrations at saints' tombs, where the classical framework of Islamic saint veneration has been infused with distinctively Hindu elements like instrumental processional bands and dancing girls who often act as sacred prostitutes, as are sometimes found in Hindu temples.[13] Mediums, used for contact with the dead and so frequently employed in Hinduism during sacred events, often perform at Islamic saints' shrines, fulfilling a role that is to be found nowhere in standard, normative Islam.[14]

Even stronger examples can be found all over India, Pakistan and Bangladesh. The so-called *Panch Pir* grouping of five saints is venerated widely on the subcontinent, and in Islamic circles includes the Prophet Muhammad, his two grandsons (Hasan and Husayn) and sometimes a Hindu goddess or two. In the mountains of Nepal, one researcher even discovered a *Panch Pir* group consisting of the Prophet, his two grandsons, the saint Madar Shah, who was the founder of the Madari Sufi order, and the goddess Sahaja Mai. Many Muslim saints are also venerated by the Hindu inhabitants of India. For example, Mu'inuddin Cisht, who is considered to be the first great propagator of Islam in India, is celebrated nearly everywhere in an annual festival, and both Muslim and Hindu pilgrims visit his tomb in Ajmer. In fact, the cults of Islamic saints and the cults of Hindu gods or saints are often so similar they bridge the theological gulf between Muslim monotheism and Hindu polytheism. Popular two-way syncretism is aware of the difference between the two religions, which is less of a problem in the domain of cultic practices, both on the local and even sometimes on the national level, than it becomes in other areas such as ritual food, marriage outside the group and political association. But the petty parcelling out of religious association is less important than the one great standard of folk religion that has a near universal reach: pragmatism. Folk religion is practised because people believe it will benefit their lives – and whether their beliefs match those of theologians is a distant concern.

Sufi mysticism, Sufi saints and syncretism

We will examine one order of Sufi mysticism that had an appeal in the Balkans, in order to view some of the trouble that a mystical tendency in Islam has had when it has begun to involve itself in the very real, present-in-the-world activity of proselytizing the faith. As we stated before, the Sufism that entered the Balkans was heavily influenced by the rootless life of the Turkic tribes that settled Anatolia. The Turks, a nomadic people practising tribal shamanism, converted to Islam but maintained the shamanic centrality of the holy man in their religious and social life. When various Turkoman tribes passed through Iran they adopted and adapted Zoroastrian ideas into their brand of Islam,[15] so the Sufism that arrived in the Balkans was already a cocktail composed of diverse elements. This faith was not shy in adopting elements into its core set of beliefs, and when it settled in the Balkans, it continued this trend, melting and merging with the folk Christianity practised in the former provinces of the Eastern Roman Empire, Byzantium.

The Baktashiyya brotherhood of Islamic Sufi mystics certainly bears out this unique and varied genealogy. Nominally a Sunni movement, it fitted well with the Ottoman Empire, which was predominately Sunni. The Ottoman state actually had a suspicion of Shi'ism, since some of its eastern neighbours were Shi'a and had territorial ambitions in Ottoman lands, but the Baktashiyya were de facto Shi'ite – outwardly Sunni but inwardly Shi'ite. Shi'a Islam, with its veneration of Ali and his martyred son Husain, is a movement that by the very nature of its hero-worship tends to invite all sorts of variations from orthodox Islam, and even from orthodox Shi'ism. The early Shi'a tradition enshrined the notion that Ali received special knowledge of the inner meaning of the Qur'an. Religious figures with special or secret knowledge have always invited wild speculation, especially of a Gnostic character.[16] Most Shi'ites are Twelve Imam Shi'ites who believe that there were twelve legitimate rulers, or Imams, in the Islamic world in a line of succession from the Prophet. A component of their belief involves the 'Hidden Imam', a ruler who is said to have disappeared, and thus started the so-called occultation of the Imam.[17] The whereabouts of this missing Imam became the jumping off point for some wild theological speculations. Supernatural, messianic interpretation abounded, and there became a tendency in this type of Shi'ism to view the Imams as physical manifestations of Allah. One of the more successful offshoots of Shi'a Islam is Baha'ism, which is an outgrowth of Babism, a Shi'a reform movement founded in 1844 by Ali Muhammad of Shiraz in Iran, who proclaimed himself the bab, or living door between Allah and the Hidden Imam. He abrogated Islamic law for his followers in 1848, and his movement was rigorously persecuted. In 1850 the Bab was executed. His movement survived in exile, but it mutated into a religion wholly separated from Islam in 1868 with the coming of

Mirza Husayn Ali Nuri, known as the Baba Ullah, who then declared himself the Chosen One. His religion, Baha'ism, is universalistic in its reach, advocating the unity of all religions, and it is syncretistic to the core, proclaiming that God has been sending his prophets as his flesh-and-blood manifestations throughout history, and that they culminated in the Baba Ullah. It is important to realize that the movement began from a tendency on the part of Shi'a Islam to venerate its ancestral heroes. Shi'a doctrine, when taken to its logical (or some would argue illogical) extremes invites heresy.[18]

The Baktashiyya pursued the tendencies of Shi'a Islam to the bitter end. They combined Shi'ite veneration of the Imams with the tendency of all Sufi orders to worship their founder – and like most Sufi orders, the Baktashiyya was founded by a single man. His name was Hajji Baktash, and he was born in Khurasan in the thirteenth century. As in most Sufi orders, the founder set the tempo of religious and organizational life for the order, and became both an individual of importance during his life, and an object of veneration after his death.

The Baktashiyya clung tenaciously to many heterodox practices and beliefs. They used Turkish during their ceremonies instead of Arabic. They believed in bird metamorphosis, as Hajji Baktash supposedly had the power to transform himself into a dove. During the sixteenth century they also added other religious elements, including the so-called *Huruf-i* doctrine, which was an extremely heterodox form of Islam incorporating many elements from Judaism's Kabbala, including its tendency to use white magic to transform and control nature, coupled with its wild speculations about the components of the godhead. Additionally, the movement clung to an element that repeatedly caused trouble for them: hypostatization, or the transformation of human beings into divinities. They took these ideas from the Shi'ites as well as from Anatolian Christian groups, who held an especially liberal proliferation of Trinitarian doctrines, or the dividing of God into three. Since there was no set or standard doctrine for the Baktashiyya (in fact, that was a central principle behind their brand of Sufism) these Trinitarian groupings changed widely from time to time and place to place. When the Baktashiyya landed in Albania, the divine trio was Allah, Muhammad and his daughter Fatima. Sometimes a lesser trio was venerated, such as Ali, Fatima's husband and one of their sons, either Hasan or Husayn. Some groups venerated a trinity of Ali, Hajji Baktash and Fazlallah Astarabadi, a Muslim heretic who was executed in 1407 for his Gnostic notions.[19] Often Ali, the prophet's adopted son and cousin, was merged with the person of Muhammad, becoming a hypostatized dual personage of high spiritual value.[20]

This veneration of Ali gave the Baktashiyya their designation as Shi'ites or followers of Ali, but of course, no Orthodox Shi'ite would accept what they did with the veneration of Ali. The Baktashiyya believed in the transmigration of souls, or metempsychosis (a belief they may have pilfered from the Kabbala, which also has notions about reincarnation). The dual person of Muhammad–Ali was believed by the Baktashiyya Albanians to be represented on earth by every grand Baba of the order, and hence the Babas were subject to veneration.

Typically, a Baktashiyya creed included belief in the divine authority of the Twelve Imams, along with Moses, Mary, Jesus and numerous saints. But worship was a secret rite, reserved for the high initiates of the order. Only those not initiated into the rites of the Baktashiyya were required to follow the *shari'a*, or Islamic sacred law. The inner, secret and true meaning of the Qur'an was reserved for the elect, and that knowledge entitled them to relax many of the orthodox standards followed by the rest of the Muslim community. This inner circle negated the *namaz*, or the five prayers, and did away with ritual bathing, and women, who were normally segregated in many Muslim communities, could participate in the services with men. This led to accusations of Baktashiyya lasciviousness, but really, that was the least of their sins of transgression against orthodoxy. One of the prime directives of the Abrahamic religions is their openness to any willing convert. As a matter of practical policy, the Abrahamic religions can be practised anywhere by anyone. Most orthodox movements generally strive not to impose intellectual and formal requirements, but mystical movements such as the Baktashiyya often cast aside this demotic inclusiveness for more exclusive standards.

The relationship between Baktashiyya Sufism and Gnosticism

We can also see this in the cult of Mithras, which was an incredibly popular pagan religion in the late Roman Empire, but which was eclipsed by the rise of Christianity as the state religion of Rome. Mithraism was a relatively late trend in Roman religion, and helped temporarily revive the declining position of paganism.[21] Like Christianity, Mithraism was a monotheistic creed and both faiths used rituals and liturgies with redemptive and cathartic elements. Like Christianity, Mithraism was a cosmic religion and it focused its energies on the personage of a single God-man. Both religions were born in lands other than the Roman Mediterranean heartland (Christianity in Judaea and Galilee and Mithraism in Persia) but both received widespread propagation along the well-travelled trade and military pathways of the Roman Empire. Like Christianity, Mithraism was adept at adopting and transforming as it travelled through the Empire. Originally a Zoroastrian religion with many Persian and Indian elements, in its journey west Mithraism also picked up Chaldaean and Babylonian doctrines and liturgies, including a detailed astrology, astralism and magico-religious disciplines of the Magusai sects.[22] Roman

Mithraism was heir to all these trends, and the syncretistic nature of the faith enabled it to take on more of a mystical and redemptive character, which were themes that apparently suited the times.

Mithras was worshipped in a constructed or natural cave known as a *specus*. Usually, the cave was adorned with images of the god and his exploits. Those images varied, but nearly all Mithraea contained a statue depicting the event that created the world: the god's slaughter of the cosmic bull, the *tauroctonia*. The specifics of Mithraic worship differed from Christianity, but since very early times, the similarities between Mithraic and Christian rites disturbed the early Church fathers. The early Church fathers attempted to slander Mithraism when they could and the secret nature of the initiation process, held deep in an underground vault, was an easy target for its enemies to mischaracterize. The Church father Tertullian called the Mithraic temple 'the kingdom of the shades'.[23]

In the end, the Gnostic character of Mithraism probably brought about its demise. Gnostic religions have the attainment of special knowledge as their cornerstone. If the attainment of knowledge is the special prerogative of the devotee of Mithras and not of Christ, then the doors to Christ open wider, while those to Mithras close to some degree. Early Christianity fought hard to destroy Mithraism, but in a great irony, the spectre of Mithraism was found in Christianity, and even in Islam and Judaism. As soon as a Jewish, Christian or Islamic group starts to practise secret rites, the Gnostic beast stirs, and the old call to Mithraic initiation is asserted. Secret Gnosticism in the Abrahamic religions led to a kind of purposeful duplicity – a public and private face for the faiths.

We see this two-faced surface in many Sufi-dervish orders, like the Baktashiyya. At least for their moderate and liberal forms, the face they turned to the public was substantially different from their private, communal face, creating a distinction between an esoteric and exoteric philosophy of religion.[24] The exoteric is the outward form of religious practice, which is open to all. For Islam, that is embodied by the five pillars: faith, prayer, charity, the fast (during Ramadan) and the pilgrimage or *hajj*. An esoteric philosophy is a hidden doctrine, open to a few and not widely revealed. The Baktashiyya had innumerable secret doctrines, which they hid with varying degrees of success or failure during their long history. Such doctrines include a belief in the divinity of Ali, a tripartite division of Allah and the relaxation of ritual standards. An allegorical reading, as opposed to a literal reading, of the Qur'an is also part of this esoteric philosophy. The Baktashiyya shared many characteristics with the Gnostic rites of Mithra, like the fourfold system of initiation, known as the four gates of admission. The first gate was the *shari'a*, or the law, the Qur'an and Hadith, which is the exoteric way of mainstream Islam. The second was participation in the *Tarika*, which were certain mystical and mental exercises, designed to purify the initiate. The third was receipt of the *Ma'rifa*, or Gnosis, which was the very dawning of the mystical consciousness on the individual seeker, and finally the fourth was the *Hakika*, or Truth, which was available only for those who had attained the very pinnacle of divine knowledge and were transformed into something decidedly different from the rank-and-file worshipper.

Finer gradations of inclusion also existed in the Baktashiyya movement. The *ashik* was an associated member of the order without the full rights of membership, the *mukhip* was an *ashik* who had passed through the ceremony of initiation and received limited rights to participate in Baktashiyya ritual meetings, and the *devsh* was a *mukhip* who had completed the stage of service to the elders of the brotherhood, and attained some skill in the practice of the way. This last group were special members and were given permission to wear the ritual accessories of the order: the *hikra*, or Sufi's cloak, and the *taj*, the ritual hat. The *Baba* was appointed as the head of the *devshs* and *mukhips* on a local level, who were the heads of smaller communities, and were allowed to wear a *taj* with a white band around its top. The *devish-I mudjarrad* were dervishes who took the vow of celibacy, and such members of the order participated in the secret rites of initiation. As a special sign of their exalted status, they shaved their heads, beards and moustaches (a marked contrast to the Muslim practice of full beards), and wore a silver or copper ring in their right ear. Finally, the *caliphas* were dervishes who controlled an entire geographical region, usually containing a number of brotherhoods.

The Baktashiyya communities took on certain characteristics that resembled those of Christian monastic houses. This tendency to mimic Christian tradition is found in Sufism in general, and has frequently brought it criticism from a wide variety of sources.[25] The Sufi cloak, worn by the Baktashiyya and numerous other orders, was made of a rough material, like a monk's habit. Often, Sufi orders of extreme ascetic inclination, like the Baktashiyya, took vows (either life-long or temporary) of celibacy, and many orders, including the Baktashiyya, lived in semi-enclosed communities, like monasteries, with separate buildings for ritual, economic and domestic use. The Sufi resemblance to Christian monks was sufficient for many Muslim clerics to declare them heretics.

Syncretism and Baktashiya Sufism: a two-sided religious experience

The syncretistic character of the Baktashiyya brand of Sufism is apparent even from this relatively brief survey. They borrowed everywhere, and from everything with which they came into contact. From their base of Turkish Islam infused with a Sufism that had been influenced by Persian Zoroastrianism, tribal shamanism and Anatolian Christianity, the Baktashiyya absorbed distinctly Balkan modes of worship, styles of dress, and, most important of all, an eclecticism that has always been the hallmark of Balkan religious life.

Movements like the Baktashiyya often mask their real heretical and unorthodox views behind the exoteric/esoteric dichotomy. Their exoteric religious philosophy is for the rank and file: the unschooled and untutored absorb basic and essential religious revelation from the Prophet, Jesus or Moses. Some thinkers, such as the tenth-century Jewish theologian and philosopher Maimonides, believed that an exoteric faith existed for the purpose of nation-building. Maimonides believed God sought to create a nation known as Israel, but first he had to separate this nation from the mass of idol worshippers who surrounded it. So he revealed a religion based on positive and negative laws, forcing people to believe and behave according to divine dictates but without any spiritual or intellectual requirements. So the Law, in a sense, is the *form* of a religion; thus an intellectual elite can forgo certain aspects of formal religion because they understand the practical strictures of divine ordinances as merely symbolic.[26] For less cautious groups like the Baktashiyya, this idea can lead to the abrogation of religious law, at least for the elite. Thinkers like Maimonides never endorsed abrogation for either the elite or the masses, but his esoteric philosophy certainly leaves room for the elite to hold beliefs about God and his law that would be considered heretical by most religious authorities.

This intellectual syncretism is a rarefied and deliberate form of what folk religion does naturally. The esoteric/exoteric distinction allows seemingly mutually exclusive or contradictory practices and ideas to exist together in formal religious settings. Popular folk syncretism accomplishes the same thing, but without the elaborate protective structures its elitist cousins utilize.

The syncretism of Saint Besse: a pagan deity in Christian garb

Popular saint veneration often carries the exoteric/esoteric distinction. Of course, the element of secrecy is missing, but it is replaced by an even more two-faced phenomenon: one face the formal, accepted religion of a region or people, and the other a syncretistic graft. In other words, the dominant religion is combined with a subservient religion creating a dual, simultaneously orthodox and heterodox religious face.

As we have seen, syncretism often involves the blending of older religious practices with newer ones. A religion only inadequately supplants another religion, and elements of the old faith persist, often in harmless ways. The manifestations can be as small and specific as the Green Man ornamentation or more profound, in ways we will explore below. Saint veneration is usually the vehicle for this unique dynamic.

Every tenth of August, in a remote valley in the Italian Graian Alps, a lesser saint is venerated whose location and function at first seems to be not deeply syncretistic at all. This saint, St Besse, has an ancient lineage. He is indigenous to the region, springing from the rocky land of the Italian Alps like a piece of natural geography. And we shall see why this is a fitting metaphor.

But first some details. St Besse is unique among the lesser, unofficial saints of Roman Catholicism, because he is not confined to any special-ized tasks. He is called the saint who gives his devotees 'firm protection in all circumstances'. Even so, he has seemed to develop some areas where he excels. For example, he is often portrayed in the guise of a soldier, and as such is considered the patron of those in uniform. The focus of his cult is a small chapel that is attached to a large, hulking block of standing stone, which rears up almost alone in the middle of the high pastures of the area. This rock is called 'St Besse's Mount', and on it stand a cross and a small oratory, behind which is a ladder, which gives access to the pin-nacle of the mount. Here, the faithful are allowed to climb the ladder and chip the rock with knives, then carry the chips home as 'stones of Besse' and keep them as if they were relics of the saint himself. During times of war, the people of this valley have worn them as talismans (amulets with special powers) for protection. During peacetime, these relics are kept in homes as tokens of safekeeping. More importantly still, the stones, when mashed into a powder and mixed with liquid, have often been consumed by people with various illnesses because of their supposed restorative and regenerative properties.

In some legends, St Besse is a Roman soldier who fought in the Theban Legion. In these legends he was a Christian, and while the rest of his band of soldiers were slaughtered in a battle, he escaped. Through various in-trigues with hostile locals, he was abused and finally handed over to the Roman legion, who viewed him as a traitor for his suspicious escape fol-lowing the massacre of his fellow legionnaires. He died a glorious martyr and his remains were interred in the rock that would eventually become the centre of his veneration.

A competing tradition portrays St Besse as a simple shepherd. As a god-intoxicated boy, spending all his time on the high alpine meadows among his flocks, he has no time for anything like proper shepherding. He mostly fasts and prays. Because of his holiness, God blesses Besse by making his flock the fattest. The jealousy of the other shepherds leads to Besse's inevitable murder and he is thrown down from the top of the mount that would later be the focal point of his veneration.

Robert Hertz, in his masterful essay on St Besse, explains the probable origin of both stories.[27] This area of the Alps is roughly divided into two groups, separated by geography and language, and they have always vied for political and cultural control of the region. Frequently devotion to

St Besse and the stories told about him reflect the varied contemporary concerns of the modern worshippers. Hertz examines the name 'Besse', and sees in it an echo of the word *bescha*, as in *Munt della bescha*, or the mountain of sheep, which is often used in the canton of Grisons to denote high pasturage. The word is most likely descended from the Latin word *bestia*, or sheep. So in one popular story of Besse, he becomes a shepherd because the etymology of his name is most likely from the dialect word for 'sheep'. In the speech of the Soana Valley, the corresponding Romansh word *besch* gives rise to *bess*. In both areas the conjunction is almost perfect: the name Besse is bound to sheep both in form and function.

Most important for Hertz are not the variations on stories told of St Besse and his supposed martyrdom, but the stable element, the rock where his martyrdom occurred, which continued to be the site of his veneration until well into modern times. Hertz reaches the conclusion that the rock of St Besse is the actual object of veneration. The clue is in the consumption of the stones – known technically as *geophagy,* which is common the world over.[28] If devotees consume St Besse's stone, then logically the stone must be viewed as sacred, or at least able to impart special power.

Other examples of stone veneration

Stone veneration is ancient. As we saw in the introduction, Islam uses the Ka'ba, the black stone employed in pre-Islamic worship, as a symbol of Allah. Similarly, stones and their sacred mounts have been worshipped in almost every culture that has one or both. St Besse's chapel, with its *geophagy* and stone veneration, points to a pre-Christian practice, most likely connected to earth deities. In this rocky Alpine area reliant on sheep for food and clothes, this sort of religion makes a great deal of historical sense and the survival of these practices after the coming of Christianity also has a certain social and historical logic.

If we think that this kind of transference of a sacred site from one religion to another is only confined to minor examples like St Besse, we need only look at some of the West's great sacred sites. As we saw in the introduction, the fixtures used in the *hajj* in Mecca have a pre-Islamic origin. The Temple Mount in Jerusalem, now home to the Dome of The Rock, Islam's third most important sacred site (and the area where Muhammad ascended into heaven)[29] was once the site of the Temple, which was Judaism's most sacred building and where ritual sacrifices were performed. The site of the Dome of the Rock is only a portion of the Temple. The rock is known is the *eben shetiyyah*, which in Hebrew means 'the stone of the foundation'. The rock was the traditional location of the Ark of the Covenant, Israel's visible symbol of their pact with God.

But we should not think that the rock's sanctity is based solely on the events that occurred around it. Just like with St Besse, these quasi-historical occurrences on the mount are only grafts. The tales are only (admittedly important) surface dross behind the sanctity of the Mount. The Hebrew term for the rock, 'the stone of foundation', refers to the widespread belief that this was the foundation stone that God used in the formation of the world. This stone was not only the keystone for creation, but also a kind of cap, holding the waters of the abyss (or the *tehom,* often depicted as a serpent's mouth, which had flowed water freely before creation) plugged. In Latin the foundation stone is known as the *axis mundi,* the world axis, and in Greek it is called the *omphalos,* or the 'world navel', the exact spot where the world was created and where all of creation is subsequently hinged. Beneath this stone is a small cave known in Arabic as the *bir-el-arweh,* the 'well of souls', which is the supposed entrance to the world of the dead.[30] So this stone, as well as being the keystone of the world, was also supposed to be a nexus between this world and the next, and the abode of the shades who inhabited an older Semitic notion of the afterlife, called *sheol* in Hebrew.

The sanctity of the rock on the Temple Mount, then, dates back to the older manifestations of Semitic religions of the region. The religions that became Judaism, Islam and Christianity, all heirs to this Semitic ancestor, have used this sacred spot to bolster their claims of divine authority.

The syncretism here is so fluid, and the historical grafting work so clever that we can barely see the seam. In Muslim tradition the cave below the rock was created when Muhammad ascended into heaven and the stone wanted to join him. Unable to fully follow, the uplifted rock created the space now known as the well of the souls. Of course, the cave existed long before Islam and long before the birth of Muhammad and we can almost strip the historical layers from the Temple Mount to the time when the Jebusites ruled the city. During David's conquest of Jerusalem, found in 2 Samuel 5.6–9 and 1 Chronicles 11.4–7, he brought the Ark to Jerusalem, but did not attempt to install it on the site of the Temple until 24 years later when David purchased the Temple Mount site, then called the *goren* of Arvana the Jebusite. The Hebrew word *goren* is traditionally translated as 'threshing floor', but the word can also mean a circular place of pagan worship. Many scholars believe that Arvana's *goren* was probably a Jebusite shrine connected with fertility worship. In fact, threshing floors are usually placed near agricultural fields or in the open spaces in front of town gates, and the Temple Mount is an elevated, rocky place, and was probably never a cultivated area. The name Arvana (or Araunah) appears in the Bible in 2 Samuel 24. The word *arvana* appears in Ugaritic texts as a general term for ruler. The Arvana of 2 Samuel was most likely not a mere peasant with a threshing floor, but the last king of the Jebusite city. He was probably a king-priest like Melchizedek of Salem in Genesis 14.18. Even when Arvana lost his kingdom to David he more than likely continued to perform the sacred functions of the priest. King David purchased the high spot of Jebusite worship and installed the Ark of the Convent on what would become the Temple Mount, both assimilating and usurping the divine claims of the Jebusite god Salem. Jerusalem, the original Hebrew pronunciation of which was like Yerushalem, means 'City of Salem', or 'City founded by Salem'. It was extremely common for cities to be named after patron deities in ancient Semitic cultures. Salem was the Semitic god of completeness and creation and of the setting sun (and most likely of peace, for his name comes from the three root letters in Hebrew for peace, as in *shalom*).[31]

So David did much the same thing that was done with St Besse's stone. The Temple Mount, originally a pagan or early Semitic place of worship, became, in the reign of his son Solomon, the site of the Temple, which became the religious fixation point for Judaism until its last manifestation destroyed by the Romans in AD 70.

Besse: a pre-Christian god in a saint's clothes

Is this really a form of syncretism? On one hand, it is the clearest expression of syncretism and on the other it is another phenomenon entirely. The 'holy site' syncretism found in the veneration of St Besse and the Temple Mount is a kind of blending of one religious tradition onto another. The stone at St Besse's has probably *always* been venerated, but the specific type of worship has depended upon several factors, the most important being how the actual, real-life veneration of the stone interacts with the religion of the region. When the veneration of the stone *was* the religion of the region, there were no problems, but when the veneration became subjected to local Christian worship in the area, syncretism began to play a role. At that point, the worship of Christ, the establishment of local parishes, and the veneration of Besse as a cover for the veneration of the old stone, merged to form a single local custom with clearly syncretistic elements.

The sanctification of the Holy Mount is a similar case. This sacred site was venerated, in turn, by the Jebusites, the Davidic monarchy-run state cult of the Temple, and Islam. The site has always been holy, and was the *axis mundi* of the Semitic peoples in the region. The stone that capped it was the literal crux of the universe, the entrance to the underworld and the keystone of the world. Everything of any importance seems to have occurred there: God fashioned Adam from its soil, Abraham nearly sacrificed Isaac on its stone, Muhammad ascended into heaven during his mystical night flight from Mecca to Jerusalem. The sanctity of the site remains throughout all the manifestations, so the stable element is the sacred stone, while the stories that are told to justify that sanctity change from time to time. The site remains holy and the stone is holy but the guise in which it is dressed changes. [32]

The syncretism of a holy place is slightly dissimilar from the syncretism of a holy practice. We saw how the Baktashiyya practise elements of an esoteric or secret cult with initiation stages and levels of holiness. The Baktashiyya have taken the normative practice of Islam and suspended it for certain of their devotees. Essentially, they allow certain of their elect members to practise a mystery cult that is completely alien to the spirit of Islam. But the higher levels of the Baktashiyya hide this aspect of their worship. The hidden side of their rites is heretical, so it must be concealed. The syncretism of a holy place can often forgo any secrecy. Quite the contrary, this type of syncretism is almost always public and nearly always local and, as in the case of the Temple Mount, national. This type of syncretism attempts to capitalize on its predecessors' holy sites in order to shore up claims of hegemony. This also happens a great deal with Christian holy days, which nearly always correspond to pagan or pre-Christian holidays. Seizing a holy site does much the same thing that changing a holiday does: it takes the power from the preceding religion and transfers it to the new one, so it strengthens the hold of the new, while lessening the powerful memory of the old. Of course this process is loaded with all sorts of unexpected ironies. It keeps the old ways alive, albeit in altered forms, and creates a taint in the bloodstream of the new creed, giving the appearance of admixture, of impurity, of syncretism. Often the very thing that the adherents of the new faith wished to eradicate winds up having a new life and sometimes that new life matures into something totally unexpected.

North African Jewish saint veneration: a unique syncretism with Islamic and Berber customs

Traditional Judaism has specific strictures against the veneration of individual people. Moses, as the literal giver of the Torah to the people of Israel, is without doubt the greatest figure in the history of Judaism. His stature is far greater than even Abraham or Noah, since his legacy lived on in written form. Later, post-biblical traditions portray the *shekinah*, or the female instantiation of God, carrying Moses away at the time of his death, and even administering the kiss that withdraws his soul from his body. In these portrayals, his body is then hidden away to prevent the people of Israel worshipping his grave. [33] The propensity for people everywhere to devote their religious energies to the veneration of holy men and women, both living and dead, has often been seen as a great danger. But for the greatest Jew that ever lived, it seemed inevitable, and only the sly stealing of his body prevented this. A man who had literally seen God 'face to face' and knew him as a friend, had to be hidden to prevent people from worshipping him as a god. But this has not prevented Jews from venerating other holy people of lesser stature, at other times and in other places. Nowhere is this more evident than in North Africa and nowhere is it more prevalent than in Morocco.

A teeming and ineradicable veneration of local North African saints, by both men and women and of men and women saints, in the Christian, Muslim and Jewish traditions, has been attested for some time. In the time of Augustine of Hippo (AD 354–430), natives in Roman North Africa had a pronounced tendency to visit shrines of holy men and women in order to venerate them and collect their holy items for special treatment.[34] This tendency probably pre-dated the arrival of Christianity in North Africa[35] and continues to this day. Most of North Africa in the West is inhabited by a people known as the Berbers. The world 'berber' comes from the Graeco-Roman word 'Barbarian'. The Berbers, however, call themselves *Imazighen* (Free Men) and speak a series of languages and dialects from the Chamito-Semitic group (called Berber, or *Tamazight*). With the arrival of Islam in North Africa, Berber peoples were progressively Islamicized, but as we have seen above, they often formed a marked syncretism that bore deep imprints of the precursor Berber practices. Again, saint veneration and worship was and is the great repository of this admixing. For the Jews of Morocco, saint veneration, learned from Berber Muslims and adopted into a Jewish framework, allowed, in a sense, for a unique and flavourful blending of Berber animism, Muslim practices and Judaism.

Certain saints are venerated during their lifetimes. Saints are almost always revered for their great learning and piety, and for their ability to control the forces of nature.[36] Saints can raise the dead, create food, control the elements, stop the sun from moving across the sky, create rain, heal sickness, and cure sterility. Some saints, by the nature of their mastery of the elements, do not die in the conventional sense but merely pass on to the other side without decaying, and even those who do die often come back to visit their disciples and those in need. While alive, Jewish saints will often have studied with holy figures from Judaism's past, particularly the prophet Elijah. Once they are dead, the saints' graves become holy sites worthy of veneration (since the dead saints can still be appealed to in the beyond). Interestingly enough, Muslim and Jewish saints' graves in Morocco are almost always associated with stones or rocks, streams or springs, and trees or plants.[37] The conjunction of saints' graves and natural elements is hardly accidental, and points to the underlying Berber practice behind the custom, which involved active worship of the things that a Berber (as a desert person) would find important in his or her environment: water, trees and unusual rocks or stones that acted as lines or markers of demarcation between groups. Animism, or the worship of usually inanimate objects in the world that have been, in a sense, rendered alive or ensouled, is a vital tribal practice of many people. In the Berber context, the pattern is quite familiar: certain sites, such as a stream, a spring, or a prominent stone or tree, are sacred to the indigenous religion, and the newly arrived faith (in this case Islam) cannot eradicate the site, so it incorporates it.[38] Universalizing creeds like Islam can make interesting compromises when they encounter an ineradicable particular.

For Islam, the veneration of saints in Morocco took decidedly un-Islamic turns in certain cases. Some examples of ritual prostitution have been observed in the rites associated with some *mussem,* or pilgrimages to saints' shrines. The majority of Muslim cultures, which usually segregate men and women according to strict codes, would look upon this with distaste. Berberized Islam, however, allows this, in certain cases, since it is an expression of a type of worship that is so old it can be looked upon as normative, even in an Islamic context.[39] It is quite easy to see the decidedly syncretistic nature of Muslim saint veneration, as Muslim saints, like saints who are venerated everywhere, often become the focus of divine energies that are usually reserved for God, or in the very least, for his deputies the angels. Saint worship de-centres cosmic powers away from God and his ministers and spreads this power to mortals. Muslim men and women seek out saints because their intervention can get them what they need or want, and because physical contact with a living saint or with his grave after death promises a residue of power that can be passed on to others. Divine energy, in a sense, flows from the saint to his devotees. The world becomes not abandoned by God but peopled with semi-divine creatures that can be appealed to, appeased, pleaded with and bribed.

Jewish Moroccan saints share some of the functions of Muslim ones, but with important differences. For example, there is not a single attested case of ritual prostitution connected with the veneration of Jewish saints in Morocco.[40] Although Jewish *hillulot* (pilgrimages to saints' shrines) are joyous occasions, they are usually more subdued than the Muslim Berber versions, which are often accompanied by music, wild dancing and sometimes drunkenness. Jewish pilgrimages tend to be more sober affairs. This is not, in any way, to accuse Muslim Berbers of licentiousness. It simply points out how a specifically Jewish context has changed the nature of a number of older Berber customs.

Saints in both cultures are venerated in festivals at certain times of the year, usually when the weather in Morocco is temperate. At these times, the pilgrimage is a family and community affair, and people of all social classes and sexes mix together, both in travelling to the tomb or shrine and once they have arrived there. Very often, the saint is buried in an inhospitable location, which does not seem accidental, as the pilgrimage is supposed to be marginally rigorous, to give the devotees a sense of accomplishment in visiting their saint. People pitch tents close to the saint's tomb, and wealthy people try to get rooms or portable shelters close to the grave, since proximity is seen as advantageous. Saint veneration in Morocco has religious, social, economic and even transnational functions and, as such, it is an intricate part of Moroccan life.

The areas of overlap between Jewish and Muslim saint veneration far outweigh the areas of disjuncture. There is something like a pan-saint veneration in Morocco, which can be seen no more clearly than in the Muslim adoption of Jewish saints and, in a more limited number, the Jewish adoption of Muslim saints. Very often, Muslims will so entirely adopt a Jewish saint that his or her religious status is blurred. Sometimes, the Islamization of Jewish saints occurs simply by long familiarity of Muslims with a specific Jewish saint's tomb. A Muslim family may become caretakers of a tomb, either because they reside near it or because they are assigned the job by local Jews, and that family will tend the grave in a hereditary capacity. Eventually, the Jewish saint becomes an object of Muslim veneration. Jewish saints are also appealed to by Muslims because Muslim saints have failed the individual petitioner in his or her request,[41] and Jewish saints are traditionally not averse to helping Muslims who have the correct attitude of respect and reverence.

The opposite tendency, for Jews to venerate Muslim saints, is less prevalent. For although Muslims, even those of a decidedly syncretistic blend like the Berbers, can view Judaism as a valid religion across a wide range of practices and beliefs, Jews cannot reciprocate by seeing validity in Islam, a religion that is supposed to supersede Judaism. Of course, in some contexts, this does not prevent a limited number of Muslim saints from becoming the objects of Jewish veneration, as there is a fascinating tendency among the Jews and Muslim of Morocco to view their saints as a common, shared heritage. This can be seen clearly in the phenomenon of the 'forgotten saint', in which no one will know where a saint is buried, either because he or she has been forgotten, or because his or her cult has fallen into disuse. The saint's tomb will be uncovered by a Muslim ploughing a field, for instance, and a Jewish saint will become a Muslim one. The opposite tendency is less common, but not entirely unknown. The forgotten saint, having been stripped of identity, seems to invite the people of Morocco to invest him or her with any religion they deem fit. For the Jews of Morocco, the forgotten saint phenomenon has national importance: it is a widely held folk belief that when all the forgotten saints of Morocco are remembered, the ingathering of Jews in the Holy Land during the messianic age will commence. Here Jews have taken a strictly local custom and given it wider messianic importance.

Chapter summary

Saint veneration is the ideal vehicle for the transmission of syncretistic practices. We see this clearly in the example of Islam in the Caucasus, where Wahhabist forms of Islam have penetrated the region. Wahhabist Islam considers Sufi practices non-Islamic, and the nativization of Islam under Sufi auspices in the region has been under attack in recent years. One reason for Wahhabi rejection of Sufism is that it often preserves native, pre-Islamic elements. This is true of saint veneration in general. The cross-cultural nature of these transfers is apparent, and points to a series of practices and folk beliefs that transcend the narrow confines of an Abrahamic religion's supposed borders. The examples in this chapter – the Baktashiyya Sufism in the Balkans, the veneration of Saint Besse in Europe, and the veneration of Jewish and Muslim saints in Morocco – point to a collision of two religious worlds: that of the transcendent, single God that exists above and beyond the world, and that of the scattered, decentralized spiritual realm that exists everywhere, but has more power in certain locations and with certain people of great holiness, power and skill – the revered saints and their grave sites. This is another case of the folk giving themselves what they need: an appeal to physical specificity in religions that have at their foundations one abstract, invisible God.[42] Saint veneration not only allows the practices of the Abrahamic religions to penetrate each other's traditions but also allows the entry of paganism and pagan practices into their midst. As we saw with the veneration of St Besse, ancient stone worship was mixed with conventional Christian saint veneration and, among the Jews of Morocco, the tombs of saints were often the older markers of pre-Islamic or pre-Jewish sacred objects, like trees, stones or springs. This transference of holy places and qualities is not uncommon in saint veneration. The next chapter will explore religious history's greatest exemplar of this trend, the Virgin Mary, and her rise from a human woman to a divine being.

Draw your own conclusions

Is there a difference between saint veneration and saint worship (hagiolatry)?

Are there differences between gods and goddesses in a 'pagan' pantheon and the notion of God, the angels, and the saints in the Abrahamic religions?

Do the saints explored in this chapter assume roles of God?

Does saint veneration (or worship) always involve syncretism?

What is the place of the 'saint' in the Abrahamic religions?

Further reading

For a view of the rise of Wahhabist types of Islam in lands where a more native Islam once flourished without rivals:
V. S. Naipaul (1981), *Among the Believers*, New York: Vintage Books.
V. S. Naipaul (1998), *Beyond Belief*, New York: Vintage Books.

For saint veneration in Sufi Islam:
Alexander Knysh (2000), *Islamic Mysticism: A Short History*, Boston: Brill.

For heterodox forms of Islam in the Balkans:
H. T. Norris (1993), *Islam in the Balkans*, Columbia, SC: University of South Carolina Press.

For a history of Gnosticism and an overview of its literature:
Kurt Rudolph (1987), *Gnosis: The Nature and History of Gnosticism*, San Francisco: Harper.

For an extended treatment of the cult of St Besse:
Robert Hertz (1983), 'St Besse: a study in an alpine cult', in: Stephen Wilson (ed.) *Saints and Their Cults*, Cambridge: Cambridge University Press.

For a history of the Temple Mount in Jerusalem:
Rivka Gonen (2003), *Contested Holiness: Jewish, Christian, and Muslim Perspectives on the Temple Mount in Jerusalem*, Jersey City: Ktav Publishing House.

For an extended treatment of the saint veneration of the Jews of Morocco:
Issachar Ben-Ami (1998), *Saint Veneration among the Jews of Morocco*, Detroit, MI: Wayne State University Press.

Notes

1 John B. Dunlop (1998), *Russia Confronts Chechnya: Roots of a Separatist Conflict*, Cambridge: Cambridge University Press, p. 3.

2 Dunlop, *Russia Confronts Chechnya*, p. 10.

3 Dunlop, *Russia Confronts Chechnya*, p. 26.

4 Vladimir Bobrovnikov (1991), 'Post-Socialist Forms of Islam: Caucasian Wahhabis' in ISIM Newsletter, March 2001, p. 29.

5 Corrigan et al., *Jews, Christians and Muslims,* p. 474.

6 Hourani, *The History of Arab Peoples*, pp. 275–8.

7 Fromkin, *A Peace to End All Peace*, pp. 424–5, for the historical connections between Wahhabism and the Royal House of Saud.

8 This is the one of the themes of Karen Armstrong's *The Battle for God*.

9 Corrigan et al., *Jews, Christians and Muslims,* for a brief discussion of the politics surrounding the Islamic Revival in Indonesia Malaysia, and Java, pp. 466–8.

10 Naipaul, *Among the Believers*. In addition to the *wayan* puppet stories in

Indonesia, Naipaul gives several examples of syncretistic practices in both his books about Islam. He shows us the Mashbad shrine in Pakistan p. 68, where supplicants tied cloth to the gates and when the cloth became untied, the prayer was granted. People entering the shrine rubbed their hands on the cloths, to cause them to fall, allowing supplicants' prayers to be answered. He also shows us how the story of the Five Pandava brothers told in Indonesia is an Islamized version of a tale told in the Hindu Epic the *Mahabharata,* p. 319. In *Beyond Belief,* he explains that the Islamic *pesantren* schooling system is a holdover from Buddhist monasteries in South East Asia. Naipaul discusses the story of Kali Juga and the spread of Islam and its thinly veiled origins in Hindu epics p. 128. He introduces us to 'Ali's Footprints' an Islamic shrine whose centrepiece is a rock supposedly bearing Ali's footprint. Naipaul sees in this the familiar lingam phallic emblem of Hinduism p. 337.

11 Ebertshäuser et al., *Mary: Art, Culture and Religion through the Ages,* p. 96.

12 Rabbinical Judaism's strictures against idolatry included saint veneration.

13 Marc Gaborieau (1983), 'The Cults of Saints in Nepal and Northern India', in Stephen Wilson (ed.), *Saints and their Cults,* Cambridge: Cambridge University Press, p. 295.

14 Gaborieau, 'The Cults of Saints in Nepal and Northern India', p. 296.

15 Norris, *Islam in the Balkans,* p. 82.

16 Hourani, *The History of Arab Peoples,* p. 31. Oddly, since he is decidedly anti-Gnostic, some read Paul as having secret Gnosis. See Elaine Pagels (1992), *The Gnostic Paul: Gnostic Exegesis of the Pauline Letters,* Harrisburg, PA: Trinity Press International, for a more extended treatment.

17 Corrigan, *Jews, Christians and Muslims*, pp. 204–7. See also Hourani, *The History of Arab Peoples,* pp. 36–7 for the origins of the Sunni–Shi'a gulf.

18 Professor O. Akimushkin and Professor Evgueny Torcehnov (trans.) 'Bektashiya', from the Russian *Encyclopaedia of Islam*, Moscow: Nauka, 1991 pp. 39–41.

19 Akimushkin, 'Bektashiya,' p. 39.

20 Norris, *Islam in the Balkans,* p. 97.

21 Ivana Della Portella (1999), *Subterranean Rome,* Venice: Konemann Press, p. 15.

22 Portella, *Subterranean Rome,* p. 16.

23 Portella, *Subterranean Rome,* p. 18.

24 Leo Strauss (1980), *Persecution and the Art of Writing,* Chicago: University of Chicago Press, pp. 22–37. For a discussion of Leo Strauss and his fascinating intellectual development within Maimonidean studies, see Keneath Hart Green (1993), *Jew and Philosopher: The Return to Maimonides in the Jewish Thought of Leo Strauss,* Albany NY: SUNY Press.

25 Knysh, *Islamic Mysticism,* p. 7.

26 Or at least understood that formal religion's expression is political, a kind of philosophy for the masses. We can see this in the work of al-Farabi, the philosophical father of Maimonides. See Ralph Lerner (1972), *Medieval Political Philosophy,* Ithaca, NY: Cornell University Press, for some of al-Farabi's more important works, particularly his commentary on Plato's *Republic* on pp. 83–95.

27 Hertz, 'St Besse: a study of an alpine cult', pp. 55–100.

28 Rafael Patai (1983), 'Earth Eating', in Rafael Patai, *On Jewish Folklore*, Detroit, MI: Wayne State University Press, pp. 174–94.

29 The Dome of the Rock is one of Islam's oldest structures. Built in AD 690, it contains the oldest extant quotations from the Qur'an.

30 Gonen, *Contested Holiness*, p. 23.

31 Gonen, *Contested Holiness*, p. 40 for Avarn's threshing floor, and p. 11.

32 Gonen, *Contested Holiness*, pp. 115–22 for the various legends surrounding the importance of the Temple Mount site, particularly of the rock.

33 For some of the fantastic stories and legends surrounding the death of Moses, see the *Jewish Encyclopaedia* entry for the death of Moses. Online version: www.jewishencyclopedia.com. The basis of the stories stems from Deuteronomy 34. This is the account of Moses' death. Here, an ambiguity in the Hebrew suggests that Moses was buried by God in Moab, in the valley opposite Beth Peor, by God himself or, alternatively, the Hebrew could mean simply 'He was buried'. The text is explicit in exclaiming that, to this day, no one knows where his grave is.

34 It seems the Donatist variety of Christianity prevalent in this part of the Roman world had, as a centrepiece to its practices, the veneration of saints' tombs and their remains. From W. H. C. Frend (1976), 'Notes on the Berber Background in the Life of Saint Augustine', in *Religion Popular and Unpopular in the Early Christian Church*, London: Variorum Reprints, Chapter 14, pp. 181–91. Frend notes the tendency of North Africans to sleep in or near the tombs of holy men in pagan, Christian and Muslim times. Herodotus noted this tendency as well.

35 Lawrence Durrell (1961), *Clea*, New York: Dutton Paperbacks. Durrell, in *Clea*, the final in his series of four novels *The Alexandria Quartet*, plays with the penchant of North Africans to regenerate saints. Scobie, the cross-dressing British official, becomes, after his death, an object of veneration among the local inhabitants of Alexandria. A tomb of a forgotten saint, El Yacoub, is found in his yard, and his identity and that of the saint are merged; his veneration is officially endorsed by the Coptic Church, although no one knows if the saint is a Jew, Muslim or Christian. Durrell, *Clea*, pp. 82–7.

36 Ben-Ami, *Saint Veneration among the Jews of Morocco*, pp. 75–83, and p. 159.

37 Ben-Ami, *Saint Veneration*, pp. 79–80.

38 Ben-Ami, *Saint Veneration*, p. 159.

39 Ben-Ami, *Saint Veneration*, pp. 164–5.

40 Ben-Ami, *Saint Veneration*, pp. 164–5.

41 Ben-Ami, *Saint Veneration*, p. 132.

42 See the latter half of Ben-Ami, *Saint Veneration*, 'The Saints, Tales and Legends', pp. 200–321, for fascinating examples of how saints worked their wonders. This is an invaluable collection of folktales.

5

The Eternal Feminine: Mary, the Christian Goddess

The Undeclarable
Here it was seen
Here it was Action
The Eternal Feminine
Lures to Perfection (Faust)

The age of Marian visitations

Despite official Roman Catholic Church reluctance to endorse visitations of the Virgin Mary, the nineteenth and twentieth centuries have been dominated by visions of the Lady. In France alone the Virgin allegedly appeared in 21 locations between 1803 and 1899,[1] while there have been 210 claims between 1928 and 1971. In 1992–3, the Virgin appeared in 120 locations, with 25 in Ireland alone.[2]

The Vatican has only officially endorsed three appearances of the Virgin Mary – those at Guadalupe, Mexico, Lourdes, France, and Fatima, Portugal. The remainder it has either rejected or ignored, depending upon the circumstances. Overall, the Church has taken a censorious approach to the Virgin Mary, trying to contain her influence, particularly the phenomenon of visitations and appearances.[3] This has not always been successful. Mary has always been a popular figure, particularly on a local level, and particularly with women. The modern Roman Catholic Church is divided between a 'progressive' approach, which tends to rationalize Mary's role, and a more 'reactionary' element, which seeks to keep Mary's traditional place of honour in the Church and even expand her role into new theological areas. This split was clearly seen in the debates that centred on Mary during Vatican II on 29 October 1963, when a bare majority vote carried the modernizers' agenda, stopping the nearly 200-year advance of Marian Catholics and placating ecumenical voices in the Roman Catholic world.[4] But Mary continues to be a potent presence in the church despite Vatican II's scaling back of her liturgy and devotion. This is particularly the case in the Church in the developing world, where Mary's influence is strong.[5]

While conservative voices in the Church have continued to denounce Marian veneration, the alleged sightings have not abated. A recent example is the appearance of the Virgin near the small town of Medjugorje in Bosnia-Hercegovina. The story is told that on 24 June 1981, on a night that many locals remember as hot and sultry, six young people were playing in a field outside of Medjugorje, when they suddenly saw a luminous figure. It was the *Gospa*, the Virgin Mary, and they knew this for certain. The figure gestured to them, and they approached. After a few remarks, the figure vanished, but not before promising to return. The youngsters hastened back to the local rectory, and told the local Franciscan priest what had occurred. Within hours, the entire village was aware of the appearance. The visitations happened repeatedly, but the young people were the only ones who could see the Virgin. The local Franciscan priests and monks, long locked in a rivalry with the bishop in Mostel, fostered the appearances and brought the seers as much as possible within the fold of normative Roman Catholicism.[6] The Vatican refused to endorse the visions, and in fact essentially ignored them. The messages the Virgin conveyed through the seers were conventional enough: she urged them to fast, to go to mass and confession, to work for peace. But what disturbed conservative voices in the Church was the sheer number of visitations, which occurred nearly daily. This, along with the perceived triteness of the sentiments of the Lady, was viewed as a progressive decay of Catholic imagination and education.[7]

But what many commentators failed to realize was that the appearances had a great revolutionary force in the Medjugorje region. In an area beset by clan and ethnic violence, the influx of thousands of international pilgrims per year had a 'civilizing' influence on the town and the region surrounding it. The physical affluence that the pilgrims brought, as well the feeling that most locals had of 'being watched' by the pilgrims, led to a cessation of a pattern of violence among local Serbs and Croats that was centuries old.[8] The appearances of Mary at Medjugorje, while appearing untidy and chaotic from the outside, were actually quite orderly, and had the kind of beneficial effect on the population that Church theology would be expected to foster. The distrust of the Marian appearances in Medjugorje seems to have more to do with lack of control among Church officials, than with the specific theological implications of the appearances. And the fact that women are the most important seers in the movement no doubt solidified the mistrust.

The Abrahamic religions, particularly in their more fundamentalist and conservative forms, have attempted to root out strong female divine elements. The veneration, and at times outright worship of the Virgin Mary in the Roman Catholic world has been the greatest expression of the need for a female in male, monotheistic worship. A form of syncretism is clearly at work here, as aspects of ancient goddess worship have often been incorporated into Roman Catholicism, as well as other Christian traditions and Judaism.

The problem of the divine female in male monotheism

There probably has been no greater stumbling block for the Abrahamic religions than female divinities.[9] Judaism, Christianity and Islam were conceived and born surrounded by cultures with robust ancient goddess religions. It seems this confluence led to great efforts to distance themselves from their neighbours – to conceive, in bold and unequivocal terms, the literal masculinity of God. Despite this self-conscious effort to make God a man, the female modes of worship continued to creep around the gates of the Abrahamic religions, and often make forays deep into the heart of masculine monotheism. This often brought curious results and strong reactions, and certainly has provided interesting material for the study of religion.

How the feminine was introduced into male monotheism depended on the time and on the particular social circumstances in which Islam, Christianity and Judaism found themselves. Each faith did (and does) flirt with the outer edge of goddess worship, but that flirtation manifests in drastically different ways.

The divine female in Judaism

Rafael Patai's book *The Hebrew Goddess* documents the long association of Judaism in every era of its history and in every manifestation of its faith (from tribal confederation to settled kingdom, from rabbinical Judaism to the Kabbala) with goddess worship. He concludes that popular Hebrew worship was based on the early Semitic model: Yahweh was the chief god in a pantheon of gods and goddesses. He had wives and sons and daughters – the chief wife being Asherah, who is much maligned in the Bible, but who was most likely worshipped alongside her husband by many of the Israelite rank and file, and also by more than one king of Israel and Judah.[10] Her worship was eradicated by the prophetic tradition, which sought to establish an all-Yahweh cult in Israel and Judah. Patai sees echoes of Asherah worship in almost every corner of subsequent Jewish history. Each male object of worship requires a balancing female entity; she was sought and found, according to Patai, in several interlocking manifestations.[11]

For Patai, the most important semi-modern transformation of Asherah is the *shekinah*. This curious concept has taken on a number of meanings in Judaism, some literal and some figurative. The word in Hebrew means 'dwelling' and most often it is translated in the Bible as a presence or indwelling. In the Bible, it was meant to describe whatever physical place in the world God chose to manifest himself. Through time, the concept began to take on a more figurative meaning. The word itself is feminine in Hebrew, so in the Jewish folk tradition and in the Kabbala, or the body of Jewish mystical lore, the *shekinah* gradually became a female. Somewhere along the interpretative byways, she came to be depicted as fully separate from God, who was alternately portrayed as her father or husband.[12] The personification of the *shekinah* led to her appearance in the Midrash, and she was frequently inserted at key moments in the history of Israel. She acts as a mediator between Israel and God, if necessary performing key interventions ensuring that sacred history moves according to divine plan. In one of her guises, as the cosmic queen, she becomes a kind of sacred prostitute, mating with God when Israel performs well, and mating with Satan when Israel sins.[13]

Another development of the *shekinah* is the *matronit* (from the Latin word 'Matron' with the feminine Hebrew suffix). As a later development of the *shekinah*, the *matronit* developed alongside the growing cult of Mary in the Latin West, and wound up absorbing many of her characteristics.[14] She was, accordingly, often viewed as a chaste virgin, and from other vantages she was the mother of God or the wife of God, a double view that corresponds to certain conceptions of Mary in the Middle Ages.[15] She also played a role similar to the fertility goddess of the ancient world, becoming a wife to not only God and Satan, but to various biblical heroes.[16]

So the *shekinah-matronit,* originally a divine presence, became a female personification and in that role provided a vital balancing element for folk Judaism, for mystical Judaism, and even, in certain cases, for its philosophical traditions.[17] That the *shekinah-matronit* performs the time-honoured functions of a goddess in a pantheon is not surprising. That the Jewish tradition, so fundamentally averse to the sundering of God into parts, should allow this myth to grow on the body of Hebrew monotheism is nearly miraculous.

The *shekinah-matronit* speculations belonged solely to the realm of Jewish folklore and its cousin, the Jewish mystical tradition. So in a sense, these potentially damaging elements to the faith were always kept in a secure location. Folk tradition could always be denigrated as shallow, simple and ignorant, while the mystical tradition could always be viewed by its adherents as a vast allegory: there wasn't *really* a *matronit*, she was merely a symbol. The literal/allegorical distinction is a snag and a release. As a snag, it could lead to heresy, the danger being that people could very well believe that the *shekinah* is real in the way that God is, and begin to worship her. As a release, it could allow heretical but psychologically necessary notions to enter a religion in a relatively harmless way. The *shekinah* was an extremely popular notion among nearly all segments of Jewish culture, from the Middle Ages until the modern era, and her variability was most likely one of the key factors in her survival. It allowed the *shekinah* and *matronit* to express the ardent need of worshippers for a female deity, without compromising the male monotheism of Judaism. In a sense, rabbinical Judaism was allowed to have the best of both worlds. It could have its masculine God and then by various acts of subterfuge, or through a form of blatant selectivity, have its female deity as well.

The divine female in Islam

It should come as no surprise that the *shekinah-matronit* seems to mimic the roles of the Virgin Mary. Mary's influence on Christianity was so vast that some inevitable spillover into Judaism and Islam was bound to occur (with some necessary transformations). Judaism, as the older revelation that does not recognize Christianity and Islam, cannot acknowledge Mary, except perhaps as a historical character. In fact, traditional Judaism does appear to acknowledge Mary, or Maryam (and Jesus) in the Talmud. There are four supposed references to Jesus and Mary in the Talmud (and many supposed minor ones). One legend attributes Jesus as the son of Mary, a Jewish harlot, and Pandaros, a Roman solider. The Talmud and Midrash, if referring to Jesus and Mary at all, is taking aim at the virgin birth and placing the event of Jesus' conception on a distinctly naturalistic footing.[18] Despite this, Jewish folklore and mysticism were not averse to taking aspects of popular Mariology and incorporating them into the *shekinah-matronit* cult.

Mary was allowed a more flattering role in the Qur'an, since Muslims believe that Jesus was a genuine prophet. The Qur'an retells the virgin birth and recounts the Christian annunciation.[19] Muslims believe Jesus was the messiah, but without the paraphernalia of Christian notions of Jesus' divine sonship,[20] the Trinity[21] and the resurrection.[22] Islamic tradition, wary as it is about dividing God into parts, could never conceive of Jesus as a divine being – and if splitting God in two would be bad enough, a Trinitarian division would be far worse. So, mainstream Islam viewed Jesus as a prophet in a line of prophets starting with the Patriarch Abraham and terminating in Muhammad and the transmission of the Qur'an. The idea of Jesus as the Christ is, from Islamic eyes, simply a point of corruption where Christianity deviates from true, Abrahamic monotheism.

Despite orthodox Islam's squeamishness, folk Islam and its sister, mystical Islam, continued to dip into Mariology to find sources of inspiration. Sufism, at various times, has played with the notion of the female as an intermediary with God, in many instances coming close to exploring one of the roles of the Levantine goddess: the consort, wife or daughter of God.

Ibn al-'Arabi. (d. 1240) is one Sufi who is well known in the Islamic tradition but virtually unknown in the West. He seems to have been well disposed to women throughout his life, and he was influenced by women throughout his career as a mystic. His mysticism was coloured with eroticism; he used the individual, corporeal beauty of a woman as an embodied medium to express and achieve union with the beloved God. Through the contemplation of a woman's essence veiled in her corporeal presence, a mystic seeks to understand the divine attribute (*sifa*) of compassion (*raham*), and through the window of compassion seeks to understand the other divine attributes (*sifat*). These other attributes are revealed by God in his compassion and because of his need to make himself known to his seeker or lover. God's attributes fall into two categories: those connected with his beauty (*jamal*) and those with his majesty (*jalal*). For al-'Arabi, the attributes of God's beauty (*al-sifat al-jamaliyya*) related to attributes of majesty (*al-sifat al-jalaliyya*) as women relate to men. Simply put, in al-'Arabi's scheme, a number of God's attributes are feminine, and since his attributes are essential to his being, there exists in God a feminine nature.[23]

Here, al-'Arabi comes close to sundering God into two (or perhaps more) parts, both masculine and feminine. As with the *shekinah-matronit*, al-'Arabi engages in speculation that comes close to creating a goddess-like figure, which the mystically adept is to contemplate, using her beauty as a mirror-image of the beauty of God. Al-'Arabi will often personify the mystical student as a biblical character. Often, he postulates a mystically seeking man as Adam, the first man, the only man who was created without a mother. That man seeks a mother, who is sometimes spoken of as a cosmic Eve. But he also speaks of the relationship of Jesus and Mary (Maryam). She becomes the heavenly embodiment of wisdom on the path to the divine and she fulfils, in al-'Arabi's mystical scheme, a function similar to the Sophia–Christos idea of Christian Gnostics. She becomes a cosmic entity with goddess-like functions and proportions – really a second God.

Other female figures are also given this role in mystical Islam. In some Shi'a circles, Fatima, Muhammad's daughter, becomes the cosmic woman, performing a nearly identical role to the sophonic Mary.[24] Mystics would often *use* an individual woman as an object of contemplation (of her beauty) for spiritual ends. The epic love tale of Majnun and Layla was used in this type of quest. In this story, Majnun becomes so obsessed with his beloved Layla that he sees her everywhere. His obsession is so strong that he is afraid that any pain he feels will affect Layla as well. Eventually, he decides to sequester himself for he fears that when he sees the actual, physical Layla again, it will shatter his vision of the ideal Layla – his incorporeal beloved. When she tries to visit him, he refuses to lift his eyes, despite her protests. For Majnun, divine beauty and compassion are hidden behind a veil that is the corporeal form of his beloved Layla. Although he began by gazing at her beauty, she became for him only a mirror that reflected the ultimate divine beloved.[25]

The queen of women: Mary in the Christian tradition

The role of Mary as the female entity through which an adept reaches
God is certainly nothing new in Christianity, but that she should receive
such a role in Islam, even in its mystical trends, is a surprising, even extraordinary idea. The impulse to apotheosize Mary, to turn her into a divinity, was one of the great scandals that the Protestant Reformation sought
to remedy. Most of the radical and even moderate branches of the Reformation saw no justification for the veneration of Mary of any kind in
the Gospels.[26] Most radical and moderate Protestant leaders viewed her
veneration as outright idolatry and her worship as a syncretistic blending of Mediterranean goddess cultic practices with Christianity (a legacy
that the Roman Church could not eradicate, and so eventually sought to
control and foster legally and officially). Like most absolute assertions,
this statement is simultaneously true and false. Its falsity comes from its
view that Mary veneration and worship arrived, in a sense, wholesale
from the pagan world. Of course, this is not true. There was much alteration of Mary's role throughout the two millennia of Christian history,
and there is also a great deal in the Mary tradition that was not inherited
directly from goddess worship, but which grew naturally in and of itself.
As we can see from Mary's treatment by al-'Arabi, even in a tradition that
denies any divine role to Mary (other than her use by God for his divine
plans) and certainly provides no supernatural role for her son, there is a
tendency for certain thinkers to follow and build upon their speculations
regarding the mother of Jesus, and turn her from a being who is purely
physical into one who is quasi-divine or divine.

The Mary of the Gospels

At first, the conclusion of Mary's divinity seems unlikely. There is little
written about Mary in the canonical Gospels, and what does exist was
written not to give centrality to Mary but merely to illustrate her role in
the divine drama of Jesus' birth. She is a bit player in most of the Gospels; the Gospel of Mark does not even show the birth of Jesus, which is
Mary's shining moment in the canonical works. Mark begins after Jesus
is born with Jesus' baptism, and in this Gospel, Jesus even appears to
reject his mother, sisters and brothers.[27] In Matthew, she is mentioned in
the context of Jesus' ancestry and Joseph's connection with the House of
David,[28] and in the slaughter of the innocents,[29] another episode where
she is shown only in relation to her son. The Gospel of Luke gives us the
wider view of Mary, and tells of the event later known as the annunciation, the Angel Gabriel's visit to Mary to announce her virginal conception.[30] John's Gospel depicts Mary at the marriage at Cana, providing
the only indication, and a brief and confusing one at that, that she was

aware of her son's special calling and perhaps endorsed it.[31] John also puts Mary present at the death and resurrection of her son, which along with the nativity sections of Luke, is Mary's other shining moment in the canonical Gospels. The letters of Paul, which pre-date the earliest Gospel by as much as 20 years, mention that Jesus was born to a human woman, but Mary is not mentioned by name.

In fact, all the events and circumstances that would explain the rise of Mary as popular subject of veneration in the subsequent centuries are missing from the Gospel record. Her birth, her exemplary life, her perpetual virginity, and her death and assumption into heaven are not mentioned in the Gospels. Only her virginal conception of Jesus is noted, and not in Mark's Gospel. Matthew alludes to Isaiah 7.14 as an Old Testament reference to Jesus' miraculous virgin birth: 'Behold a virgin will bear a son.' This section, translated into Greek from the Hebrew, is one of the famous mistranslations in the history of translation. The Hebrew word *almah* actually means young woman, not necessarily a virgin. But the Greek translators of the Bible decided to translate the word as *parthenos*: a young woman who is decidedly a virgin. So the virgin birth, the high water mark of Mary's canonical presence, is born in this stain of mistranslation,[32] and the virgin birth is the very first element that would elevate Mary to exalted status – the very physical symbol of her sinlessness. There is a staggering gap between Mary the woman who was chosen by God to bear his son, and the Virgin who would eventually be proclaimed by the Roman Catholic Church in 1854 to be immaculately conceived (i.e. born without original sin, the first of this type since Adam and Eve), and whose assumption into heaven (usually interpreted as her body and soul ascending to heaven together, without the stain of death) the Catholic Church proclaimed as dogma in 1950.

The idea of a virgin birth is not novel. Many cultures have tales of people born to virgins in order to highlight, by a fantastic feat of generation, a person's exalted, seemingly supernatural status. In some tales, the Buddha is born of a virgin.[33] Historical figures from the West, such as Plato, Pythagoras and Alexander the Great, were also supposedly the results of virgin births.[34] Virgin birth stories were often a way for exalted men to hide their illegitimate origins. As we saw, just such unflattering rumours of Jesus' paternity were told in Jewish and pagan circles.

What separates pagan virgin births from Jesus' virgin birth is what the birth came to mean in some of the theologies of Christianity. The Jewish tradition has no single way of interpreting the story of Adam, Eve, the Serpent and the fruit in Genesis 3.1–24. A plurality of interpretations has always existed about the meaning of this highly important chapter in human prehistory.[35] Christian exegetes also sought numerous approaches to understanding this tale, but eventually, Augustine's explanation dominated.[36] Sin was the inheritance of the transgression in Eden, and sex was its agent of transmission to the rest of humanity. All people, as the products of the sexual union of their parents, share in this Augustinian original sin. Jesus, God's only son, does not inherit this original stain because of his special birth. Later, in the apocryphal tradition that would evolve to fill in the *lacunae* in Mary's life, her immaculate conception was posited. The vessel that contained Christ was seen as too holy to be marred by the sin of Adam and Eve. When Mary was disconnected from the Augustinian sin of sex, the stage was set for attributing to her some of the characteristics of her son, Jesus, and her husband, God.[37]

Syncretistic Mary: Mary in the Graeco-Roman world

The missteps and *lacunae* in the canonical Gospels are telling, for they provide vital clues to transformations that occurred in the Christian imagination as the Church increasingly turned away from its Jewish roots and embraced the larger Graeco-Roman world that surrounded it. Although the scope of the Graeco-Roman world and its effect on Christianity are beyond the scope of this work, we must visit it briefly, for it is essential to an understanding of Mariology, both at the popular level and among the intellectual and spiritual worthies of the Church. Hellenism is hard to define quickly and neatly, because it was a certain attitude toward philosophy, religion and culture that allowed a wide variety of religions and philosophies to coexist and bloom as long as they did not interfere with the governance of the Roman Empire.[38] We find a bewildering eclecticism in the Graeco-Roman world: rationalistic philosophies like Stoicism, Epicureanism and Neoplatonism stood side by side with ecstatic mystery religions like Mithraism and the Orphic rites. Both reason and wild irrationalism were embraced, often at the same time, and often in surprisingly harmonious ways. The Roman world, nurtured by the intellectual and religious history of the Greeks, and tutored in a far-flung empire peopled by divergent cultures, learned to incorporate the foreign into the domestic. Even people like the Jews, who had a self-stated aversion to foreign influences, were not immune from the effects of Hellenism and Graeco-Roman modes of thought. Philo of Alexandria, a Greek-speaking Jew who lived in Alexandria during Jesus' life, left us a bewildering series of biblical commentaries.[39] These show a marked influence of Greek modes of thought on the Jews of Egypt, and probably elsewhere, both before and after the age of Roman expansion and dominance in Egypt. When reading Philo, we become aware of a Jew who, while maintaining his Jewishness, wears a distinctively Greek-coloured garb; Philo thinks about scripture significantly differently from the Pharisaic Judaism of that time or its successor, the Rabbinical tradition.[40] We also see the influences of Hellenism on the inscriptions in the Jewish catacombs in Rome, which were written in Greek, with a smattering of Latin and a tincture of Hebrew and Aramaic. The Jewish community of Rome, like other communities, was deeply influenced by the Graeco-Roman world, both linguistically and culturally.[41]

But overall, Judaism took a more restrained approach to absorbing Graeco-Roman influence than Christianity. Some of this may be due to an accident of history. The early Jesus movement was marred, in its early years, by a conflict between those members of the movement who believed that Jesus did not annul the Torah of Moses and those who believed that he did. The primary battleground of this controversy was a question about whether Gentile followers of Jesus were required to embrace Judaism, particularly through the most irrevocable male symbol of Jewishness: circumcision. The Acts of the Apostles and some of Paul's letters document these disputes.[42] The dispute between the advocates for circumcision, led by unnamed members of the early Jesus movement, and those in the Gentile camp, led by Paul, was briefly mediated by a moderate in the movement: Jesus' biological brother James, who was the first leader of the movement following Jesus' death.[43] James, along with the members of the Jesus movement who advocated remaining in the sphere of Judaism, was centred in Jerusalem, while Paul, who viewed the Law as annulled by the death and resurrection of Jesus, preached in the east of the Empire, primarily in Asia Minor. Once Jerusalem was destroyed during the first Jewish uprising from AD 68 to 72, Jewish Christianity, as such, ceased to exist. All that remains of that early branch of the Jesus movement is the historical memory preserved in Acts and Paul's letters, and some references by the early Church fathers. Interestingly, an early heretical form of Christianity, called the *Ebionites*, or rather, the *Ebionæans* or *Ebionaioi* (a transliteration of an Aramaic word meaning 'poor men') may have been a remainder of the early Jewish-Christian Church of Palestine. The early Church father Irenaeus tells us that the Ebionites believed and followed Jewish law, did not believe in the virgin birth, and considered Paul an apostate. It may simply be a historical accident, but James, the leader of the Jewish Christians, instructed Paul not to forget the poor, which Catholic history takes to mean the literal poor, but which may have been the name of the early Jewish-Christian movement.[44] There is a story – no doubt apocryphal – told by Hegesippus, a Jewish convert to Christianity, in his ecclesiastical history (written around AD 150) of the Emperor Domitian hauling the grandsons of Jude, one of Jesus' brothers (so these grandsons were Jesus' grandnephews), in for questioning. The emperor was concerned about rumours that they belonged to a Davidic messianic group that wanted to upset his reign. Jesus' grandnephews assured the emperor that they were merely 'poor labouring men' (here we have the term *poor* again associated with Jewish Christianity) and that Jesus reigns in a kingdom of heaven, and not of earth. This answer satisfied the emperor. It is not Jude's sons' answer that is telling, but rather the emperor's fear of Jewish Christianity. This tale points to this movement's continued perceived connection to political Jewish messianic movements, even at this relatively late date.[45]

Judaism and Christianity more firmly separated when Constantine embraced Christianity in AD 310. The form of Christianity he endorsed was decidedly anti-Jewish. The growing rift between the two communities became a gulf that ended in divorce between the groups, and which no one tried to breach in any serious or long-lasting sense until recently.[46]

So Christianity left its Jewish roots behind, at least in the active sense of obeying the rudiments of Jewish ritual law. Pauline Christianity, with its reliance on faith in Christ, had no need for a law that it believed Christ's coming had abrogated. Christianity's orientation to the West, away from the established centres of Judaism in Jerusalem and Babylonia, would have a profound effect on its formation, and a marked influence on the rising importance of Mary in Christian history.

Mary in the controversies over Christ's nature

Looking at Christian heresies is often an excellent way to examine the rise of normative Christian doctrine. Heresy is almost always a normative doctrine taken to a logical extreme, and it often arises as a corrective measure for another heresy. Christianity is dominated by faith: the underpinning and stated objective is a set of shared beliefs. This concern with faith and correct belief seem to have involved Christianity in heresy more often than Judaism or Islam, which are more concerned with adherence to a set of laws or codes of behaviour. We witness in Christianity a bewildering array of heretical movements, simply because Christian reliance on belief, and people's seeming inability to be satisfied with any given set of assumptions, leads to innumerable troubles.

Interestingly, heresy has often been an inclination that has merely come along too early in the development of a religion to be accepted as normative. At later times, in other social and political climates, the same specific heresy is better received. We see this with Mary. In general, the veneration of Mary in the early Church was muted and restrained. The Church fathers who spoke and wrote in Greek called Mary the *theotokos*, 'the bearer of God', a term that is literally true[47] and is a rather conservative appellation that does not necessarily carry any theological import. As the biological mother of Jesus, Mary was afforded great esteem, but early in the history of Christianity, certain groups began to give Mary a centrality that the Church would not formally recognize (in the arena of official dogma) until the nineteenth and twentieth centuries. Some groups with Marian fixations were documented by Epiphanius, the

bishop of Salamis (d. AD 403), in a work called *The Panarion*,[48] which
contains all the known heresies of that time (or at least the ones known to
Epiphanius).[49] Epiphanius wanted to illustrate how heretical movements
distort the message of Christ, and more important still, how they distort
the social fabric of the Church. He took aim against two groups of sects
called Montanists (variously named after their leaders, Quintillians,
Priscillians, and Cataphrygians) who placed an unusually strong emphasis on Marian veneration and worship. The second group was called the
Collyridians, after a word that comes from the Greek word for bread
cakes, *collyrides*. This group prepared special ritual loaves for Mary.[50]
The Collyridians were an Arab-Christian sect, and although their heresy
died out or was eradicated, their ideas concerning Mary did not; some of
their beliefs regarding the centrality of Mary in Christian worship may
have travelled from the Middle East to the west, affecting Greek Orthodox views about Mary, which would, in turn, affect the Latin West.[51]

The centrality of Mary to groups like the Collyridians seems rather
tame, at least doctrinally, when compared to Catholic dogma of Mary's
immaculate conception and Mary's assumption into heaven. But the
Collyridians started far too early on their course of Marian worship; almost 2,000 years of Christian history needed to unfold in order to bring
Mary to such a central place in Roman Catholicism.

The suppression of heresy in the early Church initially stamped out
Marian worship, but in a curious way, the efforts by the early Church
fathers to set the Christian canon and control Christian doctrine eventually steered the Church back to Mary. We will discuss this more later, but
for now it is enough to say that Mary veneration and worship, while initially not tolerated by the Church's rising power and muscle, eventually
assumed a place that would most likely not have been possible without
a strong bishop in Rome who operated a Church from a unified power
base.[52]

Mary's later power grew in two areas that seem, at first glance, to be
largely mutually exclusive. Her image and functions were controlled by a
series of Church councils beginning in the third century AD and continu-
ing until the 1950s. The early councils were dominated by the quest to define Christ's relationship to God. So Mary became, in essence, a sub-issue
of this divisive debate, and eventually from the decided-upon definitions,
her later roles would emerge. On the other front, ideas about the Virgin
were propagated by apocryphal literature that the Church councils in the
third and fourth centuries AD excluded from the canon and suppressed as
false documents. These two routes to Mary's rise – orthodox control and
heterodox literature – are not as mutually exclusive as they appear, when
we realize that it was not the books per se, that the Church sought to suppress, but selected doctrines and the ideas expressed in them, and more
importantly, some of the people who expounded and interpreted them.

Personality clashes played a surprisingly large role in the formation of early Church doctrine. Often, the animus that two warring bishops held for each other seems to have been the underlying cause of the dispute, rather than the dispute's apparent issues.

We see this clearly in the clashes between Arius and Athanasius.[53] Church leaders like Eusebius of Nicomedia defended Arius' teaching that God the Father and Son were not always contemporary, and therefore were not equal in essence, but that the Son was only a kind of divine being and the transmitter of salvation. Athanasius, the Metropolitan of Alexandria, was a proponent of the 'orthodox', anti-Arian doctrine, and Eusebius of Caesarea was a spokesman for the middle ground. Arius' doctrine was the first major heresy that the Church was forced to confront from its new standpoint as the religion of Rome. Arius did not believe that Christ was fully God but that he stood midway between God and his creation. This view was to surface quite often in the early Church, and it found expression, although in somewhat modified form, in the struggles that surrounded the next great heresy, that of Patriarch Nestorius of Constantinople.

Nestorius believed that Jesus was essentially two beings, one human and one divine. He did not agree with the 'orthodox' position that Jesus was both fully human and fully divine. Unlike the previous Arian variety, this heresy prominently featured Mary (and conceptions of Mary) as one of the centrepieces of its controversy. Around AD 430 Nestorius delivered four sermons in which he objected to calling Mary the *theotokos*, or 'the God bearer', in favour of *christostokos,* or 'the bearer of Christ'. This shift in terminology reflected his conviction that there was a gap between Christ's human and godly manifestations. His usage of this new term created a major controversy, especially in Alexandria, where the term *theotokos* had been used for the last 50 years. Patriarch Cyril of Alexandria, who was already angered by the choice of someone from Antioch to be the Patriarch of Constantinople (Nestorius was born in Antioch), took the opportunity to become involved, and during Easter of AD 429, Cyril spoke out against *christotokos* in favour of *theotokos*. The patriarchs exchanged heated letters, and the Pope eventually became involved in an open dispute. Cyril, unlike Nestorius, provided a Latin translation of the Greek texts in question for the Bishop of Rome who spoke and wrote in Latin. This gave Cyril a decisive lead, and in a synod that met in Rome in AD 430, Pope Celestine sided with Cyril. Cyril, emboldened by the Pope's backing, issued 12 'Anathemas' against Nestorius, and Nestorius issued his own Counter-Anathemas in return.[54]

The issue got so heated that in AD 431 Emperor Theodosius II called for a general council in Ephesus at Pentecost. At this third Ecumenical Council of the Church, Cyril again took the lead, purposely arriving before the Nestorians, and despite the ire of the imperial commissioners, inaugurating the Council early and issuing a blanket condemnation of Nestorius. Many intrigues followed, but eventually Cyril won out, securing his position and ousting Nestorius and his followers. Nestorius was eventually exiled and his followers established churches in the east, away from Roman centres of power and eventually outside the Roman provinces themselves. The Nestorian Church officially broke with the Roman Church in AD 483 and had its zenith from the seventh to the tenth centuries. Its diaspora even reached India and China.[55]

As we have seen, the Nestorian dispute revolved around Christ. But Mary was necessarily brought into the debate. No one in these early Church circles doubted that Jesus was the incarnate son of God, and no one denied that he was born of a human, virgin woman named Mary. It was the *relationship* between Jesus' godly and human aspects that was hotly debated. At Ephesus, a town in Asia Minor known for its worship of the Goddess Artemis (and a town said to be founded by that mythical all-female society, the Amazons), Mary was officially given the title *Theotokos*, or 'the bearer of God'; here, her role was more clearly defined, and so she received her first real official push toward deification.

The next dispute was taken up in the fallout of the Nestorian crisis, and once again Mary was brought into arguments about the nature of Christ. At the Fourth Ecumenical Council of Chalcedon in AD 451, the Fathers of the Church went one step beyond Ephesus, awarding Mary the title *aei parthenos*, or 'ever virgin'. Here, the dispute began with the so-called Monophysites, who wanted to make it an article of faith that Christ had only one godly nature. Mary comes into play here by allowing the miraculous element of Jesus' humanity to remain intact. He was born of a human woman like any man. But Mary, the vessel for God, was not allowed to be corrupted by further sundry conceptions and births. Here, Mary took another decisive step away from her Gospel role, and assumed a more mythic stance. Jesus is shown in the Gospels as having flesh and blood brothers and sisters, seemingly by his mother Mary. As we saw, his brother James is mentioned in both Paul's letters and in the Acts of the Apostles as having had a leadership role in the early Jesus movement. But this all became inconsequential next to the agenda of giving Mary a more elevated status. By degrees, Mary was transformed from a human woman who was chosen by God to play a role in a miraculous event, to a miraculous entity herself.

Mary in the apocryphal literature

The other great avenue through which Mariolatry has been promulgated is the apocrypha. The word apocrypha is from the Greek *apokryphos* (obscure) or alternatively, from *apokryptei* (to hide away).[56] This term for the vast array of non-canonical books (those that were not included in the corpus of 'authentic' Gospels and letters, both by Paul and others) is somewhat misleading. For one, many books of the apocrypha are anything but obscure, if we take that to mean an inscrutable or confusing narrative. Quite to the contrary, many of these books are straightforward religious narratives. Also, if apocryphal books are meant to be hidden, some were not well hidden at all. Many of the apocrypha dealing with Mary were well known indeed, and some of our notions about the life of the Virgin come directly from them.[57] Many Christians would no doubt be surprised to learn that we know Mary's parent's names (Joachim and Anne) not from the canonical Gospels, but from the apocrypha. The Gospel of Matthew is the only Gospel that tells the tale of the Magi. Interestingly, their number is not given in this (or any) Gospel, nor are their names or titles as kings.[58] *Magi* (*magoi* in Greek) is simply the plural of *magus*, from the old Persian word that means magician or sorcerer. The drive to make them kings was perhaps due to the squeamishness of later commentators about the word's connection to magic. Attributing the number three to them seems to have originated with the number of gifts given to the baby Jesus, but nothing precludes there having been two Magi or seven, who give three gifts among themselves. All these details about one of the more colourful episodes in Jesus' nativity came from extra-biblical, non-canonical and apocryphal sources. That apocryphal sources were extensively used to fill in the biographical details of Mary's life shows the enduring nature of their appeal. They were widely read and have a lasting legacy: modern readers who will never read an apocryphal book will probably still assume that there were three magi, and that they were kings, even though Matthew, the only apostle to mention them, is silent about these details.

The use of the apocrypha in itself did not bother key Church fathers, who were prepared to use them, albeit selectively. It seems that pilfering these books for biographical details about Gospel characters was not an endorsement of them as true, authentic revelation, and the practice caused some interesting problems. The wide use of these 'hidden, obscure' books made them far less than hidden and far more than merely confusing, as they are considered complementary to the Gospels, and in certain places, we have read the Gospels with their guidance.

There is no better example of this principle of the apocrypha's importance than Mary. Almost all of the elements the Roman Catholic tradition attributes to Mary have come from these books, and from the folk traditions that sustained them. We will look at just two examples of Mary in apocryphal literature: the *Protoevangelium of James* and *Concerning the Passing of the Blessed Virgin Mary*.[59]

The *Protoevangelium of James* has been attributed to James, Jesus' half-brother (in Roman Catholic tradition Jesus is born of a perpetual

Virgin and therefore can only have half-siblings through a former marriage of Joseph's). *Protoevangelium* means 'before the evangelists'; this gospel purports to tell the events that occurred chronologically *before* the canonical Gospels. Unlike the Gospels, where Jesus' mission is the central narrative concern, this gospel is interested in events that occur before Jesus' birth, among his maternal grandparents and his mother herself.

Initially, the gospel has a distinctly Jewish theme. Joachim, Mary's father, is wealthy and generous, and gives his offerings to the Temple and the poor in great quantities. However, at the start of the action of the *Protoevangelium*, as Joachim arrives with his offerings, he is rebuked by Reuben (presumably, the high priest) that his offering is no longer valid, because he has 'not begotten offspring in Israel'.[60] Joachim leaves the scene, understandably aggrieved. His plight calls to mind that of the patriarch Abraham who was denied children during his sexual prime;[61] we could also point out similarities to other conception stories in the Hebrew Bible: Elkanah, Hannah, and the birth of Samuel, and Manoah, his unnamed wife, and the birth of Samson.[62] The *Protoevangelium* sets the birth of Mary in the same miraculous vein as those that occurred in Israel's past history, to Israel's exalted national heroes – births by women who were seemingly unable to conceive naturally were thought to be caused by God's direct intervention and always heralded the arrival of great leaders or figures in Israel's history.

But in the *Protoevangelium*, an important distinction arises. We are told that Joachim 'did not show himself to his wife; but went into the wilderness, and there pitched his tent and fasted for forty days and forty nights, saying to himself: I will not go down either for food or for drink until the Lord my God looks upon me, and prayer shall be my food and drink'.[63] In the meantime his wife Anna is lamenting her childless state and praying that God will relieve her condition. Then an angel of the Lord appears to her and answers her prayer, telling her that she will conceive. Anna promises that the offspring will minister to God all of its days, much in the same vein as the prophet Samuel.[64] Meanwhile, Joachim is still in the desert, fasting and praying. An angel of the Lord goes to him and explains: '. . . the Lord God has heard your prayer. Go down hence; for behold, thy wife Anna shall conceive.' At this point, the narrator is very careful to tell us that once he had returned, 'Joachim rested the first day in his house.'[65] The reader is not told how long he had been gone (we don't know how many of the 40 days had elapsed), but Anna is pregnant, and although it is not explicit in the *Protoevangelium*, the implication is there: Anna conceived without a man. To use a term that would later be used to describe the same event, Mary had been immaculately conceived, or conceived without sexual intercourse.

The Church father Origen cited the *Protoevangelium* as proof that Mary was virginally conceived.[66] The fact that Origen (AD 185–254) cites the work dates it as a somewhat early apocryphal gospel, but certainly later than the last canonical Gospel, the Gospel of John (which was probably written around AD 100). Eventually, in 1854, Mary's immaculate conception would become Catholic dogma. So, we can see that ideas about Mary's miraculous birth had early currency, even if they did have a late official recognition by the Roman Catholic Church.

Some other motifs of Catholic iconography are found in the *Protoevangelium*: Joseph as the widowed old man with children by a former marriage, which necessarily ties into Mary's perpetual virginity and is repeatedly stressed in the work. Mary even (quite implausibly) lives in the Temple as a kind of consecrated virgin to the Lord.[67] We also see in the *Protoevangelium* a response to popular criticism of biblical tales. We see this reflected in the Gospels. For instance, in Mark's Gospel Jesus was simply placed in his tomb, and when opened, the tomb was found empty. In Matthew, a later Gospel, the Sanhedrin placed a guard at Jesus' tomb so that his followers could not steal the body and claim that he had risen from the dead. The author of Matthew was probably sensitive to criticism of Mark's Gospel that Jesus' body was stolen by his followers, and wrote the guards into his tale to thwart just such criticism.[68] We see a response to criticism of Mary's virgin birth in the *Protoevangelium*. A midwife is called when Mary is in labour.[69] When the baby is born without any travail, she goes out of the cave to tell a woman named Salome, who is walking near. Salome, a forerunner of Thomas,[70] does not believe what the midwife tells her. She inserts her finger into the Virgin's vagina for proof. Her hand falls off, and only a display of absolute repentance grows it back![71]

Mary's perpetual virginity and immaculate conception were definitive steps in taking a character who was merely a woman in the Gospels and making her a semi-divine being or goddess. Her unnatural and miraculous birth and her conception of Jesus through the Holy Spirit in a state of virginity (a state that would remain for her life) put Mary further away from the human realm, and pushed her decisively toward the divine. In the end Mary only needed to evade death to assume a completely divine stature.

She escapes death, for the first time, in a work called *Concerning the Passing of The Blessed Virgin Mary*,[72] a small book that chronicles the events that later Catholic doctrine would call the assumption. This rather late work was probably written in the sixth century, but the story of Mary's assumption perhaps goes back to the fourth century. *The Passing* is a full-blown homage to the Virgin Mary; she is already, in this document, the being she would become in official Church dogma in the nineteenth and twentieth centuries. The book begins with Mary asking her dead and risen son if he will remember her, and on the third day before she will die, to send an angel to announce her death. She then asks Jesus to take her soul up to heaven once her body has died.[73] Jesus answers her with a stream of devotional language: 'O Queen of all saints, and blessed above all women, before thou carriedst me in thy womb, I always guided thee, and caused thee to be fed daily with my angelic food.'[74] Here the cosmic Jesus, the pre-existent Logos, or the Cosmic Word, cared for his mother even before he was born to mortal life.[75] Even if we figuratively interpret this 'angelic food' that Jesus fed his mother, we must see this special and divine care she received as a hallmark of Mary, the mortal being – a hallmark that would change her from a mere human into an apotheosized demi-goddess. Jesus promises to raise her soul after death: 'know for certain that thy soul will be separated from the body and I shall carry it into heaven.' In the second year after the ascension of Jesus, an angel appears to Mary to announce her death: 'The Angel of the Lord said to her: Thy Assumption will be after three days. And she answered: Thanks to God.'[76] Mary prepares herself for death, washing herself and dressing 'like a queen' to wait 'for the advent of her Son, as He had promised to her.' Then, as if to mark this moment with the miraculous momentousness that it deserves, at the third hour there are 'great thunders and rains, and lightning and tribulation and an earthquake.'[77] All of the apostles are miraculously brought to the site of the assumption from the various corners of the globe where they have been preaching the gospel, and they are understandably astonished to be back in Jerusalem. As they ask questions, the transfigured Christ appears and takes his mother's soul with him, leaving her body behind. We are then told that 'all the inhabitants of Jerusalem openly saw the departure of Saint Mary.'

The Passing then assumes a decidedly anti-Semitic tone, as Satan comes into the book for the first time, and his agents, the Jews, turn their evil designs upon eliminating the body of the holy Virgin. Amazingly enough, the Jews (and the author of *The Passing*) attribute their sufferings and dispersions not to their denial of Jesus as the Christ, but to Mary, the Mother of God. The Jewish bile in attempting to destroy her sacred remains reaches near manic proportions, to the extent that an angry God intervenes to confuse them, causing in their 'blindness, [the] striking [of] their heads against the walls, and striking each other' to stop them from the sacrilege.[78]

Despite the hubbub, the apostles manage to carry the body down from Mount Zion to the Valley of Jehoshaphat, where it would be entombed. Once again a Jew meddles, trying to throw the holy body onto the ground. His arm withers, and only through radical repentance and baptism to Christianity is it regenerated. Once the apostles successfully entomb Mary, a bright light shines, and her body is 'taken up by angels into heaven.' The narrative does nothing to prepare us for Mary's bodily assumption; we are told quite explicitly by Jesus that her *soul* will be taken. That her body was also assumed seems an addition, but perhaps one that should have been expected in this book. In *The Passing*, Mary

has usurped many of the roles of her son: she is responsible for the perdi-
tion of the Jews, the apostles pay her homage as they did her son, and she
is a focal point and fixation of divine energy, as all manner of miracles
and transformations occur through her and around her. Even plots by
Satan and the calumny of the Jews, which are certainly also a problem in
the Gospels for Jesus, are present in *The Passing*.

Syncretistic Mary: from human woman to Christian goddess

Mary's trajectory is easy to plot: she moves, by historical fits and starts,
from a human woman to a Christian goddess. Understanding the complex reasons for her journey is not so simple a task. Mary would go from
being the recipient of a virginal conception to being *aei parthenos*, forever a virgin, in two Church Councils – a time period of a little over
two centuries. Official movement of her cult lay dormant for centuries
until eventually the papacy picked it back up again in the nineteenth and
twentieth centuries, with the promulgation of the dogma of Mary's immaculate conception by Pope Pius IX in 1854, and Mary's assumption
into heaven by Pope Pius XII in 1950. In 1854, an idea that had existed
about Mary very early in her tradition – that she was conceived without
original sin – was finally accepted. Mary's assumption into heaven, another early tale about the Virgin, proclaims that she did not die like every
other mortal, but was subsumed, in some interpretations both in body
and soul, into heaven. Mary escapes the standard human dilemmas of
birth and death, and despite (or perhaps because of) her exalted status,
Mary has continued to be seen as an *intermediatrix*: an exalted saint who
may be appealed to for succour or favours. Probably the most radical fate
for Mary is that she will become a co-redemptrix – she will not merely
be an intercessor between Christ and God and humanity, but she will be
a deity, belief in whose intercession will lead to salvation itself. This may
have been the status of Mary with the Collyridians in the early days of
the Church. That she moves back toward this status is a testimony to the
time-bound nature of heresy: one generation's abomination is another's
mainstream belief.

Mary is now the pinnacle of the saints, and like many saints, she is
a repository for religious syncretism. But, unlike some of the saints we
have examined, she does not merely adopt local customs that have a pre-
Christian origin and mould them into a Christian milieu, she becomes a
goddess in her own right, a distinction that Christianity had sought to
eliminate. Mary has a long history of association with cults of the goddess
from the Mediterranean, and aspects of the worship of the Egyptian goddess Isis, who is enthroned with the man-god-king Horus, were directly
infused into Marian worship.[79] Mary was also associated with that old

symbol of fertility, the moon, as late as the start of the Gothic Middle Ages.[80] In the tradition of cosmic deities, Mary is related to nature in the portrayal of the *hortus conclusus* or the rose bower, an endorsement of which is given in the long laudatory poem to Mary, the *Litany of Loreto* (officially approved by the Church in 1587, but probably much older) where she is called, among other things, *mystica rosa*, the mystic rose.[81] Ultimately, Roman Catholicism endorsed views of Mary that cannot be called anything but Mariolatry – the worship of Mary. She comes close to equal status with the Father and the Son. In medieval art and elsewhere it is implied that she married the Father and gave birth to the Son, and since the Son *is* the Father, in a sense she married her own offspring – which grants her an interesting semantic supremacy over both God the Father and his Son. This kind of divine incest would not be strange on Olympus, but for Abrahamic monotheism, which normally eschews such characterizations, it is odd and revealing of Roman Catholic flexibility and willingness to adopt syncretistic ideas when their time is ripe. We see here Christianity endorsing a pagan mindset that it had originally vilified and then sought to eradicate. The history of Mary is strange – folk beliefs have always clung to her, and she has had an amazing way of transforming those into official doctrine. The syncretism of Mary is easy to discern: here is a goddess who has certainly been altered, changed, subdued and even constrained to fit a Christian milieu, but she is a goddess nonetheless – and despite Vatican II, she is still gaining power.[82] We see precedents for this tendency of a younger, usurper deity gaining power over an older one, possibly even a father or mother, in earlier religions as well. The young Zeus toppled his father Kronos and the Titans to become the primary Greek god. Baal, in the Canaanite tradition was originally a lesser deity as the son of El, the main god of the Semantic pantheon[83] – until his cult became paramount. Even Mithras, whom we met earlier, was once a lesser deity who rose in the ranks of the Zoroastrian pantheon to gain his own cultic supremacy.[84]

One of the keys to Mary's success is her adaptability. The ambiguous nature of her title, 'Mother of God', allows for endless speculation and transformation. She is the Mother of Jesus, who is, according to doctrine, God. Because Mary gave birth to God, in some sense she supersedes God as the generator of God. But Jesus as God existed before the world was made, so in a sense, Jesus was around before Mary. From this dizzying logic comes the tradition of the adult Jesus marrying the adult Mary – she becomes the wife of Christ and, by Christ's nature as 'true God and true man', a wife or consort of God. If Mary continues her ascent, Catholic Christianity, at least, will have allowed a female deity to assume a stature not seen since the era of the great pantheon of Roman gods and goddesses. She will be no less central than the goddesses found in those sacred quarters of Rome, a sacred compound supposedly usurped by Christianity.

Chapter summary

Over the centuries, the cult of the Virgin Mary has assumed a growing power in the Roman Catholic world. From the human mother of Jesus in the Gospels, she became, in Church tradition and folk imagination, the immaculately conceived eternal Virgin, who was assumed into heaven at the conclusion of her life. She did this despite periodic attempts by Church authorities to halt her progress. The Virgin Mary has alternately been embraced, rejected and ignored by the Roman Catholic Church, and this has been particularly true of visitations, which are an arena where the Church has little formal control. The appearances of the Virgin in Medjugorje, Bosnia-Hercegovina, are a case in point. The appearance in 1980 of the Virgin to local people (mainly women) and her subsequent, near daily appearances, were events that were not under Vatican control, and were only under the sporadic control of the local Franciscan priests. Fundamentalist elements in the Church, or 'modernizers' working under the guidelines of Vatican II, have little room for Marianism, and particularly for the phenomenon of visitations, which often fall beyond Church control, and are often seen by women and children.

Despite this, Mary became a de facto goddess for normative Roman Catholicism, and a powerful presence in the folk imagination. She started as a largely passive presence in the canonical Gospels, but through historical developments at Church Councils, and in the folk imagination and its expression through apocryphal literature, she began to take on increasingly more divine roles. She evaded original sin, the common human patrimony. She evaded death – another fate shared by all people. She became the very pinnacle of saints, her importance just below that of the persons of the Trinity. Hers has been a bold syncretism: after several centuries a goddess has been ushered into a major Abrahamic religion. With Mary as Bride of Christ and Mother of God, Roman Catholicism comes so close to aspects of a pagan pantheon that some have argued she should receive the greatest honour possible: a position of co-redemptrix to Christ himself.[85]

Draw your own conclusions

How is the *shekinah* similar to Mary? How is she different?

How do traditional Muslim conceptions of Mary affect al-'Arabi's visions of her?

What is Mary's role in the Gospels? How does that role change in each of the four books?

How did historical debates over Christ's nature influence ideas about Mary?

What was more important in influencing Mary's development: her portrayal in the apocryphal literature, or the Church Councils?

Is Mary a co-redemptrix in the Roman Catholic tradition? Does this make her a goddess?

Further reading

For views of the divine female in Judaism:
Rafael Patai (1990), *The Hebrew Goddess*, Detroit, MI: Wayne State University Press.

For a summary of the variations on Mary from the Gospels to Vatican II:
George H. Tavard (1996), *The Thousand Faces of the Virgin Mary*, Collegeville, MN: Liturgical Press.

For an overview of Mary as she is depicted in art and culture:
Caroline Ebertshäuser, Herbert Haag, Joe H. Kirchberger and Dorothee Sölle (1998), *Mary: Art, Culture, and Religion through the Ages*, New York: Herder & Herder.

For Mary and the incorporation of elements of Graeco-Roman goddess worship:
Stephen Benko (1993), *The Virgin Goddess: Studies in the Pagan and Christian Roots of Mariology*, New York: E. J. Brill.

Notes

1 Tavard, *The Thousand Faces of the Virgin Mary*, p. 178.
2 Tavard, *The Thousand Faces of the Virgin Mary*, p. 186.
3 Charlene Spretnak (2004), *Missing Mary: The Queen of Heaven and Her Re-emergence in the Modern Church*, New York: Palgrave Macmillan, p. 145. The first recorded 'vision' of the Virgin Mary was relatively late. Gregory of Nyssa (d. 385–386) reportedly saw her along with Saint John. They commanded him to accept the bishopric of Neocaesarea and the Blessed Virgin recited the creed he was to profess. Richard Fletcher (1997), *The Barbarian Conversion*, New York: Henry Holt, p. 36.
4 Spretnak, *Missing Mary*, p. 48.
5 Spretnak, *Missing Mary*, p. 116.
6 Max Bax (1995), *Medjugorje: Religion, Politics and Violence in Rural Bosnia*, Amsterdam: VU Uitgeverij, p. 17.

7 Tavard, *The Thousand Faces of the Virgin Mary*, p. 7.

8 Bax, *Medjugorje*, p. 106.

9 Benko, *The Virgin Goddess*, p. 14.

10 For example, *NJB*, 2 Kings 21.3, 21.7; 1 Kings 16.33.

11 Patai, *The Hebrew Goddess*, chapters are as follows: Asherah, Astarte-Anath, the Cherubim, the Shekina, the Kabbalistic Tetrad, the Matronit, Yihudim, Lilith, the Sabbath-Virgin, Bride, Queen Goddess.

12 See Patai, *The Hebrew Goddess,* Chapter 4, 'The Shekina'. For the Shekina in the *Bahir*, see Gershom Scholem (1987), *The Origin of the Kabballah*, Philadelphia: Jewish Publication Society, Chapter 8, 'The Symbolism of the Feminine; the Jewel', pp. 162–80.

13 Patai, *The Hebrew Goddess*, pp. 128–9.

14 Patai, *The Hebrew Goddess*, pp. 151–3.

15 Ebertshäuser et al., *Mary: Art, Culture and Religion through the Ages*, p. 177.

16 Patai, *The Hebrew Goddess*, p. 139.

17 David Bakan (1991), *Maimonides on Prophecy: A Commentary on Selected Chapters of the Guide of the Perplexed*, Northvale, NJ, London: Jason Aronson, p. 32, p. 85.

18 Some of the places that supposedly mention Mary and Jesus in the Talmud are: *Talmud Shabbat* 104b; *Talmud Sanhendrin* 67a; *Talmud Sanhendrin* 107b; *Sotah* 43a; *Talmud Sanhendrin* 43a and *Tosefta Chullin* 2.23. The so-called Balam references, i.e. texts where Balam is supposedly a code name for Jesus, which are *Shabbat* 104b, *Sanhendrin* 106b, *Sefrei on Deuteronomy* 34.10, *Avot deRabbi Natan* 2.5m *Mishnah Avot* 5.19, *Talmud Gittin* 56b–57b. All from *The Jesus Narrative in the Talmud,* by Gil Student (www.angelfire.com/mt/talmud). Pagan sources from the early Christian centuries also had similar criticisms of Christianity, particularly Celsus, who provided a name of the man who fathered Jesus through Mary, Panthera. This name is close to the Greek word for virgin, *parthenos*. Robert L. Wilken (1984), *The Christians as the Romans Saw Them*, New Haven, CT: Yale University Press, pp. 109–10.

19 *Koran*, 19.15–21, p. 215.

20 *Koran*, 19.34, p. 216.

21 *Koran*, 112.14, p. 473.

22 *Koran*, 4.155–157, p. 76.

23 Jamal Elias (1988), 'Female and Feminine in Islamic Mysticism', in *The Muslim World,* 78, Duncan Black MacDonald Center: Hartford, CT, p. 216.

24 Elias, 'Female and Feminine', p. 218.

25 Elias, 'Female and Feminine', pp. 219–20.

26 Tavard, *The Thousand Faces of the Virgin Mary*, Chapters 7 and 8.

27 *NJB*, Mark, 3.31–35.

28 *NJB*, Matthew, 1.18–27.

29 *NJB*, Matthew, 2.14.

30 *NJB*, Luke 1.26–38.

31 *NJB*, John, 2.1–11.

32 Nickelsburg, *Ancient Judaism and Christian Origins*, p. 23.

33 Ebertshäuser et al., *Mary: Art, Culture and Religion through the Ages*, p. 172.

34 Ebertshäuser et al., *Mary: Art, Culture and Religion through the Ages*, p. 172.

35 For a discussion about the formation of Augustine's influential view of this story, see Elaine Pagels (1988), *Adam, Eve and the Serpent*, New York: Random House, particularly 'The Politics of Paradise', pp. 98–126 and 'The Nature of Nature' pp. 127–50.

36 Pagels, *Adam, Eve and the Serpent*, pp. 98–126.

37 Benko, *The Virgin Goddess*, p. 204.

38 Benko, *The Virgin Goddess,* Chapters 1, pp. 1–19, and 2, pp. 20–82, and Bowersock, *Hellenism in Late Antiquity*, Chapter entitled 'Paganism and Greek Culture', pp. 1–13.

39 Philo of Alexandria, C. D. Yonge (trans) (1993), *Philo's Collected Works*, Peabody, MA: Hendrickson Publishers.

40 Whether Philo's work reflects Greek or Jewish concern was an overriding fixation for several scholarly works, including: Erwin R. Goodenough (1935), *By Light, By Light: The Mystical Gospel of Hellenistic Judaism*, New Haven: Yale University Press. Samuel Belkin (1940), *Philo and the Oral Law: The Philonic Interpretation of Biblical Law in Relation to the Palestinian Halakah*, Cambridge, MA: Harvard University Press. Lester L. Grabbe (1988), *Etymology in Early Jewish Interpretation: The Hebrew names in Philo*, Atlanta: Scholars Press.

41 Harry J. Leon (1995), *The Jews of Ancient Rome*, Peabody, MA: Hendrickson Publishing. See the final section, which contains an exhaustive list of translations of catacomb inscriptions, pp. 263–6.

42 *NJB*, Acts 15.22–31; Galatians 2.1–21, 4.12–20.

43 Eusebius, G. A. Williamson (trans.) (1981), *The History of the Church*, New York: Penguin Classics. Eusebius mentions James several times in his *History of the Church*. See Book Two, p. 72. For his martyrdom, see Book Two, p. 81. Eusebius makes the extraordinary assertion that James' presence in Jerusalem was all that prevented its destruction following Jesus' death, in Book Three, p. 118.

44 *NJB*, Galatians 2.10.

45 Eusebius, *History of the Church,* Book Three, pp. 126–7. Interestingly, Eusebius tells us they later became leaders in the Church.

46 In our times this impulse is represented by the so-called Jews for Jesus, or the calliope of groups that call themselves Messianic Jews.

47 Mary is the literal bearer of God, since she carried Jesus in her body.

48 Epiphanius, Phillip Amidan (trans.) (1995), *The Panarion of St Epiphanius, Bishop of Salamis: Selected Passages*, New York: Oxford University Press. Panarion means 'medicine chest' or remedies for the poison of heresy. See pp. 353–4 for the entry on the Collyridians.

49 The number of heresies in the *Panarion* is 80.

50 This was also the case with the cult practices of Demeter.

51 Ebertshäuser et al., *Mary: Art, Culture and Religion through the Ages*, p. 162; Benko, *The Virgin Goddess*, p. 170.

52 Benko, *The Virgin Goddess*, pp. 245–62.

53 Athanasius, Robert C. Gregg (trans.) (1980), *The Life of Antony and the Letter to Marcellinus*, New York: The Paulist Press. Athanasius, in his biography of the Egyptian monk Antony, even puts anti-Arian sentiments in the mouth of his mendicant holy man. See pp. 82, 91, 93, 95 and 97.

54 Ebertshäuser et al., *Mary: Art, Culture and Religion through the Ages,* pp. 163–4.

55 Michael Pollack (1980), *Jews, Mandarins, Missionaries,* Philadelphia: Jewish Publication Society, p. 7.

56 *The American Heritage Dictionary of the English Language,* Fourth Edition 'Middle English apocripha, *not authentic,* from Late Latin Apocrypha, *the Apocrypha,* from Greek Apokrupha, neuter pl. of apokruphos, *secret, hidden,* from apokruptein, *to hide away* : apo-, apo- + kruptein, kruph-, to hide.'

57 Of course, many were literally hidden, like the cache found buried at Nag Hammadi in 1945. See http://www.gnosis.org/naghamm/nhl.html for the works online.

58 In the West, they are usually named Balthazar, Melchior and Gaspar.

59 J. K. Eliot (trans.) (1993), 'The Protoevangelium of James', in *The Apocryphal New Testament: A Collection of Apocryphal Christian Literature in an English Translation,* Oxford: Clarendon Press, pp. 48–67.

60 Eliot, 'The Protoevangelium of James', p. 57.

61 *NJB,* Genesis 17.19–21.

62 *NJB,* 1 Samuel 1.28, Judges 13.1–23.

63 Eliot, 'The Protoevangelium of James', p. 57.

64 *NJB,* 1 Samuel 1.22.

65 Eliot, 'The Protoevangelium of James', pp. 58–9.

66 Ebertshäuser et al., *Mary: Art, Culture and Religion through the Ages,* p. 20.

67 Eliot, 'The Protoevangelium of James,' p. 60.

68 Janice Anderson and Stephen Moore (eds) (1992), *Mark and Method: New Approaches in Biblical Studies,* Minneapolis: Fortress Press, pp. 75–81, explores the various ways that the author of Matthew's Gospel was dissatisfied with Mark's Gospel, including the grave scene.

69 Eliot, 'The Protoevangelium of James,' p. 64.

70 Or, in the chronology of the *Protoevangelium,* a precursor of Thomas.

71 Eliot, 'The Protoevangelium of James', pp. 64–5.

72 'Concerning the Passing of the Blessed Virgin Mary', First Latin Form, in Alexander Roberts and James Donaldson (eds) (1951), *The Ante-Nicene Fathers: Translations of the Writings of the Fathers down to A.D. 325,* Grand Rapids, MI: Wm. B. Eerdmans Publishing Company, pp. 592–3.

73 Roberts, 'Concerning the Passing', p. 592.

74 Roberts, 'Concerning the Passing', p. 592.

75 Roberts, 'Concerning the Passing', p. 592.

76 Roberts, 'Concerning the Passing', p. 592.

77 Roberts, 'Concerning the Passing', p. 592.

78 Roberts, 'Concerning the Passing', p. 593.

79 Ebertshäuser et al., *Mary: Art, Culture and Religion through the Ages,* p. 228.

80 Ebertshäuser et al., *Mary: Art, Culture and Religion through the Ages,* p. 240.

81 For The Litany of Loreto, see the entry in the *Catholic Encyclopaedia,* http://www.newadvent.org/cathen/09287a.html

82 The modern strength of Mary is illustrated in her appearances, both

officially and unofficially recognized. For a largely negative view of this phenomenon, see Tavard, *The Thousand Faces of the Virgin Mary*, 'Mary in Visions',
Chapter 10, pp. 171–89.

83 Frank Moore Cross (1973), *Canaanite Myth and Hebrew Epic*, Cambridge, MA: Harvard University Press, pp. 17–18.

84 Portella, *Subterranean Rome*, p. 16.

85 This is Mary's most controversial potential role, since it places her, in some
definitions, close to Jesus in the role of redeemer, i.e. it gives Mary a vital role in
the salvation that Jesus' death and resurrection brought about. The definition of
co-redemptrix is variously defined, however, from the more drastic, where Mary
is equal to Jesus in redemptive qualities, to a lesser status, where she plays a role
in redemption, but is not the redeemer herself.

6

The Practical Kabbala: How to Build a Golem

Gnosticism or the lore of secret knowledge-systems is an extremely insidious parasitic growth, which attaches itself like a poisonous ivy to the healthy trunk of a major religion. (Paul Johnson, *The History of the Jews*)

The Holy Land and the Holy Kabbala

In Israel, in February 1974, a group of rabbis, hawkish young secularists, and followers of the militant rabbi Zvi Yehuda Kook formed the Gush Emmunim, or the 'Block of the Faithful'. It was a momentous occasion. Secular Zionism and religiously conservative orthodox Jewish groups were often at odds about the creation of a Jewish state. Gush Emmunim was composed of many ultra-orthodox groups, whose support of the Jewish state was unwaveringly firm, but Gush Emmunim was not designed to be a proper political party in Israel's parliamentary democracy. Rather, it was created to put pressure on Israeli politicians, and secular Israelis in general, to move the Jewish state and Israeli society toward a more religiously Jewish orientation. Gush Emmunim's main preoccupation was the establishment of what it viewed as Israel's ancestral and God-given borders. This group wanted the territories that Israel had won in the Six Days' War in 1963, in particular the West Bank, which they called by its biblical name, Judaea and Samaria, to be incorporated into the Jewish state.

Later in 1974, a group that would later work under the umbrella of Gush Emmunim decided to create a seed settlement in a railway depot near the Palestinian town of Nablus. This site was important because it was the area where the ancient, biblical city of Shechem had been located. The settlers were attempting to 're-sacralize' the land, which they believed had been profaned by the Palestinian Arabs. They called their settlement Elon Moreh, another biblical name for Shechem, and attempted to set up a yeshiva in the railway depot.

The settlement was illegal, and the then Prime Minister Shimon Peres tried to forcibly evict them. There were clashes with the Israeli Defence Forces, but there was also widespread support for the settlers' move among the more conservative Likud party. Peres feared a loss to Likud in the upcoming elections and eventually caved in, allowing the settlers in Elon Moreh to stay. The pressure that illegal settlers put on the Israeli government was highly effective and it was a pattern Gush Emmunim would repeat in the next 30 years. The seizing of Palestinian land by members of Gush Emmunim proved just how powerless Israeli secular officials could be at the hands of a small religious minority intent on having its way.

To the members of Gush Emmunim, the settlement of Elon Moreh – later renamed Kedumim – was steeped in religious significance. To them it was an outward symbol of the divine presence in the world: what Isaac Luria called a *tikkun*, or an act of restoration that would help to one day repair the cosmos.[1] Members of Gush Emmunim often couched their militant settlement activities in just such Kabbalistic language. This in itself is extraordinary, since the Kabbala, which is the esoteric mystical lore in Judaism, is quite often antithetical to practical action, particularly of a military or political nature. That it has become meshed with militant Messianic Zionism illustrates some of the Kabbala's inherent plasticity, but it also reveals a deep misunderstanding about the nature of the Kabbala. Rather than supporting a parochial view of Judaism that is connected to a strictly monotheistic God and his concern with sacred lands, the Kabbala is cosmic in its proportions and wildly plural in its concerns. In fact the Kabbala creates outlets for the rigidly monotheistic rabbinical tradition through the fracturing of God into parts and personalities, and even sexes. The essential dogmatism and ideological approach to Judaism of groups like Gush Emmunim is alien to the spirit of the Kabbala, which actually approaches a free form of spiritual speculation. As we will see, conceptual religious fundamentalism is nearly alien to the Kabbala, both in theory and especially in practice.

Paganism and monotheism compared

We have stressed the importance of pagan influences on Islam, Christianity and Judaism. For the student of syncretism, there are possibly no clearer well-springs of influences, both directly and indirectly, than the pagan religions and their encounters with the Abrahamic religions. But for such an important influence, sources are amazingly silent. That Jews, Christians and Muslims worshipped without the influence of the pagan creeds that surrounded them was taken as true by several generations of religious scholars.[2] Until recently it was an important principle to Western scholars of Christianity, Islam and Judaism to maintain the doctrinal integrity of each respective religion[3] and that Christianity, Islam and Judaism could be nurtured and influenced by pagan religions has only recently been accepted.

We have already seen[4] that, in a strict sense, paganism refers to the inhabitants of rural regions of the Christianized Roman Empire, but Roman paganism actually survived as an urban phenomenon well into the fourth century. Calling a worshipper of the old Roman gods and goddesses a pagan may have had a derogatory function: in other words, it was a way of ridiculing someone's backwardness no matter where they lived. Other interesting theories of the origin of 'pagan' have also been proposed,[5] but 'paganism' as a *term* has many meanings. And when we throw time into the mix, we complicate factors even more, for paganism has been transformed through time. We can continue to work out a definition as we move forward in our examination of the Kabbala, Judaism's mystical branch of knowledge, lore and practice, since in many ways the Kabbala brings a type of pagan polytheism into the heart of an Abrahamic, monotheistic religion. This is a huge area of study, so we will confine ourselves to some of the areas where obvious syncretism comes into play.

Rabbinical Judaism demythologizes the God of the Bible

It has long been noted that rabbinical Judaism attempted to remove 'mythological' ideas about God from Jewish theology.[6] By 'mythological', we mean God having a body, emotions, and all the concomitant interactions with the human and natural realm entailed by having a body. For most Westerners, interactions such as these are usually associated with the gods of the Greek pantheon. The Jewish God was divested of these functions by the rabbinical tradition, which viewed God as formless, bodiless and abstract. The terms used to connote God, including the gender terms, were seen as mere symbols of an entity that could not be couched in language.

Reducing God to an abstract deity had a profound impact on the formation of the Kabbala. As we have seen in this study, many heresies begin as counter-trends to dominant religious notions. They start as reactions against prevailing religious ideas and try to balance them with opposing tendencies. We can see this nowhere more clearly than in the Kabbala's opposition to some of rabbinical Judaism's doctrinal excesses.[7] The bloodless God of the Rabbis was an early casualty of the Kabbala's revolution. Whereas rabbinical Judaism attempted to abstract the Jewish God out of his body, the Kabbala poured him into a body with gusto.[8] Not only was God embodied and engendered, he was also split into parts. Jewish theologians often spoke of God's powers in a figurative sense as self-sustaining entities. Judaism's wisdom tradition spoke and wrote about God's wisdom as separate from him, and often as female. The Kabbalists, however, began to speak of those powers and essences as if they were self-sustaining, separately existing beings. This had a profound effect on the Kabbala, and allowed its devotees to make statements about God that in any other contexts would have been deemed blasphemy and considered heresy.[9] That this was allowed to occur is interesting, partially because the Kabbala, despite all its questionable content, never denied the importance of following the strictures of rabbinical Judaism. In fact, some of its exponents were great Halachic scholars (i.e. scholars of Jewish law). Indeed, most of the Kabbala's branches and trends supported the Halacha – or the nuts and bolts of Jewish practice, like keeping kosher or the laws regarding what kind of work was permitted or forbidden on the Sabbath. Regardless of what mystically inclined Jews said about God, the way they behaved always conformed to religious authority.

The first major Kabbalistic book: the *Bahir*

There are three important books that have had a major influence on the mystical branch of Judaism: the *Bahir,* the *Sepher Yetzirah* and the *Zohar.* Both the *Zohar* and the *Bahir* derive their names from terms for light, illumination or brilliance.[10] The *Sepher Yetzirah* can be translated from the Hebrew as 'The Book of Creation'. The *Sepher Yetzirah* is not necessarily a book with Kabbalistic content, but it became one from its frequent use in Kabbalistic speculation.

The *Bahir* is an odd and innovative book. It is unusually structured, if we can say that it is structured at all, and it is interesting because its subject matter is indicative of a break with much of rabbinical Judaism's thinking about certain cherished topics. It is extremely short and difficult to read but it remains important to understanding many of the formative ideas in the Kabbalistic tradition, which are distilled and compressed in its brief text. For modern readers, or readers who are not well-versed in the problems and concerns of traditional Judaism, the *Bahir's* revolutionary nature will go unnoticed. But for the Jews at the time of its widespread dissemination, its unorthodox subject matter was noted and commented upon, sometimes vociferously. In an early epistle from around 1230–5 Meir ben Simon, a staunch opponent of the Kabbala, raised doubts about the *Bahir's* authenticity. He believed that the *Bahir* was not an ancient document, but was of recent provenance, and more damaging still, that it was made up. He derides those who speak:

> blasphemously of God and of the scholars that walk in the way of pure Torah and who fear God, while they themselves are wise in their own eyes, invent things out of their minds, lean toward heretical opinions and imagine they can bring proof for their opinions from the words of the haggadoth, which they explain on the basis of erroneous assumptions . . . and they have a book that has already been written for them,

which they call *Bahir*, that is 'bright' but no light shines through it ... it is the work for someone who lacked command of either literary language or good style, and in many passages it contains words that are out and out heresy.[11]

What was so upsetting in the *Bahir* to men like Meir ben Simon? The *Bahir* makes repeated references to a tree that God created and, in a different interpretation, to a tree that is an expression of God's creative forces in the universe. The tree as a symbol of the universe has a very old genealogy, Assyrian art and royal iconography depicted a tree as the symbol of the universe, with its numerous branches representing various potencies or powers of the gods of the Assyrian pantheon.[12] For the *Bahir*, this tree, with its numerous branches, represented specific attributes of the divine that took on lives of their own. In the *Bahir* God says:

I am the One who planted this tree in order that all the world should delight in it. And in it, I spread All. I called it All because all depend upon it, all emanate from it, and all need it. To it they look, for it they wait, and from it, souls fly in joy. Alone was I when I made it.[13]

At times, this tree takes on the structure of the universe:

The Blessed Holy One has a single Tree, and it has twelve diagonal boundaries: The northeast boundary, the southeast boundary; The upper east boundary, the lower east boundary; The southwest boundary, the northwest boundary; The upper west boundary, the lower west boundary; The upper south boundary, the lower south boundary; The upper north boundary, the lower north boundary; They continually spread forever and ever; They are the arms of the world.[14]

At other times, the Tree is seen as Israel:

Israel is holy, taking the Tree itself and its Heart. The Heart is the beauty of the fruit of the body. Similarly, Israel takes 'the fruit of a beautiful tree.' The date palm is surrounded by its branches all around it and has its sprout in the centre. Similarly, Israel takes the body of this Tree which is its Heart.[15]

We may very well ask why this tree imagery is so radically different from what came before it in the Jewish tradition? Simply stated, the tree becomes the jumping off point for some radical speculation about the nature of God. The *Bahir* takes notions like evil and places them within the active power of God, all within the imaginative world of the branches on a cosmic tree. The *Bahir* creates the tree of existence, as a multilayered entity that can explain everything about the cosmos: from the dimensions of God's physical body, to God's creative role in existence. At times, the tree is represented as a body – often as the divine incarnation of Adam, the first man. In a certain sense, Adam, the tree and God are depicted as cosmological equals, as there is no attempt in the *Bahir* to allegorize its imagery. Nor is there any apology offered for its departures from normative Jewish thinking about the separations between the cosmos, God and human beings. Here, we come close to theological pantheism: that God and the cosmos are identical.

We can see this nowhere more clearly than in the *Bahir's* interpretation of the creation story in the first chapter of Genesis. Initially Judaism had a variety of notions about the creation of the world, but eventually one of the principle notions of rabbinical Judaism was that God created the world *ex nihilo*, or from nothing. This concept is important to traditional Judaism, because it divorces God from the physical context of the world: God literally created the world from a free act of absolute power, without dependence on matter. He creates – he merely forms the universe from his supreme will. Mythological notions of the creation of the world (known as cosmogony) very often depict a creator God grappling with the forces of chaos, usually, but not always, envisioned as a sea creature. Creation scenarios such as these were often viewed as diametrically opposed to the one depicted in Genesis. God's creation *ex nihilo* is an act of absolute power, while a mythological struggle between opposing forces, on the other hand, depicts a god that is less than omniscient and anything but omnipotent. God grapples with *tohu* and *bohu* in Genesis, two words that were most likely associated with beings that ruled the primal waters and darkness of the pre-creation cosmos. In other places in the Bible we find vestiges of earlier stories. In Psalm 74.14 we find: 'You crushed Leviathan's heads, gave him as food to the wild animals.' This is, perhaps, an echo of an early creation story where Yahweh defeats a primal sea creature in his attempt to subdue creation. Similarly, in Job 40.25 we find: 'Leviathan, too! Can you catch him with a fish-hook [like God] or hold his tongue down with a rope?' These passages may well be a reference to a creation story different from the one told in Genesis, a titanic struggle for control over the primal world between Yahweh and a sea creature, which was a personification of atavistic chaos.[16]

What the Bible only alludes to, hints at, or otherwise contains as mythological holdovers, the *Bahir* outrageously displays. We are told, rather early on in the book:

Rabbi Berachiah said: It is written 'The earth was Chaos (tohu) and Desolation (bohu).' What is the meaning of the word 'was' in this verse? This indicates that the Chaos existed previously [and already was]. What is Chaos (bohu)? Something that confounds people. What is Desolation (Bohu)? It is something that has substance. This is the reason that it is called Bohu , that is, Bo Hu – 'it is in it.'[17]

In the *Bahir, tohu* and *bohu,* usually translated as 'void' and 'chaos', develop a more substantial incarnation. We are told that rather than being nothing, *tohu* and *bohu* are in a sense something that has an existence and a substance. We even receive a folk etymology: the writer breaks down *bohu* into its component syllables to come up with an origin for the word: 'it is in it'.

The existence of *tohu* and *bohu* become, in the *Bahir,* the platform for all sorts of novel speculations regarding the existence of evil. Evil, in the rabbinical tradition, is often associated with Satan and is seen as separate from God and his realm. In the *Bahir* this system is turned on its head, as we see in this intriguing passage:

A king had a beautiful daughter, and others desired her. The king knew about it, but could not fight those who wanted to bring his daughter to evil ways. He came to her house and warned her, saying, 'My daughter, do not pay attention to the words of these enemies and they will not be able to overcome you. Do not leave the house, but do all your work at home. Do not sit idle, even for a single moment. Then they will not be able to see you and harm you.'[18]

So far we have been told about evil and given an example: those who desire the King's daughter. Then the text refines itself. We go from specific example to general principle:

They have one Attribute which causes them to leave aside every good way and choose every evil way. When they see a person directing himself along a good way, they hate him. What is [this Attribute]? It is the Satan.[19]

It is hard to know, at this point, who are the entities that have one attribute that causes them to leave the good and choose the evil. Perhaps 'they' are an idealized humanity, or the fallen heavenly host.

We are next told that the attribute of evil is Satan, which is certainly a notion that fits with rabbinical interpretations. But in the next section we veer off the track of rabbinical Judaism:

This teaches us that the Blessed Holy One has an Attribute whose name is Evil. It is to the north of the Blessed Holy One, as it is written (Jeremiah 1:14), 'From the north will Evil come forth, upon all the inhabitants of the earth.' Any evil that comes to all the inhabitants of the earth comes from the north.[20]

Nothing in the preceding section prepares us for this statement: 'the Blessed Holy One has an attribute whose name is Evil.'[21] It would be hard to conjure a statement that diverts more from traditional rabbinical or Jewish philosophical notions of God. In Judaism's philosophical tradition, evil was always explained away as non-existent, or at best, as an error in human perception.[22] The rabbinical tradition had a variety of responses to the existence of a supremely good God and the seeming presence of evil in the world, one of which suggested that hardship and suffering were products of the failure of Israel to follow the commandments. That God should have an attribute of evil is a radical notion, to say the least.[23]

Why does the *Bahir* set out to divest rabbinical Judaism of some of its most treasured notions about God? The answer is far from simple. In many ways, we can only understand it in light of the later development of mystical Judaism. Whoever wrote the *Bahir* set about, with a series of quite obvious intentions, to upset treasured Jewish notions about God. This was done, we can only imagine, from a desire to provide some alternative images in order to allow the reader of the *Bahir* to totally reconceptualize God in a way that rabbinical Judaism would not allow. Ideas of God become more like certain Eastern concepts: God is not seen as totally divorced from evil, but in a real sense includes evil as part of his essence. And the world was not so much created from nothing, nor did it spring from neutrally and formless void, but was instead populated with mythically potent beasts that God was required to defeat in order to gain hegemony.

These bold moves made in the *Bahir* allowed a mythologically invested God to return to Judaism, a crack was opened, and a type of polytheism was allowed to enter Judaism. Many later trends in the Kabbala take some of these notions of God and transform them into more boldly formulated visions of the divine. For example, the branches of the tree depicted in the *Bahir* become aspects of God that develop an existence of their own, called the *sephiroth* in Hebrew. They become invested with gender and personality, and they begin a long journey of struggle and strife with their mystical brothers, sisters and lovers.

The *Zohar*'s syncretism: the creation of a Jewish pantheon of gods and goddesses

The work that would eventually accomplish most of this is called the *Zohar*. The most important work in the Kabbalistic movement, it is gigantic, numbering nearly a million words! And the impressiveness of its quantity is equalled by that of its content. Its five books are nothing less than a recapitulation and reformulation of the entire Torah of

Moses. *Zohar* can be translated as 'The Book of Splendour', with the word 'splendour' having purposeful connotations with light. Though the *Zohar* was attributed to a remoter antiquity, it was written by a Spanish Jew named Moses de Leon in about 1286.[24] The *Zohar* had a wide and lasting impact on Judaism. Its dissemination to the greater Jewish world after the expulsion of the Jews of Spain in 1492 brought it within the sphere of the larger currents of Jewish mysticism, and allowed it, while so formally and technically a work of Andalusian Jews, to develop wider meaning in the Jewish world.

Here it is worth examining an example in order to underscore the book's importance to the entire Jewish world. The Kabbala is heavily reliant on speculations about God's name. The *Zohar* follows this trend, doing some interesting interpretative work with God's most holy name, Yahweh. The ancient biblical name for God, known as the Tetragrammaton, is read by the *Zohar* as an abbreviation for the four divine elements that compose a part of the deity: *Hokhma,* or Wisdom, *Bina,* or Understanding, *Tif'eret,* or Beauty, and *Malkhut,* or Kingship. Wisdom is identified with the Father, Understanding with the Mother, Beauty with the Son, and Kingship with the Daughter. These four concepts form a Kabbalistic tetrad, a grouping of four. One passage in the *Zohar* explains this: 'the letter Y in the name YHWH is called Father and stands for wisdom; the first H is the Supernal Mother, called Understanding; and the W and the second H are the two children, a son and a daughter, who were conceived by the mother'.[25] Further passages are even more explicit about this family relationship:

> Wisdom spread out and brought forth Understanding, and they were found to be male and female, Wisdom the Father and Understanding the Mother . . . Then these two united, and lighted up each other, and the H [i.e. the mother] conceived and gave birth to a Son. Through the birth of the Son the Father and the Mother found perfection, and this led to the completion of everything, the inclusion of everything: Father, Mother, Son and Daughter.[26]

The *Zohar,* which abounds with duplicate explanations and episodes, also offers the genesis of this family relationship in this way:

> The Y brought forth a river which issued from the Garden of Eden and was identical with the Mother. The mother became pregnant with the two children, the W who was the Son, and the second H who was the daughter, and she brought them forth and suckled them. . . . These two children were under the tutelage of the Father and Mother . . . After the Mother gave birth to the Son, she placed him before her, and this is why the first H in the name YHWH must be written close together with the W. The Son received a double share of the inheritance from

his Father and Mother, and he, in turn, nourished the Daughter. This is why when writing the Tetragrammaton in sacred texts, one must bring the W and the second H close together.[27]

Here the Jewish God has been divided into four. This is not unlike the numerous examples of just such tetrads from the world of mythology. In the Greek mythology familiar to most Westerners, Kronos, Rhea, Zeus and Hera formed the original tetrad. Kronos castrated his father Uranus (Sky), seized the throne, and married his sister, Rhea. Zeus, in turn, castrated Kronos and married his sister Hera.[28] In Hindu mythology, Shiva is the generative principle of the universe: he is the four-legged and four-armed great god of procreation – the symbolic Phallus who lives in the Himalayas, where he dwells in marital harmony with his wife, Parvati, the Great Mother. This divine couple has two children: Ganesha, god of wisdom and remover of obstacles, and Karikeya, god of war and patron of thieves.

Just as in Hindu and Greek mythology, the Father and Mother of the Kabbala's tetrad function as separate persons, or gods in a pantheon. Their relations, particularly regarding sex, would be familiar to anyone reading Greek, Roman or Indian mythological tales, but for these to exist in a Jewish book is startling. In the *Zohar* we are told that:

> Never does the inclination of the Father and the Mother toward each other cease. They always go out together and dwell together. They never separate and leave each other. They are together in complete union.[29]

Here is the paradigm of the earth mother and the sky father that we can see in Kronos and Rhea, and Shiva and Parvati. The embrace of the Kabbalistic Father and Mother engenders the sky (the universe) and earth. And the sexual nature of this union is not veiled:

> When the seed of the Righteous is about to be ejaculated, he does not have to seek the Female, for she abides with him, never leaves him, and is always in readiness for him. His seed flows not save when the Female is ready, and when they both as one desire each other; and they unite in a single embrace and never separate . . .[30]

The Father and Mother are companions and partners, but their offspring, the Son and Daughter, can be viewed as lovers. At first, the Father dallies with the daughter, and an incestuous union results. The Mother becomes jealous, and responds by suckling and fondling the Son. Eventually, as in other mythologies, the siblings take a more prominent role and leave behind their parents, the older deities, who retreat into the background. In the *Zohar*, passages involving the Mother and Father are few, while those involving the Son and Daughter are numerous. The Son and Daughter take on many guises, but usually, the Son is known as the King, while his sister-wife is known as *Malakut*, kingship, or the *Shekinah* or *Matronit*. She is also identified with the community of Israel, and female images like the Earth, the night, a well and the moon. While the relationship of the Mother and Father is rather placid, that between the Son and Daughter is more tempestuous, and they are more often than not called 'lovers', or *dodim* in Hebrew. The reason for the difficulties lay primarily with the identification of the Daughter with the community of Israel. When the community is holy, the King and Queen are together and mate, usually in their bedroom in the Temple in Jerusalem. When Israel sins, they are torn apart. The most dramatic expression of this was the destruction of the Second Temple, which led to their permanent estrangement. The great exile caused by the destruction of the Temple by Rome becomes, in the *Zohar's* mythological world, an act of estrangement without parallel in the history of the universe. Only if Israel is holy can the union be re-established.

As we can see, the rank polytheism of these tales is astonishing. The natural question is how could a tradition that fosters so grave and bold a polytheism be allowed to grow on the body of Judaism?[31] One answer is that the traditions expounded in the Kabbala were reputed to be old and therefore held in esteem even among the most orthodox sages of the Talmudic period. The so-called mysticism of the Account of the Beginning, which represents the mechanics of the creation of the world as recorded in Genesis, and the Account of the Chariot, which is the vision of the heavenly host by Isaiah and Ezekiel, are the two main branches of Jewish mysticism and they have quite venerable genealogies.[32] There is also a famous passage embedded in the Talmud that warns of the dangers of the mystical pursuit:

> Our Rabbis have taught, four entered into Pardes [paradise]. They were Ben Azai, Ben Zoma, Aher, and Rabbi Akiba. Ben Azai gazed and died. Of him it is written 'precious in the eyes of the Lord is the death of the pious ones.' Ben Zoma gazed and went insane. Of him it is written, 'have you found honey, eat your share lest you become full and vomit it up.' Aher became an apostate. Rabbi Akiba entered and exited in peace.[33]

This enigmatic passage has been interpreted in a variety of ways, almost all of which stress the rigours of the mystical pursuit, and act as a warning to those who set about studying these topics. This passage from the Talmud also shows how venerable such pursuits were, the great sages of the Talmud often engaged in them – even if they were frowned upon for the masses and considered just for the elite.

Jewish medieval 'rationalism' and the nature of God's sexuality

Even Maimonides (1135–1204) the arch-rationalist medieval Jewish philosopher and theologian considered these topics so important that he wrote *The Guide of the Perplexed* to document his discoveries in these areas, even though writing this knowledge down was strictly forbidden.[34] *The Guide of the Perplexed* was considered by generations of scholars an archetypal example of medieval rationalistic theology. Maimonides was under the influence of such Arab philosophers as al-Farabi (AD 870–950), who wrote commentaries on Plato and Aristotle and was under the sway of the renaissance of philosophical thought brought about by Arab exposure to Greek intellectual culture. These thinkers were mainly influenced by Aristotle, but they read Plato as well, and their unique fusion of Platonic and Aristotelian philosophy was the hallmark of the age. Maimonides was called a rationalist since he sought to find rational or explicable bases for Judaism wherever possible. One part of *The Guide* explains the historical reasons for some of the more obscure laws found in the Torah.[35] The book devotes a considerable amount of space to lexical exegesis – for example, explaining that the terms used in the Torah for God's physical body are used allegorically. Overall, Maimonides expends a great deal of energy explaining the universe and God to the extent that the human mind can explain it, mostly in Aristotelian terms. In the Latin West, where copies of Aristotle's work had been lost or were in short supply for centuries, Latin translations of *The Guide* were considered to offer access to Aristotle's thinking, and had an influence on Church theologians of the High Middle Ages.[36]

But the rational basis of *The Guide* is partially a smokescreen. The book was written not as a systematic treatise of theology (in fact, its structure thwarts most attempts to systematize it), but to explain the two areas of Jewish mystical thought: The Account of the Beginning, *Maaseh Beresith*, and the Account of the Chariot, *Maaseh Merkabah*. Maimonides waits until Part II, chapters 30 and 31, to begin his explication of the former, and Part III chapters 1 to 7 for the latter, in his large three-volume work. He waits a long time to explain these forbidden topics, and sandwiches them between other materials, to fatigue and confuse less qualified readers, as he believes the material under consideration should not be told to everyone. He says: '. . . as I have explained several times in our commentary on the Mishnah, none of those who know [something of these matters] should divulge it.'[37] Then he gives the reader a hint of what is not to be revealed in this topic:

> And they say explicitly: as from the beginning of the book up to here, the glory of God [requires] to conceal the thing, they say it at the end of what is said concerning the sixth day [of the beginning]. Thus what we have said becomes clear.[38]

Maimonides is referring here to what the sages of the Mishnah have to say about the creation of the first man and woman. The secret is the bisexual nature of God. If God created man and woman in his image, and the man and woman in Genesis 1 are created at the same time, then God, in a sense, possesses characteristics of each sex. So here, Maimonides makes a bold move: he invests the bloodless and abstract God of the rabbinical tradition with gender. Further, he suggests that God created man and woman in his image through some sort of procreative act, and that primal man may have been an androgyne, or may have had both male and female sex organs on one body. We find these ideas in Aristophanes' speech in Plato's *Symposium*, but they are also found in the Jewish tradition:

> When the Holy One, Blessed be He created Adam, He created him an androgyne . . . He created him double faced, then He split him and made him two backs, one back on this side and one back on the other side.[39]

God in Genesis also takes this creature and splits him in two. The androgyne becomes Adam and Eve in the second creation story told in chapter 2 in Genesis. Before they ate the fruit from the tree of the knowledge of good and evil, a kind of lawless sexual state existed in the Garden of Eden. Maimonides, the arch-rationalist, explained some very old and odd stories about the procreative activities of the first man and the first woman in the Garden of Eden, before they partook of the fruit. The serpent, called Sammael (the Blind God) had relations with Eve, and spawned all manner of half-demon children. The world before the knowledge of good and evil was a world devoid of intellect, and hence all reflections about forbidden and prohibited activity were impossible. The concourse between a sexualized God, his creatures, the heavenly host, and the fallen angels, was far greater in the Garden than in any other time in human history, for indeed we can say that human history had not even begun yet. The Account of the Beginning documents the sexual nature of God's creation of human beings. Here, Maimonides, the supposed rationalist, uses distinctly mythological images to explain how the God of Genesis did his work.

When Maimonides gets to the other topic of Jewish mysticism, the Account of the Chariot, he sets out to explain the visions of Ezekiel and Isaiah. In order to do this, Maimonides once again buries the chapters in a sea of other topics, to confuse less devoted and worthy readers. Ezekiel and Isaiah's famous vision was of a divine chariot composed of the likeness of four living creatures, one that looks like an ox, one a lion, one an eagle and one a man. They all have straight feet 'and the sole of their feet was like the sole of the foot of a cal [*kaf egel regel* in Hebrew] and they sparkled like burnished brass' (Ezekiel 1.4–7). The creature's feet become very important for Maimonides' interpretations, as does a substance, called *hasmal* in Hebrew, which emanates from the man. 'Foot' is often used as a euphemism in Hebrew for 'penis'. In colloquial Hebrew there is an expression for urination: *meme reglayim* or 'waters for the feet'. The vision that both Ezekiel and Isaiah see, but in slightly different forms, is one of the boldest mysteries of the Torah: it is God's generation of the souls of men and women. The act of procreation is accomplished by God through the cherubim, or angels, whose union creates the soul of every person born on earth. The *hashmal*, usually translated as 'amber', is the divine seed issuing from the cosmic phallus, generating souls.[40]

The stories told in these sections of *The Guide* have an obvious sexual connotation, and this kind of lore was always seen as inherently dangerous to disseminate, so it was told only to scholars and sages who met certain requirements.[41]

The Kabbala becomes popular: the Kabbala of Isaac Luria

When the great age of Jewish rationalism ended in the thirteenth century, the great age of the Kabbala began, and the proponents of the Kabbala took these stories and embedded them in their own unique view of the universe. If the rationalist branch of Judaism in the Middle Ages saw validity in mythological stories about God, mysticism and folklore, areas of Judaism unhindered by the demands of reason did so as well, and often without restraint. The initial reaction to the widespread dissemination of such stories was shock, dismay and condemnation.[42] But the popularity of the Kabbala was not negatively affected by this material, and in fact, the content actually helped actively promote it. As we said, one reason why the Kabbala was so widely successful, even though some Kabbalists uttered statements about God that in other contexts would be deemed heretical, is that instead of eroding the foundations of rabbinical faith, most of its branches and versions supported them.

The most influential movement in the Kabbala was that founded by Isaac Luria (1534–72), who is known in the Jewish tradition as the Holy Lion. The fact that his version of Jewish mysticism came to dominate the field is extraordinary, as he left no writing of his own, except for a few short poems. His disciples wrote down his teachings and passed them among themselves. He was born in Egypt but early in his life moved to Safed, a city in the hills of northern Palestine, where he died in a plague before he was 40. This man, who lived for a short time and left no substantial written record of his own, would a few years after his death dominate the world of Jewish mysticism and, in the decades that followed, his would be nearly recognized as the only form of Jewish mysticism on the block.[43]

If we couple these facts with the actual content of his teaching, his popularity is even more amazing. Luria's doctrines are extremely abstruse. Gershom Scholem, the great modern scholar of the Kabbala, was the first to recognize that Luria owed a great deal of his doctrine to Gnosticism, which at various times exerted an enormous influence over Judaism, Islam and Christianity. Gnostic religions competed with Christianity in its formative years, and flourished alongside Judaism in the lands of Jewish exile, particularly in the east, in such places as Babylonia. As we have seen, Islam also came under its sway, especially among its mystics. Most Gnostic movements had secret, esoteric components that were taught to upper-level adepts, and many saw the creation of the universe as the result of a 'fall' from a primal harmony to a lower, darker state. The message was that individual souls, or even God, could and did fall from their heights, and the result of such calamity is the sorry state of the world: the inherent tension of life and death, the struggle with illness and disease, the pain and suffering of existence. The more radical movements in Gnosticism, like the Manichaeans, saw the world under the control of a creator god called a demiurge, while the higher god – the true God – sits above creation and is somehow trapped or incapable of exerting his power. In fact some Christian Gnostics equated the Jewish God in the Old Testament with the demiurge, and viewed the Christian God, with Christ as his representative, as the true God.

Indeed in the Lurianic Kabbala we find some of these general Gnostic trends. First a cosmic drama unfolds that would not be out of place in a Gnostic creation account. There is a catastrophic fall and a failed attempt at ascent by holy entities. Luria's Kabbala speaks about a nongodly power, and comes close to creating a basic dualism in the concept of God himself; it sees the souls of human beings as trapped in the matter of the lower regions of the universe (our world). Freeing the soul from this prison became one of the Lurianic Kabbala's prime directives.[44]

The main characters in the Lurianic myth are God, the cosmos, and human beings. In the beginning there was nothing but God. God, in fact, was the universe, stretching limitlessly in every direction. There was no time or location. There was just God and extension. Then, movement began. A space opened up in this non-existent realm, and it was as if God contracted himself, resulting in an area that was empty of God. This first part of the Lurianic drama is called *tzimtzum*, or contraction or withdrawal.

In the next part of the drama, God tried to re-enter the vacated space, to restore, it seems, its condition. But he did this only partially, and only a line, or charge, from the divine was extended into the empty space. This was called *hitpashtut* and was the opposite of the first act. *Tzimtzum* was likened to God breathing out and *hitpashtut* likened to God breathing in.

What happened next was the subject of much discussion among Luri-anic Kabbalists. Something went wrong with the space that God had vacated and attempted to reinhabit. The space that had just been formed could not stand the pressure of God trying to reinhabit it, so it shattered. The outer husks of this form were scattered in all directions. They are known as holy sparks in the Lurianic diction. Some of these sparks re-turned upward to their source, God, while others became entangled with the shattered husks that held them, which are called *klipot,* and which fell with them. Divine harmony had been broken. Things in the universe were now out of order, and the stage was set for the entry of human beings.

The sparks and husks that fell from the divine space yearned to re-turn to their place with God. For the Lurianic Jew, every positive work enacted on the earth helps to lift the sparks to heaven. Even ploughing a field can help, since it releases the sparks trapped in the soil and lifts them heavenward. But mostly, the performance of the *mitzvoth,* or command-ments given to Moses and written in the Torah, perform this vital cosmic function. The performance of the *mitzvoth* with the correct intention, or *kavannah*, helps to cure the world and promote the primal lift. This is known as *tikkun,* and the individual acts of a Jew in conformity to the Laws of Moses are but a prelude to the Great *Tikkun*, when all the sparks will be gathered, and the Messianic Age will be ushered in.[45]

We have stressed that Judaism is a religion that places more emphasis on correct behaviour than on correct thinking or belief. It is just this distinction that allowed the Lurianic Kabbala to have such a popular appeal. The fractures and divisions in the divine life, created due to the incredible pressures on the structure of the universe at creation, led to the breaking of the primal vessels that held the world's substance. So the righteous Jew becomes a hero in the divine drama.

The Lurianic Kabbala often had unequivocal heretical content. Many heretical tendencies and movements lead to schisms within religious communities, and the Kabbala certainly took its toll on Jewish commu-nal life. It has been recognized that two of the greatest schisms in the history of Judaism, those of Shabbeti Zevi and Jacob Frank, could not have occurred if it were not for the Lurianic Kabbala's unique epistemol-ogy.[46] But with the notable exception of these two important events, this version of the Kabbala worked to promote Jewish observance, and not undermine it. This was the true genius of the doctrines moulded by Isaac Luria and his followers: the Kabbala worked to shore up the *minutiae* of the rabbinical tradition, so that each act of the observant Jew, when practising the *mitzvoth* with the correct intention, acquired a stature of mythological importance.

The Lurianic Kabbala places a great deal of emphasis on individu-al worship and its cosmic significance. An unintended consequence of this was the rise of magic. The idea of a crippled or damaged God who requires the help and succour of worshippers led to an inflated idea of the power of the worshipper. This is the idea of *kavannah*, or intention, pushed to its logical extreme. The Kabbala began as a set of abstract speculations on the nature of God, the universe and the human place in that universe. The inflated notion of the individual Jew's actions in the divine drama of the Kabbalistic universe helped foster the rise of magic in the Kabbala in the late Middle Ages.

The breaking down of barriers: the relationship between the Bible, the Kabbala and magic

The borders between superstition and magic on the one hand, and religion and revelation on the other, are not nearly as clear as they are supposed. In a famous passage in the book of Samuel, Saul visits the witch of Endor, who successfully conjures up the ghost of the prophet Samuel to seek his advice (1 Samuel 28). Also in 1 Samuel 23.9–12, David relies upon the priest's ephod, or vestment worn by an ancient Hebrew priest, to predict the future; for the ephod seemed to contain some sort of mechanism that could respond to questioners' enquiries. Again in 1 Samuel 14.41 we see Saul using the Urim and Thummin, also somehow a part of the priest's ephod, and casting lots to predict God's will. These practices – the conjuring up of a ghost, the use of divinatory techniques, and the practice of casting lots to assign guilt or innocence – in any other context than the Hebrew Bible would be labelled magic. There are specific prohibitions in the Bible against sorcery, magic and divination:

> There must never be anyone among you who makes his son or daughter pass through the fire or sacrifice, who practises divination, who is soothsayer, augur or sorcerer, weaver of spells, consulter of ghosts or mediums, or necromancer, (Deuteronomy 18.10–12; NJB)

But despite these prohibitions, biblical heroes did employ these techniques. Even in the later version of Judaism, the rabbinical tradition, the sages and wise men of the Talmud and Mishnah often employ magic or magical techniques. In one passage of the Talmud, Rabbi Joshua ben Hananai performs a magical incantation. He scatters flax seeds on a table and they instantly take root and grow. He then reaches into them to pull out the head of a witch who was casting an evil spell upon him. In another passage, Rabbi Jannai turns the tables on a witch who attempted to turn him into an ass, only to turn her into an ass.[47] So despite the biblical prohibitions against wizardry of all kinds, the rabbis of the Talmud often practised magic. They justified it by making distinctions between types of magic: they contrasted the black magic of wizards, which had destructive intent, with the magic of the rabbis, which was protective in nature. In fact, they argued that magic should only be used in defence, and not as an offensive weapon.[48] The rabbis of the Talmud, according to their customary predilections, divided magical practice into many categories, permitting some while banning others. Two main types of magic where forbidden: that which produced 'the performance of an act', and that which created an illusion, or 'captured the eyesight'. The first was an offence punishable by death. The second, creating the appearance of magic but not actually performing a magical act, was forbidden, but the penalty was less dramatic. One type of magic was allowed: that which involved 'The Laws of Creation', a term that was later interpreted to mean invoking the mystical names of God and the angels.[49] Both traditional Judaism and its folk versions believed in the existence of demons. One tradition even saw the origins of demons in the creation of the world on the sixth day: as God rushed to complete his tasks, he began to create human-like creatures that would have had bodies. But he ran out of time, and only created their souls, which wander about the earth, and cause all sorts of mischief.[50] They employ magic to bedevil people, whom they envy, and often a Jew must protect him or herself by counter-employing magic.

A venerable demon in the Jewish pantheon of evil is Lilith. She probably began her long and distinguished career as a Near Eastern goddess. Her name has Semitic roots in the word for night[51] and became established in the Jewish world with a host of images derived from the Bible and from extra-biblical sources. Lilith began her adventures as a demon as Adam's first wife. The Bible contains two creation stories: the first is the account of the creation of the world in six days in Genesis 1, and the second is the retelling of that story in Genesis 2. Human beings are created in Genesis 1.27 in a single act: 'God created man in the image of himself, in the image of God he created him, male and female he created them.' In this first creation story, it appears that the man and the woman were created in a single moment and at the same time. Genesis 2 contains the more detailed story of the creation of a man from the dust of the ground, God's blowing the spirit of life to animate him, and eventually, after failing to satisfy his man with the creatures of the earth, God making a woman from 'his side' to act as his helper and mate (Genesis 2.18–24). Traditional Judaism viewed the man created in both stories as identical. He is, in fact, called Adam in both tales, which is the Hebrew word for 'man' and also, through repeated use, the proper name of 'the first man'.

Similarly the woman of the first creation story is merely called 'female' in Hebrew, which is a word that can be used for any female animal.[52] But in Genesis 2 the woman is called the Hebrew word for woman, and given a personal name. The 'discrepancy' between the two stories led later interpreters to postulate a first wife for Adam who was different from Eve. Eventually, she became identified with Lilith, the Near Eastern goddess of the night. Oddly, although Eve's intransigence leads to the expulsion from the Garden, it is Lilith who was pictured as the wife who cannot be controlled. She resisted Adam's attempts to dominate her, particularly sexually, and fled from him. God attempted to capture her by sending three angels to her cave retreat, but she resisted them. She vowed, as revenge for Adam's insults, to hinder women in childbirth and strangle babies in their cribs. In later medieval tradition she would also assume the roles of witch and temptress. According to popular legend, Lilith would visit men sleeping alone and entice them with her beauty into sexual unions. From these unions would issue her half-demon, half-human offspring, who were particularly powerful creatures in the demonic world and who often assumed leadership roles.[53] Lilith, as both the hinderer of human procreation and the inspirer of male lust, seems to engender mutually exclusive elements. And so she became, in the Jewish folk tradition, a standard repository for both male fantasies and fears about women and women's sexuality. She was eventually joined, in the pantheon of evil spirits, by Asmodeus, a demon found in the apocryphal book of Tobit.[54] He becomes, in later tradition, the king of the demons with Lilith as his queen. It was against this couple and their offspring, and their intentions to harm Jews with the use of magic, that Judaism fully armed itself with its own versions of magic.

The word and magic in the Kabbala

Traditional Judaism, with its reliance on the inherent power of the spoken and written word in the Torah, was already prone to magic, and the Kabbala simply nudged the cult of the name of God to its logical extreme. The keeper of the holy name derived power from his secret knowledge of God's name, and could perform all kinds of miracles, including raising the dead, practising exorcism, transforming into animals or other people, and generating life from lifeless matter. Kabbalistic magic gave its adepts the ability to understand different languages, including the languages of animals. They could also make intelligible the murmuring of the sea, the rustling of the wind, and the language of demons and angels, and perform many of the functions that are usually reserved for God or his ministering angels.[55]

The use of the holy names of God and his angels for magical purposes was performed by the rabbis of the Talmud and the adepts of the Kabbala, so we should not be surprised that the vast and sprawling folk tradition of Judaism also employed them. Like the variety of folk Islam we saw in the Balkans, folk Judaism often made dramatic compromises away from the lofty monotheism of its more fundamentalist or normative cousins. We can see this most clearly during the Middle Ages, and most strongly in the transformations of some of the traditional objects used in Jewish worship. These objects, venerated as sacred, began to take on a magical character. The Torah scroll has probably always been an object of extreme veneration for most traditional Jewish communities, and there is a host of laws concerning the proper procedures in producing, handling, using, and discarding scrolls of the Law.[56] The Torah scroll was so sacred that it could not be leaned on, nothing could be placed upon it and unclean hands could not touch it. So sacred was the physical scroll that inevitably, it began to be used for magical purposes. It was believed that placing it upon a sick child would cure her. It was also thought that if a woman was in labour, bringing a Torah into the room, or even to the doorway, would help alleviate her pain.[57] The Torah became so powerful in the popular folk imagination that practices of actually drinking or eating portions of the Bible became common.[58] Verses of the Bible were recited for their magical effect and entire books were circulated that advertised particular verses' magical usages. For example, for a recently circumcised boy, one recited Genesis 48.20: 'He blessed them that day and said, "In your name will Israel pronounce this blessing: 'May God make you like Ephraim and Manasseh.'"' To drive off demons and evil spirits, one recited Numbers 6.24–27: 'The people rise like a lioness; they rouse themselves like a lion that does not rest till he devours his prey and drinks the blood of his victims.' Exodus 22.17 was used to counteract magic: 'If her father absolutely refuses to give her to him, he must still pay the bride-price for virgins.' Isaiah 41.24 was useful for the same purpose: 'But you are less than nothing and your works are utterly worthless; he who chooses you is detestable.' To win someone's favour, one recited Genesis 47.16: 'The sons of Asher: Imnah, Ishvah, Ishvi and Beriah. Their sister was Serah. The sons of Beriah: Heber and Malkiel.'

Often, the verses recited seem to have no bearing on the subject at hand, and were merely recited because they sounded exotic. But often the incantations were quite specific: for fever, one recited Numbers 12.13: 'So Moses cried out to the LORD , "O God, please heal her!"' For consumption, one called upon Leviticus 5.19: 'It is a guilt offering; he has been guilty of wrongdoing against the LORD.' Verses were even recited for seemingly frivolous reasons: to fatten a fowl one recited Deuteronomy 22.6: 'If you come across a bird's nest beside the road, either in a tree or on the ground, and the mother is sitting on the young or on the eggs, do not take the mother with the young.' Isaiah 10.14 produced the same effect: 'As one reaches into a nest, so my hand reached for the wealth of the nations; as men gather abandoned eggs, so I gathered all the countries; not one flapped a wing, or opened its mouth to chirp.' Unsurprisingly, to arouse someone's love, one recited from the Song of Songs 1.3: 'Pleasing is the fragrance of your perfumes; your name is like perfume poured out. No wonder the maidens love you!' The list continues. Verses are cited to make flocks thrive, to cause an enemy to drown and die, to be invisible, to thwart robbers, pursuers, highwaymen and slanderers, to cause a man who has sworn falsely to die within a year, and for good luck on entering a new home or beginning a new piece of work.[59]

Wearing amulets with written incantations on them was closely allied with the phenomenon of the magical incantation. The most famous is the 'Abracadabra' formula, which means, most likely, 'Flee like these words' and is an example of the firm link in the Kabbalistic tradition between word and deed. This phrase was eventually transferred to the public lexicon, and has become a kind of generic magic formula whose Kabbalistic provenance most people do not recognize.[60] The writing of amulets was closely linked to the mezuzah, another sacred item in the Jewish tradition that often assumed magical properties. A mezuzah is a box that contains a parchment with Deuteronomy 6.4–19 and 11.13–20 written upon it. Like most objects in the Jewish tradition with a sacred function, there are specific strictures about its creation and its display.[61] For most Jews, affixing a mezuzah to the doorpost of one's home was (and is) one of the premiere signs of Jewishness. But this simple box quickly took on magical properties among some Jewish groups. First and foremost, having one affixed to one's doorpost was seen by Jewish rank and file and luminaries alike as the most efficacious way of warding off Satan.[62] Meir of Rothenburg (c.1215–93), a communal leader of German Jews in the Middle Ages, had this to say about the power of the mezuzah: 'If Jews knew how serviceable the mezuzah is, they would not lightly disregard it. They may be assured that no demon can have power over a house upon which the mezuzah is properly affixed. In our house I believe we have close to twenty-four mezuzoth.'[63] In the popular imagination, affixing the mezuzah to one's house was also a way of assuring long life. There is a pun in the *Zohar* that splits the word mezuzoth (the plural of mezuzah) into two words: *zaz mavet*, or 'death departs.' This was viewed as a promise that longer life would visit homes with mezuzoth properly affixed to their doorways. In more recent times, when a community was threatened with a plague, leaders would inspect the mezuzoth to see if anything about their display or the parchments within was ritually wrong. During the Middle Ages there were reports that non-Jews recognized the power of the mezuzoth and used them, albeit in ways that orthodox Jews would not condone. But even for Jews, there began a gradual encroachment on the traditional usages of the mezuzah, as they began to be employed in novel ways, and even their contents were tampered with.

One of the host of rules involving preparing, making and displaying mezuzoth centred on the preparation of the scroll. In keeping with the biblical dictum that nothing is to be added or subtracted to the text of the Torah, mezuzah scrolls were always scrupulously prepared to copy exactly the text of Deuteronomy that the box was made to contain. Then, near the conclusion of the Geonic period (AD 650–1250), some features we see in amulets began to encroach upon the production of the mezuzah. The face of the scroll was not altered, but its back, about which there was no prohibition, began to see tampering. The name Shaddai was inscribed there, which is probably best translated as 'Almighty', and a tiny window was created in the box to view the letters, in particular the equivalent of the 'S' in Hebrew. Shaddai was considered a particularly efficacious name in driving away demons, and Jews the world over adopted the custom of displaying it on the outside of their mezuzoth. Even so conservative a commentator as Maimonides saw no harm in the custom, and it prevails today.[64]

So it was only a matter of time before the text of the mezuzah itself was altered. Following the Geonic period, names, verses and figures were added to the text. These types of alterations were roundly condemned by most authorities, but the practice was widespread in most Jewish communities, and did not wholly disappear until modern times. Mostly, the alterations involved the special names of God and his ministering angels: El, Elohim, YhVh, Shaddai, Yah, Ehey, and the seven names of angels: Michael, Gabriel, Azriel, Zadkiel, Sarfiel, Raphael and Anael, which were added to the margins of the scroll. These were often accompanied by special symbols that meant to convey the power and significance of the names, and hence give the people who displayed the mezuzah even more protection from evil spirits. Often, the hexagram, or six-pointed star, was prominently featured in such altered mezuzoth. In the later Jewish tradition it became known as the Star of David, or the *magden David* in Hebrew. When it was first used, it had no specific connection with the most famous king of Israel, and the hexagram had an unusually wide geographical range: the Pythagoreans, who practised a philosophy that venerated numbers, considered the figure especially holy, and it also had mystical or sacred significance in Peru, Egypt, China and Japan. It probably entered into Judaism via magical papyri from Hellenistic times, most likely from Egypt.[65] The inclusion of these elements in the mezuzah, and its use for protection and cures for illnesses, pushed this ritual object directly into the realm of the amulet. It had been transformed from an object with sacred significance into a magical object with sacredness ingrained in its very physical being.

Playing God: creating a golem

The most dramatic expression of Kabbalistic magic is the creation of a golem. The word 'golem' is derived from the Hebrew word for 'matter' or 'embryo'. For the most part, a golem is considered a kind of Jewish Frankenstein's monster, and this description is not far from the mark.

But whereas the creation of the monster in *Frankenstein* can be related to certain trends in the Romantic tradition,[66] the creation of a golem has deep Jewish roots. Stories about golem-making always related, both in more official rabbinical literature and in folktales, to events taking place inside well-prescribed Jewish religious contexts.

The golem tradition stretches back to the Talmud. One of the earliest references is found in the context of a discussion about proscribed and permitted magical practices and behaviours:

> Rava said: If the righteous wished, they could create a world, for it is written: 'Your iniquities have divided you from your God' (Isaiah 59:2). Rava created a man and sent him to Rav Zeira. The Rabbi spoke to him but he did not reply. He [Rav Zeira] said: You are from the fellow scholars. Return to dust! Rav Hanina and Rav Oshyaya spent every Sabbath eve busy with the *Sefer Yezirah*. A three year old calf was created by them and they ate it.[67]

This passage contains many puzzling elements. Whether we are meant to accept or condemn the magical, esoteric practices presented here is unclear. When coupled with the quote from Isaiah the fact that 'if the righteous wished they could create a world' implies that if it were not for humanity's sinfulness, nothing would prevent us from appropriating powers from God. Rava creates a man and sends him to another sage, Rav Zeira; the rabbi speaks to him and he does not reply. Despite Rava's power, he cannot create a man with the power of speech, which is a defining element of a human being's psychological makeup. At the rabbi's request, the creature returns to the dust from which it was made.

The connection of golems to speech is paradigmatic. In the history of golem tales, a lack of speech usually leads to the golem's destruction. The moral is simple: language and reason are the special human endowments given by God, and the golem, as a lesser creation by the hands of humans, can never share in these gifts. The golem is traditionally created by the employment of a special mystical language and is never able to partake in ordinary discourse. It becomes a creature both created by the divine word and silenced by it, and even in this brief passage, there is some evocative wordplay that illustrates the connection between language and golem construction. In the Aramaic original, 'Rava bara gavara', translated as 'Rava created a man', we can hear a mantra-like sequence of transformations of the letters in *bara*, the word for 'create'. In their various permutations, these letters not only generate Rava's name and the verb 'to create', but also the Hebrew word *eiver*, meaning 'limb'. Kabbalists drew heavily on such connections. The *Sepher Yetzirah* contains many passages that equate the use of language with God's creative power. So letters, the constituent parts of language, came to be seen as the atomic elements of material creation as well. Bezalel, the architect of the biblical Tabernacle, is described in the Talmud as knowing the secret combination of letters that created the world.[68] In *The Sepher Yetzirah*, God's techniques for creating the world are further elaborated:

> He placed in a circle like a wall with 231 gates. The circle oscillates back and forth . . . He permuted them, weighed them, and transformed them: *alef* with them all and all of them with *alef*; *bet* with them all and all of them with *bet* . . . And we find that all that is formed and all that is spoken emerges from one name.[69]

The person engaged in golem construction acts much the same way and imitates God, chanting the correct sequence of letters to correspond to the various limbs and organs of the human body. In this way, it was believed that the initiate could create a very real human being piece by piece.[70]

Elaborations of the golem-building ritual were written by Rabbi Eleazar of Worms in his commentary on the *Sefer Yetzirah*:

> It is incumbent upon him [the golem builder] to take virgin soil from a place in the mountains where no one has ploughed. And he shall knead the dust with living water, and he shall make a body [golem] and shall begin to permute the alphabets of 231 gates, each limb separately, each limb with the corresponding letter mentioned in *Sefer Yetzirah*. And always the [divine] name with them.[71]

The physical aspect of the golem-making ritual is probably derived from the imagery of sexual intercourse, as the male principle (the living waters) merges with the female (virginal soul) to create new life. Eleazar of Worms (1165–1238) was bold enough to write down many of the formulae for creating a golem. He supposedly wrote on the forehead of his golem the Hebrew word for truth: *emet*. When he finished with the golem, and wanted to de-animate him, he simply rubbed out the 'e' to spell *met*, which means 'dead'.

The thirteenth-century German *Hasidim*, or pietistic mystics, were especially engaged in the work of golem-making. Rabbi Samuel, the father of Judah the Pious, was said to have created a homunculus that accompanied him on his travels and could not speak.[72] Then in the middle of the sixteenth century Elijah of Chelm was said to have created a golem so large and fearsome that he grew wary of it, and only by erasing the secret name he had written on its forehead, did it die away. Many of the wonder-working rabbis of the sixteenth, seventeenth and even the eighteenth centuries were said to have created golem. They did this, more often than not, to protect their communities from Gentile aggression. The remains of the famous Golem of Prague are said to be still mixed with the debris in the attic of that city's *Altneushul*, Europe's oldest synagogue.[73]

The syncretism of the Kabbala, its pagan nature, and its impact outside of Judaism

The speculative elements of the Kabbala received a major renovation with the work of Gershom Scholem. His groundbreaking studies of the Kabbala not only created an entire branch of historical study for the discipline of Jewish studies, they also rehabilitated the mystical branch of Judaism, which had been denigrated, both systematically and from neglect, by modern Jews in the nineteen and twentieth centuries.[74]

The practical elements of the Kabbala, including its magic, have not received this beneficial treatment, but the speculative Kabbala, with its connections to Neoplatonism and its points of contact with various Eastern religions, has been viewed as a bridge between uncompromising Western monotheism and Eastern pantheism. The magic of the Kabbala has often been seen as a corruption or degradation of the lofty idealism of its speculative branch. That some men had the temerity to attempt to put into practice the lore they learned from the *Bahir*, the *Sepher Yetzirah* and the *Zohar* was too much to stand, and that this branch of the Kabbala became entangled with magic made it unpalatable for much scholarly discussion. Magic seemed un-Jewish, and hence, not worthy of serious study.

Magic in the scholarly imagination stinks of certain cardinal sins: a base and formless superstition, a fantastical body of cause and effect relationships that defy common sense and rational perception, and most of all, an influx of ideas and practices into a religion that views them as largely alien to its tradition. Of course, the word Kabbala literally means the '*tradition*', but the Kabbala radically altered certain time-honoured Jewish religious notions. The central genus of the Kabbala was that its radical nature was hidden by a cloak of historical respectability, so ultimately, the speculative Kabbala was embraced by modern Jewish thought and religion, and it is now the darling of New Age Jewish groups and many Hasidic sects.[75] But the practical Kabbala's mixed and syncretistic heritage was considerably more difficult to digest. The raw profusion of the magical elements of the Kabbala was bewildering, so in the hands of ordinary people, the Kabbala has had the same fate as many of the trends we have examined in this work: it has become the repository of other religious traditions' ideas, practices and influences. The Kabbala's magical branch borrowed heavily from pagan religions, particularly those from the Near East, and later from German folklore. In some of the magical incantations written by the practical Kabbalists, some scholars have even seen names of Greek gods and goddesses,[76] as well as deities from the Babylonian, Assyrian and Egyptian pantheons, and figures and deities from German folk tradition.[77]

All in all, a kind of arch-magical religious tradition was created out of the matrix of the Kabbala, which we can see very clearly in the reliance of Christian thinkers on ideas found in Jewish mysticism in such diverse branches of study as alchemy and medieval Neoplatonism, where the borrowing was heavy and the exchange of ideas and practices was not one-sided. The Kabbala had a certain impact on Christian thinkers and Christian movements. Notably, the heretical group the Cathars (tenth century to around the fourteenth century) employed the Kabbala in their speculations. But more mainstream Christian humanists in the Renaissance also admired its diversity and pluralism, and from them, the Freemasons borrowed heavily from the Kabbala's thick stock of imagery for their rites. Alchemy in the Middle Ages would have been nearly impossible to practise without the Kabbala's influence, and eventually, a Christian Kabbala was created. The Renaissance humanist Pico della Mirandola (1463–94) was perhaps the first Christian student of the Kabbala.[78] Christian mystic Johann Kemper (1670–1716) was heavily influenced by its doctrines, as were modern spiritualist movements like the Swedenborgians, and modern theosophy like that of Madame Blavatsky (1831–91).

Whereas the speculative Kabbalists easily cloaked their syncretism in the veil of tradition, the magicians of the Kabbala took fewer pains to do so. The net effect has been a drastic devaluation of the practical Kabbala by both modern Jews and contemporary scholars of religion. While some can view this study as a receptacle for trash, it can just as easily be seen as a robust response to complexity and change in Jewish culture, which has had a lasting and profound impact on spiritual discovery in other faiths and movements.

Chapter summary

Far from being the narrow ideology that groups like Gush Emmunim have defined, the Kabbala is extremely pluralistic, and its exuberant system of images is difficult to reduce to one set of political or theological definitions. Far from endorsing a rigidly political and fundamentalist version of Judaism, the Kabbala allows rabbinical Judaism to flirt with ideas and concepts that are effectively alien to its traditions. The Kabbala deviates from accepted Jewish definitions of the nature of God, God's unity and the language used to denote God's aspects and powers. The early book, the *Bahir*, speculated on the creation of the universe, the nature of God and the status of evil in ways that deviated from normative, rabbinical Judaism. In some of the strongly figurative language of the *Zohar*, God was split into 'parts', and these parts, or aspects of God, behave much like gods and goddesses in a pagan pantheon. The *Zohar*'s speculations about the nature of God allow Orthodox Judaism to have aspects of a pagan pantheon without sacrificing orthodox practice. The syncretism produced here is one of adoption and absorption of pagan ideas about divinity, and harks back to several sources, most likely from the Middle East, including Assyrian notions of a divine tree. We saw how radical was this transformation by discussing how religious Jews used the Kabbala for magical purposes, and how in effect, the wonder-working rabbis' knowledge of the secret lore of the Kabbala allowed them actually to usurp some of the powers of God. The rabbis of the Kabbala often behaved like the demi-gods of a pagan pantheon, in essence sharing in the divine power. On a folk level, this trend manifested itself in the transformation of Jewish ritual objects into magical paraphernalia: such sacrosanct objects as mezuzoth, Torah scrolls and biblical verses recited as incantations were employed for their magical qualities. These 'pagan' practices crept into Jewish monotheism as objects became invested with supernatural or magical qualities. This is particularly the case with the cult of the word, already strong in normative Judaism, as it was taken to its logical extreme in folk Judaism and the Kabbala.

Draw your own conclusions

How does the Kabbala's notion(s) of God differ from that of rabbinical Judaism?

How do the creation stories in the *Bahir* and Genesis differ? How do their varying cosmogonies affect our view of creation?

Is there an essential difference between mythological notions of God in the Kabbala and God as depicted in Genesis?

What is the difference between sacred objects and magical objects? How is the notion of divine power affected by each view?

Is there a difference between symbolic language of God and literal language of God?

Is there a difference between mythology and religion?

Further reading

For a general introduction to the Kabbala:

Erich Bischoff (1985), *The Kabbala: An Introduction to Jewish Mysticism and its Secret Doctrine*, York Beach, ME: Samuel Weisner Inc.

For more detailed accounts of the Kabbala, see some of the many works by Gershom Scholem, especially:

Gershom Scholem (1987), *The Origins of the Kabbalah*, Philadelphia: Jewish Publication Society.

Gershom Scholem (1991), *On the Mystical Shape of the Godhead*, New York: Schocken Books.

Gershom Scholem (1996), *On the Kabbalah and Its Symbolism*, New York: Schocken Books.

For an excellent account of modern Kabbalistic Jewish mystics:

Herbert Weiner (1992), *9½ Mystics: The Kabbala Today*, 1992, New York: Collier Books.

For a more extended discussion of Jewish magic:

Joshua Trachtenberg (1961), *Jewish Magic and Superstition: A Study in Folk Religion*, Philadelphia: Jewish Publication Society.

Notes

1 Karen Armstrong (2000), *The Battle for God*, New York: Alfred A. Knopf, pp. 280–4. Kedumim is still an active settlement and, as of the time of this writing, they have their own webpage that contains information about their settlement and ideology: http://www.kedumim.org.il/kedumim/

2 An opposite and contemporary approach can be found in Frank Moore Cross's *Canaanite Myth and Hebrew Epic* (1973, Cambridge, MA: Harvard University Press), which places Israelite religious writing firmly in the tradition of its Near Eastern neighbours.

3 We can see this at work even in the recent *The History of the Jews*, by Paul Johnson. Rather than contextualize Jewish literature, Johnson seeks, more often than not, to highlight its supposed uniqueness. See pages 91–6 for examples of this in Johnson's work. Read his *Quest for God* to see his Christian agenda, all but hidden in the pages of *The History of the Jews*. Paul Johnson (1988), *The History of the Jews*, New York: Perennial Library, Harper & Row.

4 See page 54.

5 Jane Prentence and Nigel Pennick (1995), *A History of Pagan Europe*, London: Routledge, p. 1. The authors introduce an alternative meaning for the term pagan. See also Bowersock, *Hellenism in Late Antiquity*, particularly the essays 'Paganism and Greek Culture', pp. 1–13, and 'Dionysus and his world', pp. 41–53, for examples of paganism's continued existence even after the rise of Christianity as the state cult of Rome.

6 Howard Eilberg-Schwartz (1994), *God's Phallus and Other Problems for*

Men and Monotheism, Boston: Beacon Press, for a provocative, if not always plausible, look at the web of difficulties that are associated with God's male body, Chapter 5, pp. 110–32.

7 And, to some degree, the excess sterility of philosophical Judaism. However a fundamental misunderstanding exists in discussion of this topic. The supposed gulf between irrational and rational elements in Jewish Medieval philosophy is not as neat as we would like it to be. We will explore this later. See David Bakan (1991), *Maimonides on Prophecy: A Commentary on Selected Chapters of the Guide of the Perplexed*, Northvale, NJ, London: Jason Aronson Inc., pp. 39–42.

8 Gershom Scholem, *On the Kabbalah and Its Symbolism*, 'The Kabbala and Myth,' pp. 87–117.

9 Scholem, Gershom, *On the Mystical Shape of the Godhead*, pp. 38–55.

10 The *Bahir* probably derives its title from the first verse quoted in the text (Job 37.21) 'And now they do see light, it is brilliant (*bahir*) in the skies.'

11 Gershom Scholem, *The Origins of the Kabbalah*, pp. 42–3.

12 Simo Parpola (1993), 'The Assyrian Tree of Life: Tracing the Origins of Jewish Mysticism and Greek Philosophy', in *Journal of Near Eastern Studies*, Vol. 52, 3 (July 1993), pp. 161–208.

13 Aryeh Kaplan (trans.) (1989), *The Bahir*, York Beach, ME: Samuel Weisner, Inc., p. 9.

14 Kaplan, *Bahir*, p. 34.

15 Kaplan, *Bahir*, p. 36.

16 George W. E. Nickelsburg (2003), *Ancient Judaism and Christian Origins: Diversity, Continuity and Transformations*, Minneapolis: Fortress Press, p. 63 for a brief discussion of Tohu and Tiamat, the ancient dragon(s) of Chaos.

17 Kaplan, *Bahir*, p. 1.

18 Kaplan, *Bahir*, p. 60.

19 Kaplan, *Bahir*, p. 60.

20 Kaplan, *Bahir*, p. 60.

21 These interpretations are from Scholem, *The Origins of the Kabbalah*, 'The Book Bahir', pp. 49–199.

22 See Chapters 8 and 9, pp. 430–7, Part three of Moses Maimonides, Shlomo Pines (trans.) (1963), *The Guide of the Perplexed*, Chicago: University of Chicago Press, for Maimonides' view of evil, a view not atypical of Jewish medieval rationalist philosophy.

23 The biblical tradition does capture vestiges of a 'trickster' or demonic incarnation of the Jewish god; in Jacob's wrestling with God in *NJB*, Genesis 32.22–30, and in God's assault on Moses with Zipporah and Gershom in *NJB*, Exodus 4.24–26.

24 Rafael Patai (1990), *The Hebrew Goddess*, Detroit, MI: Wayne State University Press, p. 114.

25 Patai, *The Hebrew Goddess*, p. 116.

26 Patai, *The Hebrew Goddess*, p. 117.

27 Patai, *The Hebrew Goddess*, p. 117.

28 Patai, *The Hebrew Goddess*, p. 120.

29 Patai, *The Hebrew Goddess*, p. 123.

30 Patai, *The Hebrew Goddess*, p. 124.

31 See, Patai, *The Hebrew Goddess*, Chapter 5, pp. 112–34, 'The Kabbalistic Tetrad', for a wider treatment of polytheistic elements in the classic Kabbalah. Here, specifically in the nearly universal religious phenomenon of divine tetrads (groups of four deities).

32 These references are found scattered in the Babylonian and Palestinian Talmud. *Tosefta Hagigah* 21, 2.2; *PT Hagigah* 2.1; *BT Hagigah* 14b; *BT Hagigah* 11b; *BT Hagigah* 13a. Most of these references are presented with prohibitions on the teaching of sexual matters, highlighting the sexual nature of this secret knowledge.

33 See *Tosefta Hagigah* 2.3–4 for the famous passage about the four scholars entering paradise.

34 Maimonides follows the Talmudic injunction cited above, but then makes significant alterations as he proceeds to break most of them in the writing of *The Guide of the Perplexed*.

35 Part III, chapters 33–50, pp. 532–617, of *The Guide of the Perplexed* contains Maimonides' explication of the historical and, where necessary, rational basis for the commandments.

36 For an in-depth discussion of the relationship of Maimonides' thought to Western philosophy and ethics, see Raymond L. Weiss and Charles Butterworth (eds) (1975), *The Ethical Writing of Maimonides*, New York: New York University Press. In particular, the introductory essay by Raymond Weiss, pp. 1–26.

37 Bakan, *Maimonides on Prophecy*, p. 132; Maimonides, *The Guide*, section 3, 417.

38 Bakan, *Maimonides on Prophecy*, p. 133; Maimonides, *The Guide*, section 3, 347.

39 Bakan, *Maimonides on Prophecy*, p. 171.

40 Bakan, *Maimonides on Prophecy*, p. 217. The Israeli Hebrew word for electricity is *hashmal*. Eduard Yechezkel Kutscher (1982), *A History of the Hebrew Language*, Jeruslam: The Magus Press, Hebrew University, p. 199.

41 See reference 32.

42 We saw the strong reaction of Meir ben Simon. The irrational elements of the Kabbala made it run foul of mainstream rabbinical Judaism in the early years of its propagation. The Kabbala was later embraced by the Hasidic movement; it appealed to their sense of pietism. As the large segments of the Jewish world moved in more secular directions in the early nineteenth century, Hasidism became increasingly identified with the Orthodox Jewish world. The Kabbala came along for the ride and was viewed as yet another quaint Oriental custom of the Hasids, but not lacking some authenticity. For an account of the Kabbala in the traditional world of Yiddish-speaking, Ashkenazi culture, see Dovid Katz (2004), *Words on Fire: The Unfinished Story of Yiddish*, New York: Basic Books, Chapter 5, 'Yiddish and the Kabbalah', pp. 113–30.

43 Weiner, *9½ Mystics*, p. 70.

44 Weiner, *9½*, pp. 70–1.

45 Weiner, *9½*, pp. 70–1.

46 See Gershom Scholem (1973), *Sabbatai Sevi: The mystical Messiah, 1626–1676*, Gershom Scholem and R. J. Zwi Werblowsky (trans.), Princeton, NJ: Princeton University Press.

47 Howard Schwartz (1988), *Lilith's Cave*, New York: Harper & Row, p. 2.

48 Schwartz, *Lilith's Cave*, p. 2.

49 Trachtenberg, *Jewish Magic and Superstition*, p. 19.

50 Trachtenberg, *Jewish Magic,* p. 29.

51 From the Hebrew root *l-y-l*, which means night, F. Brown, S. Driver and C. Briggs (2004), *The Brown-Driver-Briggs Hebrew and English Lexicon*, Peabody, MA: Hendrickson Publishing, p. 538.

52 The Hebrew words in the verse are *zakar ve nekeva*, male and female, *JPS Hebrew English Tanakh* (2003), Jewish Publication Society: Philadelphia, p. 2.

53 Schwarz, *Lilith's Cave*, p. 7.

54 Tobit is not found in the Hebrew Bible. The Hebrew original is lost, and only Aramaic fragments and a Greek translation exist. Despite their absence from the Jewish canon, stories about Tobit and its characters continued to be told in Jewish folklore during the Middle Ages. Sir Lancelot C. L. Breton (1992), *The Septuagint with Apocrypha*, Peabody, MA: Hendrickson Publishing, 'Tobit' in the Apocrypha section, pp. 23–35.

55 Erich Bischoff (1985), *The Kabbala: An Introduction to Jewish Mysticism and its Secret Doctrines*, York Beach, ME: Samuel Weisner Inc., 'Magic of the Kabbala', pp. 51–68.

56 The great care with writing and preparing Torah scrolls stems from the biblical injunction that 'Whatever I am now commanding you, you must keep and observe, adding nothing and taking nothing away', *NJB*, Deuteronomy 13.1.

57 Trachtenberg, *Jewish Magic*, p. 57.

58 Trachtenberg, *Jewish Magic*, p. 112.

59 Trachtenberg, *Jewish Magic*, pp. 110–1.

60 Bischoff, *The Kabbala*, p. 59.

61 Trachtenberg, *Jewish Magic*, p. 146.

62 Trachtenberg, *Jewish Magic*, p. 146.

63 Trachtenberg, *Jewish Magic,* p. 146.

64 Trachtenberg, *Jewish Magic*, p. 148.

65 Trachtenberg, *Jewish Magic*, p. 140–1.

66 Frankenstein is deeply tied to the Romantic Movement. The novel is not a statement about technology gone astray, as modern film incarnations portray it, but is really about the Romantic spirit derailed. Victor Frankenstein, in his act of creation, is aping nature and nature's god; he harnesses the irrational forces of nature, and becomes like God. Like the golem stories, there is an element of transgression here. Golem stories no doubt received some influence from the Romantics, but they have a much older lineage; they are tied to Jewish folklore and Jewish theological assumptions about the world in a complex web of interconnections.

67 *Babylonian Talmud, Sanhedrin*, 65b.

68 *BT Berakhot,* 55a.

69 Aryeh Kaplan (trans.) (1997), *Sepher Yetzirah: The Book of Creation in Theory and Practice*, York Beach, ME: Samuel Weisner Inc., 2.4–5, pp. 108–31.

70 Kaplan, *Sepher,* p. 127.

71 Kaplan, *Sepher,* p. 127.

72 Trachtenberg, *Jewish Magic,* p. 85.

73 Trachtenberg, *Jewish Magic*, p. 85.

74 Harold Bloom (ed.) (1987), *Gershom Scholem: Modern Critical Views*, New York, New Haven and Philadelphia: Chelsea House Publisher, for multi-faceted views of his influence on the study of mysticism and beyond.

75 For an example of New Age uses of the Kabbala, see any book by Daniel C. Matt, particularly *God and The Big Bang: Discovering the Harmony Between Science and Spirituality* (1996, Woodstock, VT: Jewish Lights Publishing), an investigation of similarities between modern cosmology and the Kabbala. For an excellent work on the use of the Kabbala by modern Hasidic and Ultra-Orthodox, see Weiner, *9½ Mystics*, Chapter 6 on 'The Lubavitcher Movement', pp. 155–96, and 'Bratzlow – The Dead Hasidim', Chapter 7, pp. 197–226, are particularly informative.

76 Trachtenberg, *Jewish Magic*, pp. 92–3.

77 Trachtenberg, *Jewish Magic*, pp. 87–8.

78 Kutscher, *A History of the Hebrew Language*, p. 175. Here we are told that the word 'Kabbala' was absorbed into many European languages, notably German, *Kabale*, French, *cabale*, and English, *cabal*, taking on the pejorative meaning of a secret plot.

7

Akbar: One Man's Syncretism

... the King cares little that in allowing everyone to follow his religion he was in reality violating all ... (A Jesuit Missionary, commenting on Akbar's religious tolerance)

The destruction of the Babri Masjid mosque

The Babri mosque was one of the oldest and largest in the city of Ayodhya, in the Uttar Pradesh province of India, which is home to some 13 million Muslims. It was reputedly built by Babur, the first Mughal ruler of northern India, in the sixteenth century. A significant architectural achievement, the mosque was perhaps best known for the deep well in its central courtyard. Both Hindus and Muslims visited the well to drink from its waters, which were known for their curative and restorative effects. This was particularly true during the annual festival celebrating the birth of Rama, a Hindu demi-god who was reputedly born on the site of the Babri mosque. Babur reputedly tore down a temple dedicated to Rama when he constructed the mosque, in part to assert Muslim hegemony in the area. The mosque was an active centre of worship for hundreds of years, until in 1949, during the aftermath of Indian independence, Hindu activists broke into the mosque and set up statues of Rama within it. Fearing sectarian violence, the state government closed the mosque to all and had it sealed. Then in 1986 the mosque was reopened by a lower court at the request of the Hindu charitable organization Vishwa Hindu Parishad (or VHP, 'World Hindu Council') to allow Hindu worship there. The campaign to build, or as they saw it, rebuild the Rama temple, became a rallying call for many ultra-orthodox Hindu fundamentalists.

On 6 December 1992, a crowd of nearly a million people, comprised primarily of activists from the VHP and other fundamentalist groups, gathered around the Babri mosque. Fired up by inflammatory speeches, the crowd destroyed the mosque completely. Many saw the destruction as a premeditated act on the part of the VHP and other groups with a radical Hindu-Nationalist social, political and religious agenda.

The destruction of the Babri mosque had both a practical and a symbolic importance. Practically, a great treasure of early Mughal architecture was lost forever. Symbolically, the forces of Hindu fundamentalism asserted their growing power for India and the world to see. The Babri mosque's destruction illustrated Indian secular democracy's increasing peril in the face of pressure from radical groups like the VHP. And as we saw with the movement of Israeli settlers among such groups as the Gush Emmunim, radical groups' actions can politically and socially polarize entire societies.

This polarizing element is at odds with the wide diversity of Hinduism, with its dozens of branches and offshoots, and its wide divergence of cultic practices and theological opinion. The anti-Muslim stance of the VHP and other groups ignores the nativization of Islam in India – and also ignores sheer demographics. After Indonesia and Pakistan, India is the most populous Muslim country. Interestingly, the kind of polarization this wide diversity can create can just as easily lead to great harmony. The creation of the Sikh religion in northern India in the seventeenth century is such an example: it has been seen as a reaction to the Mughal invasions, and representative of a desire to create a religion that bonded elements of Islam and Hinduism. A less well-known attempt at creating a syncretistic faith was made by the Mughal ruler Akbar (Babur's grandson) who tried to create a religion that combined elements of nearly all of India's religions. He called the new religion *Tawidi-i-Illahi*, or 'The Divine Faith'.

Before we discuss Akbar's important religious innovation, we need to explore some of the groundwork laid prior to this eclectic religious outlook. Therefore, we will briefly look at the history of the Mughals both in India and in their native lands in central Asia.[1]

The Mughal invasion of India

A curious, often cruel irony sometimes guides history. Akbar, who is considered the greatest Mughal ruler of India, demonstrates this principle. He created and fostered, as a central pillar of his programme of governance of much of northern India, a conspicuous act of apostasy from Islam. After his death, there were rumours that this, the greatest Muslim ruler of India, had received versions of the last rites in the Jain faith, in Zoroastrianism, in Christianity and in Islam. The confusion over so fundamental an element as a great ruler's religion is a testimony to an eclectic religious life. In many ways, Akbar's was the first syncretistic religion created by a single person and as such, it is a unique and important product.

Like the Ottoman syncretism in Anatolia and the Balkans, Akbar's religious syncretism harked back to his ancestral heritage, as well as reflecting the contemporary realities of his rule. The Mughals (sometimes called the Moguls) were an incarnation of the Mongols: a nomadic people from central Asia who wreaked havoc in the Middle Eastern Islamic kingdoms of the medieval period.[2] So intimately associated with India, the Mughals had actually been imports, and when they began their rise to power at the beginning of the sixteenth century on the subcontinent, India was comprised of a vast number of Hindu and Muslim states, often at odds with each other.[3]

India was affected early on by the rise of Islam. While the south remained relatively stable at this time – Tamil was controlled by the Chola kingdom, while the Rashtrakutas dominated Maratha country – the north was the scene of bickering rivalries between Hindu clans, so there was no uniform Indian front to confront the Arab generals who invaded the Sind, the western region of the subcontinent, in AD 750. It quickly became an Arab state. In the south, port cities in India were exposed to Islam by Arab traders. The advance of Islam profoundly affected the Indian political, social and religious scene, as Muslim states had been set up in north, west and central India by Muslim Turks from Central Asia. These kingdoms quickly acclimatized themselves to India, providing a model the Mughals would later follow in steering their kingdom through the complicated scene of Indian political and religious culture.

The Mughals began, like the Turks, as a nomadic people in Central Asia. Their homeland was in the hinterlands of Central Asia, also like the Turks before them. And by Akbar's time (the late fourteenth and early fifteenth centuries), the Mongols were no longer the marauding hordes of old. They were largely Muslim, largely settled, and had embraced the civilizations that they had originally sought to conquer and destroy.[4] If they invaded other lands, they did so with a more genteel urbanity than their ancestors, and they absorbed Persian culture with sponge-like voracity – especially the brand of Shi'a Islam known as Imamism, which we discussed in a previous chapter.[5] Like the Ottomans, the Mughals began small and started a slow but inexorable rise to power and legitimacy in central Asia, Persia and northern India. Along the way, they adopted and adapted the languages, cultures and even the architectural styles of the people they conquered, adding those elements to the eclectic mix they carried with them. The Mongols have a somewhat justified reputation as marauders, but what is not generally known is that their rule was, overall, religiously tolerant. They tended to leave the religious lives of their subjected peoples alone – and this image of the tolerant Mongol is at odds with the popular and historical perception.[6]

The Mughal line began with Timur, nicknamed Leng, or 'The Lame'. In the West, his name was bastardized to Tamerlane. He was born in 1336 in Kesh, to a family in the tribe of the Barlas, who were Turkized Mongols who had joined Genghis Khan during his conquests in the thirteenth century. Timur's rise to power, from a simple warlord to a great political leader, was quick. In 1370 he gained control over Transoxiana, and then turned his attention to north India, where in 1398, he defeated the army of the sultan of Delhi. Timur entered the royal city and completely destroyed it. He returned to central Asia following the expedition, and took with him some of the best craftsmen of the city.[7] But most importantly, he established a line of succession over this area of India that would become key to Mughal hegemony in north India. He bequeathed the entire area to his grandson Muhammad, and it was this promise that his descendant, Babur, later used as his excuse to conquer the territories of north India. On his mother's side Akbar was descended from Genghis Khan. His ancestral line also included Zahiruddin Muhammad Babur, also known as 'The Leopard', who was the great grandson of Tamerlane on his father's side. In 1483, Babur ruled a modest-sized state in Turkistan. At first he confined his ambitions to central Asia, defeating some of the states that surrounded him, including parts of modern Afghanistan.[8]

In 1526 Babur was invited by Alam Khan, the uncle of Ibrahim Lodi, the sultan of Delhi, to assist in his struggles against his nephew.[9] Babur defeated him, even though there were superior numbers of the Indian forces. This was a victory largely due to a new innovation: firearms. But we should always be as careful of our allies as our foes for, much to the consternation of his allies, Babur stayed in India and founded the Mughul Sultanate. He reigned from 1526 to 1530, and when he died he ruled a state that stretched from Deccan to Turkistan, including all of Hindustan. Although a Muslim, he displayed a tolerance that would be a hallmark of most of his descendants. As a semi-nomadic ruler from central Asia – a region exposed to most of the cultures and religions of the world at that time – he was not known for excessive zeal in the enforcement of Muslim doctrine.[10]

When Babur died, he left a vast but fragile state. He was a great military leader, but lacked the gifts of a civil administrator, and so there was no effective central government, taxes were not regularly collected, and governors of the region, appointed by Babur, effectively controlled their states in independent and corrupt ways. He was succeeded by his son, Humayun, who did not have his father's martial prowess, and in ten years of concurrent rebellions, he lost most of the lands his father had conquered. He retreated to Persia to regroup, and then in 1555 he mounted a successful counter-offensive, restoring his father's empire to its original borders. While in exile, and even after his reconquest of his father's lands, Humayun was a patron of Persian arts. He encouraged painters to come to the Mughal court, establishing a style of painting that would become a hallmark of Mughal rule: his painters drew prominent human figures with facial detail, in violation of Islamic custom.[11] He also imported architects from Persia who began to develop a new style that incorporated Persian and Indian elements, and that would reach its apogee in the Taj Mahal, built by Akbar's grandson. Humayun was also an avid student of astronomy, geography and mathematics, and spent much time studying the stars. Legend tells us that this was his undoing, for in January 1556, while observing Venus, he was caught off guard by a call to prayer, and tangling his feet in the folds of his robe, he fell down a flight of stairs to his death.[12]

Akbar's early career: the moderate relaxing of anti-Hindu laws

He was succeeded by his 13-year-old son Akbar, whose full name was Jalaludden Muhammad Akbar Padshah Ghazi, who became, at this tender age, ruler of the empire under the stewardship of Bairam Khan, who had been the military and political advisor behind Humayun's successful reconquest of Hindustan. With his aid, the young king conquered even more territory. During his reign, from 1556 to 1605 (which coincidentally corresponds exactly to Queen Elizabeth's), his empire was far greater than his grandfather Babur's, including the old ancestral lands and encompassing almost all of northern India.

The details of the Mughal conquests are interesting to us as background, but what is really important is the scene: we see a people who were already prone to eclecticism and syncretism, conquering and administering a region that was home to diverse and settled peoples. This is the cultural background that formed Akbar's unique heritage. As the offspring of a Sunni and a Shi'ite, and a Mughal and a Persian, mixing was literally in his blood. Still, certain elements of Akbar defy our abilities to form a neat cause-and-effect relationship between his environment and his response to that environment, as certain aspects of Akbar's life remain enigmatic. He became one of the most cosmopolitan men of his age, yet remained illiterate for his entire life. He appeared to be a carefree youth who enjoyed the outdoors, and he was an avid hunter who was not averse to taking physical risks on the hunt, but he supposedly had a scientific, positivist bent, even performing experiments with animal husbandry.[13] Even though illiterate, he studied philosophy,[14] and was said to have had a keen analytical mind. But he had a darker side. Akbar was subject to fits of melancholy that grew so overpowering that they caused him to black out. He viewed these fits as spiritual in aetiology.[15] During his greatest and final fit, in 1578, he was unconscious for some time, and some of his companions thought he was dead. When he woke, he reported having seen visions and heard voices.[16]

Part of Akbar's complexity may have been due to his exile in Persia. When he retreated with his father following the collapse of the empire, he spent his formative years in Persia, in a rich atmosphere of intellectual and religious diversity. Like all great cultures, Persia at its zenith was able to prosper while balancing seemingly mutually exclusive elements and ideas in harmony, and this tension was a great source of social creativity and religious wealth, which we can see reflected in Akbar's personal complexity. He absorbed Persian culture, and when he returned to India

to administer his father's and grandfather's land, we can see that orthodox Islam was loosening its hold on him.

The tolerant, adult Akbar has been contrasted with the religiously
intolerant youthful Akbar.[17] It seems that after he entered into a series
of strategic marriages with the daughters of Hindu notables, his stance
slowly softened. He was seen performing the *hom*, or fire ceremony, with
his Indian wives, and his domestic tolerance soon transferred to the public
realm. On the reimposition of his dynastic power, one of his first major
acts was outlawing the taking of slaves in war.[18] In a land of continual
strife, this was an extremely popular decree. He followed this with the
abolition of the so-called Pilgrim's tax in 1564,[19] which had been a much-
despised tax whereby Hindu pilgrims were required to pay the Muslim
government of India for the privilege of visiting their own shrines. Shortly
after he banned the *jizya*, the tax that non-Muslims were forced to pay
the Muslim government of India. His leniencies concerning Hinduism
were accompanied by a series of conquests of the Hindu empires that
surrounded him, and part of his desire to become integrated into Hindu
India was motivated by his consolidation of power.[20] He introduced a
series of Hindu customs into his courtly ceremony, the most important of
which was the weighing of his body with gold, silver and precious objects,
along with his appearance at the window of the palace every day for 'in-
spection' by his subjects.[21] He also relaxed orthodox Muslim standards of
entertainment. He was especially fond of song and dance[22] and his court
became a magnet for artists of every kind, allowing painting, textile art,
and monumental and religious architecture to flourish during his reign.[23]

Akbar's ecumenical debates: the Ibadat Khana

Akbar's softening of anti-Hindu laws was eventually followed by an examination of Islam. In 1575 he established the Ibadat Khana, or House of
Worship (or Adoration), where under his sponsorship, members of various Islamic sects debated issues related to Muslim theology and religious
practice.[24] According to contemporary reports and legend, the debates in
the House of Worship were cantankerous and ugly – the Muslim clerics
who competed for Akbar's favour appear to have had a limitless capacity
to insult each others' positions and engage in endless polemic and personal insult. Once more, legend informs us that Akbar was so disgusted
by this all-too-human display of bigotry and personal animus within the
ranks of Islam that he opened the floor of the Ibadat Khana to other
religious persuasions. The House of Worship now became an arena of
inter-religious discussion and debate. Akbar invited, by turns, Hindu,
Jain, Zoroastrian and Muslim (Shi'a, Sunni and the various Sufi sects)
theologians and scholars to discuss major and minor points of their faiths

in the open and under his tutelage. The pantheistic philosophies of Sufism appeared to hold a particular fascination for this mystically inclined king and the philosophy of Ibn al-'Arabi, which we examined before, held his attention for some time.[25] The Emperor could now listen to ecumenical debates from the various religious sects of India. Eventually, Portuguese missionary priests from their colony at Goa also attended the Ibadat Khana. The king allowed the priests to open churches in the realm, to preach,' and to gather converts. In fact he was so enthusiastic that the Europeans were certain he would soon convert to Christianity.

Akbar strengthens his hold on Indian Islam: the Infallibility Decree

But Akbar was not interested in joining another faith. Instead, his next move was to consolidate his hold on Islam in India, and in 1579 he issued the so-called Infallibility Decree.[26] In essence, the role of the Muslim king or Caliph had always been to defend the faith.[27] But with the rise of an organized clergy, or *ulema*, the various political rulers of Islam had begun to exercise a primarily political and military role,[28] as their power as religious leaders waned, and the Islamic clergy held the power to interpret divine law and issue religious decrees.[29] Akbar's short decree overturned this tradition. The Infallibility Decree gave him extraordinary and nearly unprecedented powers for a Muslim ruler.

The decree begins with a litany to the peace and stability of Akbar's state: '. . . Hindustan has now become the centre of security and peace in the land of justice and benevolence, so that numbers of the higher and lower orders of the people, and especially the learned men possessed of divine knowledge . . .' dwell within its borders. We are then told that to this congenial and prosperous state, many men of learning from 'Arabia and Persia' have immigrated, so that the principal *ulema*, or Muslim religious community, now dwells in Hindustan. This statement is meant to impress upon its audience that the decree has the stamp of approval of Islam's most esteemed scholars and theologians. We are told that the Muslims of this realm are known for their 'piety and honest intentions' and that they have duly considered the words of the Qur'an, where it says 'Obey God and obey the Prophet, and those who are invested with authority among you.' We are then told that this group of scholars also obeys the traditions regarding the Prophet, or the *hadith*, which says 'Surely the man that is nearest to God on the Day of Judgment is the just leader; whosoever obeys the *amir*, obeys me, and whosoever rebels against him, rebels against me.' A further justification is offered, not from divine inspiration, but from reason: 'we have agreed that the rank of the Just King is higher in the eyes of God than the *Mujtahid* (the religious judge).' The just Muslim ruler is the highest judge of religious matters.

The Qur'an and the tradition support this, as does the testimony of reason. After all that justification, the decree itself is spelled out:

> Further we declare that the King of Islam, the Asylum of Mankind, the Commander of the Faithful, Shadow of God in the World, Abul-Fath Jalal-ud-din Muhammand Akbar, Padisha-i-Ghazi, is a just and wise king, with a knowledge of God.
>
> Should, therefore, in the future, religious questions arise regarding which the opinions of the Mujtahids are at variance, and His Majesty, in his penetrating understanding and clear wisdom, be inclined to adopt, for the benefits of the nation and in the interests of good order, any of the conflicting opinions which exist on that point, and should he issue a decree to that effect, we do hereby agree that such a decree shall be binding on all his people and all his subjects.

In other words, what Akbar says, goes. And just to hammer the point home, he adds:

> Should his Majesty see fit to issue a new order in conformity with some text of the Qur'an, and calculated to benefit the nation, all shall be bound to it, and opposition to it will involve damnation in the next world, and loss of religious privileges and property in this world . . .[30]

For a man who had ended the taking of slaves in war and lifted the burdensome pilgrim taxes for Hindus, this decree, which is draconian to a radical decree, seems out of character. In some of the anti-Islamic literature written about Akbar, the decree is portrayed as his attempt to wrestle power away from a corrupt and petty religious authority that was more interested in preserving its privileges and special rights than exercising justice. No doubt there is some truth to this allegation, but the wider implications of the Infallibility Decree are hard to ignore: Akbar was investing himself with supreme authority on all religious matters. In a sense, he was bucking Islamic history, which had developed a strong clerical class, by giving himself a degree of religious power only found at this time in some rulers of Protestant Europe. Couching the ruling in terms of state welfare was honest enough, but the pretence of basing it on precedent was disingenuous, for there was nearly none. And the third-person point of view of the decree, which makes it seem a unanimous decision reached by all the important Muslim rulers in Hindustan, is simply bald duplicity.

Akbar founds a new faith: the *Tawidi-i-Illahi*

Akbar's liberalism was circumscribed by his will to rule. If the latter had to cancel the former, he was prepared to curtail his liberalism, though the tenor of time gave Akbar's moves a flavour of liberalism that some people in our time may appreciate. Muslims have long accused Akbar of being anti-Islamic, and there is some legitimacy to this point. His next move, the formation of the so-called *Tawidi-i-Illahi* (translated as the Divine Faith or Divine Monotheism)[31] seems to encourage that as a foregone conclusion.

There is probably no area of Akbar's reign that has been more examined or misunderstood than the development of the Divine Faith. In a dramatic sense, the earlier Infallibility Decree was an expression of absolute power exercised with despotic inevitability. But in another and equally compelling sense, it was a document expressing a liberal stance towards Islam – almost a reformed expression of the faith. By claiming the power of religious ruling (or at least, the right to decide its ultimate expression), Akbar took one of the more powerful tools for governance out of the hands of individuals with a strict religious agenda who often persecuted the dominant faiths of India. In a sense, Akbar's despotism preserved liberty. The Infallibility Decree was distressing to Muslims, but at least it was clothed in Muslim garments. But the founding of the Divine Religion – Akbar's personal court creed – truly scandalized Muslim authorities. The Infallibility Decree had certainly deviated from Islamic precedent, but in key ways, it attempted to maintain its ties to Qur'anic intentions. On the other hand, the founding of a new faith – a conspicuous act of apostasy – was totally incongruent with Islam. And one of the reasons the Infallibility Decree seems to exhibit un-Islamic principles is that people often wrongly couple it with Akbar's founding of a new faith.

The Divine Faith's characteristics

The Divine Faith was a mélange of elements from the religions that surrounded Akbar, or which he had encountered on his youthful travels – and of course, it was heavily influenced by the interfaith discussions that he had heard during the sessions of the Ibadat Khana, starting in 1575. First and foremost, the religion's name implies its deep-rooted connection to Islam: the Divine Faith, or Divine Monotheism, took as its central core the lofty moral sentiment of Islam's prime tenet that there is but one God and that the order of the world springs from this God's just governance. In this way, the Divine Faith always had an Islamic theoretical underpinning, even when its rites deviated from Islamic practices.

Akbar was supposedly guided by a rationalist spirit. But in Akbar's case, the word 'rationalism' is a slippery and loaded term. That Akbar based his new religion on careful investigation is certain. He listened to the doctrines and theories propounded in the Ibadat Khana and, using a rubric that he considered rational, he appropriated elements of the different faiths that he believed to be the most highly efficacious and most deeply grounded in human reason. But at certain times Akbar seems to confuse a sense of symmetry with reason, and the aesthetic goal of balance is not necessarily identical with reason. Perhaps we can forgive Akbar this confusion, since his goals were so grandly impossible to reach, but it is because of this inconsistency that the Divine Faith often resembles, in an analysis of its form and functions, a simple and crass political statement. It tried to please everyone with its massive scope, but by doing so accomplished the inevitable: it pleased hardly a soul.

The practices of the Divine Faith show both its majesty and its inherent flaws. An individual was admitted into the Divine Faith by appearing before Akbar with his turban in his hands, and prostrating himself at his feet. Then Akbar placed his hand on the supplicant's head to symbolize that the emperor has now ended the impure life of this person, and was raising him to pure intentions and a new life. Akbar then placed upon the novice the *Shast*, which was engraved with the words *Allah Akbar* ('God is Great'). One commentator, who did not wish to flatter Akbar or his new religion, claimed that rather than a spiritual genealogy, which was often given during initiations into religious orders, the novice was given an image of Akbar that was meant to be worshipped. When they greeted each other, the members of the new faith said *Allah Akbar*, and responded with *Jalla Jallaluhu* ('May his glory be extolled'). Akbar's new religion also endorsed a kind of astral veneration: the stars, moon and (taking a cue from Zoroastrianism) the sun were all viewed as legitimate avenues through which to approach God.[32] It was said that Akbar also incorporated Persian fire ceremonies into the Divine Faith. Some sort of belief in reincarnation, or the transmigration of souls, was also part of the Divine Faith's structures of belief,[33] so in order to maintain a state of ritual purity and ensure a favourable reincarnation, members were enjoined to avoid eating flesh, refrain from religious persecution, and shun marriage in childhood, all of which were deemed practices that would not be beneficial for a favourable reincarnation.

The Divine Faith has often been called a fellowship of believers rather than a religion,[34] but the Divine Faith certainly did not lack the accoutrements of an organized religion, and it was an organized enough movement to incur the wrath of certain Muslim authorities. In 1580 a *fatwa*, or religious decree, was issued against Akbar by Mullah Muhammad Yazdi.[35] The decree was backed up by an attempt to dethrone Akbar and replace him with his brother, Mizra Muhammad Hakim. Some of the provinces of northern India rose up in a revolt which was quickly suppressed. Without an army to back up their decree, there was little that hostile religious authorities could do to stop the syncretistically minded emperor. Akbar was powerful enough to do whatever he saw fit to do, and Muslim clerics could do little but sit and brood and wait for his death, hoping his successor would be more disposed to a more orthodox agenda.

One reason we can say that Akbar founded a faith, and not a simple fellowship, lies in his response to the coup. Like some religious leaders, he responded to persecution by persecuting those who persecuted him. He issued a series of anti-Muslim ordinances, and unlike his opponents, he had the power to enforce them. Akbar banned the killing of cows and universally commanded the practice of *sijdah,* or prostration to the emperor (which until then had been practised by those in the Divine Faith but not those outside it). He banned or exiled several prominent mullahs from the realm and adopted some Hindu customs that infuriated Muslims, including wearing the *tilak* or Hindu mark, on his forehead. Akbar was even said to have desecrated mosques and Muslim holy sites during the years of persecution (1591–1601). Still, a great deal of debate surrounds this issue. Gestures that appeared to be persecutions were carried out by Akbar with his left hand, while his right hand shored up Islam by building mosques and supporting Islamic fellowships.[36]

Akbar's legacy: the Divine Faith dies with Akbar

When Akbar died, his peculiar legacy died with him. Just as the mullahs had hoped, his heirs did not have his same enterprising spirit, and the Infallibility Decree's strictures were not enforced by his offspring. The Divine Faith died with Akbar. The anti-Muslim ordinances were abandoned. Some of his heirs flirted with his broad-mindedness and his son Jahangir kept the custom of the *jharoka,* the daily appearance of the sovereign at the window of the palace.[37] But in 1611 this emperor fell in love with a Persian woman named Mihr un-Nisa, and as he grew old and enfeebled, she installed relatives in the court, and pursued a more orthodox Islamic agenda under Jahangir's ageing nose. Jahangir was the son of a Hindu princess, and also knew and understood the doctrines of Christianity. He appears to have been tempted to convert to Catholicism, but decided against it in order to avoid allying himself too closely with Portuguese power.[38] His successor, Shah Jahan, who was Akbar's grandson, went on a campaign to destroy Hindu temples in 1632, largely at the prodding of his religious advisors. He followed up these acts with discriminatory policies against Hindus, including banning Hindus from cremating bodies near cemeteries, a practice most Muslims found abhorrent. Hindus were forced to wear their tunics buttoned on the left, while Muslims wore them on the right. He also peeled back some of his grandfather's liberal decrees and Hindu court practices, like prostration in front of the emperor.[39] It was Shah Jahan who built the Taj Mahal as a monument to his most beloved wife.[40] But it was his heir, Aurangzeb, who conformed most rigorously to Muslim orthodoxy. In 1679, he reimposed the *jizya* and the tax levied on non-Muslims when they visited their shrines. He supposedly knew the Qur'an by heart, and had all known Sufis and their masters expelled from his lands. By the time the British came to India in the early 1700s, Mughal power, as well as tolerance, had effectively ended.[41]

Unlike the other, more organic syncretistic movements we have examined, Akbar's syncretism contains a strong element of narcissism. Here was a man with unlimited power, and with it he attempted to mould a world in his own image and to his own likeness. That the world budged imperfectly is no surprise. Even the powerful must deal with necessity, and necessity obeys its own dictates. Some may find the narcissistic element of Akbar's religion unsavoury, but the fact that his religion was founded on a self-guided and self-referencing impulse does not mean that it did not have wider, positive repercussions beyond the fortress of Akbar's self. One person's narcissism need not become a complete abomination when we can garnish our lives with the fruit this person grows. Akbar's powerful impulse to arrange life and religion to meet his own aesthetic ends can be looked at as a peculiar, inspiring example. The example can be cautionary or bold, but the benefits of arranging a religious life cannot be supplanted or ignored. Akbar's syncretism was indeed bold and his failure was just as dramatic, but that failure came only after he died in his bed – he never saw it coming.

Chapter summary

The destruction of the Babri mosque in 1992 is but one illustration of the tensions between Muslims and Hindus in India. The rise of Hindu nationalism and fundamentalism has exacerbated tensions between Hindus and Muslims on the subcontinent, and also between Hindus and other religious minorities. Various attempts have been made to suppress Indian society's religious and ethnic polarities. For example, the Sikh religion was a response to the Muslim invasions of India, and tried to meld aspects of Hinduism and Islam into a new religion. But even Sikhism has seen a rise in fundamentalism. The causes of Hindu and Sikh fundamentalism are similar to those of fundamentalism in the Abrahamic religions in the West. Mostly, India's fundamentalist groups are reacting to the rise of a world culture, and the advance of secularism, and the Westernization of Indian society.

Akbar responded to the great diversity of India's religious landscape not by resorting to fundamentalism, but with a response that was almost opposite to that: he created a new religion that was a mélange of most

of the faiths already present in India and nearby Persia. His new religion
was morally informed by Islam: it claimed to be both a summary and
a fulfilment of all that came before it. Practically, it was a religion that
incorporated many of the cultic practices of India's native or near native
faiths, with Zoroastrianism and Hinduism looming large among these.

Akbar was born into a religiously eclectic family. His ancestors were
relatively recent converts to Islam, and were widely travelled. As residents of central Asia, they encountered many of the world's religions,
so the Islam they practised was varied, and was also influenced by Shiʻa
doctrines and, later, Sufism. Akbar gained a cosmopolitan stature in Persia, where he was influenced by the refined culture of Persian painting,
poetry and architecture. Zoroastrianism, still a vital religion in Iran even
after the coming of Islam, was an early influence on Akbar. After coming to power, he came under the influence of his Hindu wives, whom he
married for strategic alliances, and probably because of their influence,
he soon relaxed anti-Hindu laws; soon after, he wrestled control of Islam
with the Infallibility Decree. The founding of the *Tawidi-i-Illahi*, the
Divine Faith, was Akbar's final act of religious significance, and it was
one fraught with political motivations. It was syncretistic by design and
to the core, and its main objective was to harmonize India's religious
traditions.

Akbar's syncretism was bold and self-conscious. He practised accommodation not due to ignorance or coercion, but due to a deep psychological need. The results were astonishing, and at a time when religious
affiliation was tantamount to individual identity, they were also presciently modern.

Draw your own conclusions

What were the political motives for Akbar's creation of the Divine Faith?
Whom was it meant to satisfy?

What does the creation of the Divine Faith tell us about the diversity of
religions in a plural society?

How does the Divine Faith blur the line between polytheism and
monotheism?

Could Akbar's syncretism be a 'cure' for the kind of radical fundamentalism witnessed in the destruction of the Babri mosque? Or would Akbar's
kind of syncretism cause more problems than it would create?

Further reading

For a general history of Mughal India, including its magnificent art and architecture:
Valerie Berinstain (1997), *India and the Mughal Dynasty*, New York: Discoveries Harry N. Abrams Publishers.

For specific accounts of Akbar and his reign:
Irfan Habib (ed.) (1997), *Akbar and his India*, Delhi, India: Oxford University Press.
S. R. Bakshi and S. K. Sharma (1999), *The Great Moguls: Akbar*, Vol. 3, New Delhi: Deep and Deep Publications.

Notes

1 Malise Ruthven (2004), *Fundamentalism: A Search for Meaning*, Oxford: Oxford University Press, p. 42, pp. 180–2. As of this writing, violence continues to erupt at the site of the destroyed Babri mosque.

2 For a brief treatment of the rise of the Mongols, see W. H. McNeil (1963), *The Rise of the West: A History of the Human Community*, New York: New American Library, pp. 542–6.

3 Berinstain, *India and the Mughal Dynasty*, p. 14.

4 Bakshi and Sharma, *The Great Moghuls*, Vol. 3, p. 39.

5 The concept of the Hidden Imam is discussed on page 74.

6 Irfan Habib (1997), *Akbar and his India*, Delhi, India: Oxford University Press, p. 82.

7 Berinstain, *India and the Mughal Dynasty*, pp. 18–19.

8 Berinstain, *India and the Mughal Dynasty*, pp. 19–20.

9 Bakshi and Sharma, *The Great Moguls*, pp. 24–6.

10 Berinstain, *India and the Mughal Dynasty*, pp. 30–1.

11 Berinstain, *India and the Mughal Dynasty*, p. 35.

12 Bakshi and Sharma, *The Great Moguls*, p. 3; Berinstain, *India and the Mughal Dynasty*, p. 35.

13 Habib, *Akbar and his India*, pp. 83–4.

14 Apparently, friends and tutors read aloud to Akbar.

15 R. Krishnamurti (1961), *Akbar: The Religious Aspect*, Baroda India: Baroda Press, pp. 70–2.

16 Habib, *Akbar and his India*, p. 83.

17 Habib, *Akbar and his India*, pp. 84–5.

18 Bakshi and Sharma, *The Great Moguls*, p. 13.

19 Bakshi and Sharma, *The Great Moguls*, pp. 14–15.

20 Berinstain, *India and the Mughal Dynasty*, p. 54.

21 Berinstain, *India and the Mughal Dynasty*, p. 56.

22 Berinstain, *India and the Mughal Dynasty*, p. 56.

23 Berinstain, *India and the Mughal Dynasty*, pp. 58–68.

24 Berinstain, *India and the Mughal Dynasty*, p. 68.

25 Berinstain, *India and the Mughal Dynasty*, pp. 86–7.

26 Krishnamurti, *Akbar*, pp. 30–1.

27 For the formation of the caliphate, see Albert Hourani (1991), *The History of Arab Peoples*, Cambridge, MA: The Belknap Press of Harvard University Press, chapter 'The Formation of an Empire', pp. 22–37.

28 For a short treatment of the rise of the *ulema*, see W. H. McNeil (1963), *The Rise of the West: A History of the Human Community*, New York: New American Library, p. 474. Also see Hourani, *The History of Arab Peoples*, p. 36 and p. 67, for an explanation of the creation of the office of the judge or *qadi*, which had no political or fiscal functions at all. Understanding this makes Akbar's grab at absolute power seem all the bolder.

29 Hourani, *The History of Arab Peoples*, p. 36.

30 Bakshi and Sharma, *The Great Moguls*, pp. 41–2.

31 Bakshi and Sharma, *The Great Moguls*, p. 45.

32 Bakshi and Sharma, *The Great Moguls*, pp. 49–50.

33 Bakshi and Sharma, *The Great Moguls*, p. 50.

34 Bakshi and Sharma, *The Great Moguls*, p. 186.

35 Bakshi and Sharma, *The Great Moguls*, p. 107.

36 Bakshi and Sharma, *The Great Moguls*, p. 189.

37 Berinstain, *India and the Mughal Dynasty*, p. 77.

38 Berinstain, *India and the Mughal Dynasty*, p. 78.

39 Berinstain, *India and the Mughal Dynasty*, pp. 90–1.

40 Berinstain, *India and the Mughal Dynasty*, p. 98.

41 For a short but detailed history of the Mughal reign in India in its entirety, see Berinstain, *India and the Mughal Dynasty*.

8

Living with Religious Complexity: Syncretism in its Golden Age

Naught upon earth is wrought in thy despite, O God
Nor in the ethereal sphere aloft which ever winds
(Cleanthes, 'The Hymn to Zeus')

A pagan challenge to the Abrahamic faiths: Santeria in the New World

The Abrahamic religions' collision with the 'pagan' world, both during their formation and during their historical development, has been a recurring motif of this work. But secular culture in Europe and the United States often carries an unstated or understated Judaeo-Christian value scheme, so often, pagan religions are not accorded the same cultural standing as the Abrahamic religions.

Such was the case with Santeria, a religion practised in the Caribbean and Latin America, which very much fits into the patterns of syncretistic religions that have been under examination here. The word Santeria means 'The Way of the Saints'. Its adherents often call it 'Regla de Ocha', or the 'Rule of Ocha'. It is also called Lukumi, which is from the Yoruba language of West Africa, and means 'Friend'. And in Brazil, Santeria is typically called Candomble Jege-Nago.[1] Whatever it is called, all forms of Santeria exhibit certain common features. Brought with slaves from their West African homelands, Santeria can be traced to the traditional Yoruba belief in a supreme deity known as Oloddumare and his innumerable helpers, who are supernatural beings known as orishas. In addition, Santeria relies heavily on animal sacrifice, and maintains a belief in possession and exorcism, as well as the veneration of ancestors – all very persistent ideas in Africa even today.[2] When Africans were brought to America's Spanish colonies, they were often, immediately upon arrival, baptized to Roman Catholicism. This abruptness ensured a certain continuity of West African religious ideas and practices in the New World, as Roman Catholic saints simply became the orishas, or the ministering 'angels' or helpers of Oloddumare. Their favours were curried through animal sacrifice and ritual. Some Catholic saints became firmly identified with Yoruba orishas: Babalz Ayi became Saint Lazarus, patron of the sick and dying; Chango become Saint Barbara, who controls the weather; and Elegba (or Eleggua) became Saint Anthony, the controller of roads, gates and destiny.[3] Saint veneration is a major route for syncretism, as we have seen in previous chapters, and Santeria's blatantly syncretistic character flourishes in Latin America and the Caribbean.

But despite its wide appeal, Santeria has been persecuted and denigrated, even as it is still rapidly growing, and moving beyond its traditional bounds and into the United States. Hialeah, Florida, is a prosperous community of over 200,000 people in Miami-Dade County. Founded by millionaires at the turn of the century, it was a playground for the wealthy, featuring horse racing and *Jai Alai* as its chief distractions. With the influx of Cubans and other Latin Americans into the southern United States in the 1980s, the nature of Hialeah began to change. In the late 1980s a group of Santerians began to organize their religion in a way that few Santeria groups had ever done. They pressed for formal recognition in the Hialeah community, which responded in 1987 with the passing of a series of ordinances banning animal sacrifice in the city. In 1988 the Santeria group, organized as the Church of Lukumi Babalu Aye, moved into a new storefront directly across from the Hialeah City Hall. Members of the group claimed that the police entered their church nearly every day and confronted members as they exited. Christian groups protested in front of the church, demonstrating against its practices. Even animal rights activists became involved, claiming that Santeria's ritual slaughtering was inhumane.

The church sued the City of Hialeah, a lower court ruled in favour of the city, and the case went through a round of appeals before it reached the Supreme Court in 1993. In *Church of Lukumi Babalu Aye v. City of Hialeah*, 91-948 Supreme Court of the United States, the Court upheld a court of appeals decision that the City of Hialeah's laws were unconstitutional. The court found that the ruling placed an unfair burden on the Santerians, who could not practise their religion without animal sacrifice. The city had stated that other types of animal killing in the City of Hialeah were permissible: it was ruled 'self-evident' that killing animals for food is important, the eradication of insects and other pests is 'obviously justified', and the euthanasia of excess animals in the city's animal shelters 'makes sense'. The city failed to make the case as to why the Church of Lukumi Babalu Aye should alone bear the burden of the ordinances, while other groups, like slaughterhouses, pounds and veterinary clinics, did not.[4]

The Supreme Court's decision allowed the Church of Lukumi Babalu Aye to become a fully recognized member of the Hialeah community. For example, Lukumi priests and priestesses began in 1997 to marry people according to the rites of the religion in unions recognized by the State of Florida. The court case exposed a strong element of antipathy in the community, and points to a wider aversion among members of the Abrahamic faiths and secular, Western culture toward 'pagan' religions and their practices and philosophies. This aversion exists despite the deep debt that the Abrahamic religions owe to pagan religions, particularly Christianity's debt to Graeco-Roman paganism of the first two centuries of the Church's existence. This chapter will explore syncretism's golden age in the West, and will conclude that Christianity owes a debt to it. First, however, we will summarize some points discussed previously.

One definition of religion

Religion is the search for the ineffable. It is bound, on one side, by the structures of a community of faith that provide the physical and spiritual tools for organized religious life. It is bound (or more accurately *un-bound*) on the other by the figurative horizon of human imagination, thought and will – and these need not have boundaries at all. The human mind strives for the ineffable, and some people will do anything to reach it, mixing and blending according to the dictates of the quest. Human desire tends to pull people in two directions: some seek to unite, while others struggle to separate.

Reactions to admixture in religious traditions have differed radically from time to time and place to place, and this book has shown some of those reactions, and has outlined a few of those times and places, and their rich and varied legacies. We have come across one assumption again and again: Islam, Judaism and Christianity are monotheistic creeds, and as such they posit one god as the creator of the universe. They are also revealed faiths: God gave the religions to Moses, Jesus and Muhammad in divine exposés, which were enshrined in sacred writing and the interpretations of which became the basis for religious communal life for Jews, Christians and Muslims. According to this formula, the formative processes of Islam, Judaism and Christianity were then concluded. Judaism received its initial formation starting with Abraham, culminating with Moses, and receiving minor, but important, amendments from the prophets. Rabbinical Judaism refocused and refined this heritage in its hermeneutical works, creating modern Judaism, but the coming of Moses and his legislation effectively concluded the formation of Judaism. All else was to be interpretation and commentary. Christianity followed a similar path: after the disputes about the canonicity of books in the first three centuries of the Jesus movement, no one seriously doubted the veracity of the Gospels or the Pauline and apostolic letters until the late eighteenth and early nineteenth centuries. Islam's veracity revolves around Muhammad's revelations in Medina and Mecca and an accurate transcription of those revelations in the Qur'an. Eventually, the tales told

of Muhammad and his early followers were enshrined in a type of orthodoxy (the *hadith*) outside the Qur'an. The Islamic tradition, in a sense,
was closed, and only interpretation was still open.

Syncretism redefined: our examples, re-examined

In part, syncretism is a response to this orthodox closure; it offers a type
of open-endedness in order to respond to change and crisis. As such, it
has a marked flexibility that is not often found in orthodox traditions.
Orthodoxy, in a compelling sense, is an anti-syncretism. Orthodoxy
seeks to put an end to religious 'mutations', or at least to radically control
them. Syncretism *is* the process of religious mutation; it is at the opposite
pole to static orthodoxy, and it is often its enemy.

But we have run into problems. In a certain sense, all religions are syncretistic: they develop from antecedents and accrue influences from other
faiths and add them to their own.[5] This happens to such a great extent
that the word *syncretism* is almost useless as a defining term, so the best
approach to exploring syncretism is to interpret it as a process, rather
than a specific entity or definition. As such, we can develop and display
many elements at once. Syncretism can employ opposite elements with
different faiths at the same time or with the same faith at different times.

There is nothing more frustrating than working with a concept that
can include virtually everything, because universal concepts risk becoming toweringly empty. The essence of meaning is hard definitional work:
we try to set a standard of measure above or below which an object
or concept can fall. If we hold something to mean too many things, it
deserves to mean nothing at all, and if life is to have meaning, we must fit
it into the conceptual world that we draw and the concepts we trace with
words. Syncretism defies these attempts, and as such, it is tied to a type
of conceptual anarchy that the orthodox mentality can never accept. It
is not simply a question of political, physical or theological control, for
often, syncretism in the hands of rulers has been a powerful tool to promote unity and control, rather than a fractious element that has inspired
anarchy and independence. Syncretism can become a defining parameter
in a people or group, and a wise ruler can use the intelligent blending of
religious elements for his own ends. Indeed, as we have seen, the unintended consequences of a forced uniformity can be more interesting than
the motivations for the enforcement of purity.

With the phenomenon of Marranism, the attempt to create a uniform
Roman Catholic culture in Spain initially backfired. The drive for an
enforced purity led to an increasing fear of impurity. The vibrancy and
strength of multicultural Spain was replaced by a Catholicism that was
nominal for many Jews and Muslims for at least 200 years following

their supposed conversion in 1492. By that point, time had eroded much of crypto-Jewish and crypto-Muslim practice until all that was left were vestiges. The survival of Marranism in rural Portugal until well into the twentieth century is more a testimony to the power of syncretism than to the impulses of Judaism. Secretiveness can become a habit long after it has lost its function as a mechanism for group survival.

As practised in the Balkans, Islam provides an example of an opposite kind of syncretism, which even when it barely resembles orthodoxy, is used by rulers to spread a faith that maintains a marginal control and uniformity. Here we have seen an example of folk Islam practised in an area where there is little interest in enforcing orthodox uniformity. Most of the reasons for this are social and historical: this is a land that has never known adequate, real or lasting orthodox control. In fact, the Balkans were the area of the Islamic and Christian world into which were deposited so-called undesirable people, who could not properly integrate into the normative world of their cultures. The armed struggles of these castaways, protracted as they were over the generations, led to a culture of syncretism that became a lasting legacy of the Balkan region. The fruits of this syncretism are singularly fascinating. Rather than becoming greater than the sum of its parts, the result often accentuates the parts that composed it, without overwhelming them into incomprehension. Initially, the Balkans was home to robust Slavic and Greek pagan religions. The Church, both Orthodox and Roman Catholic, came relatively late to the region, and when it did a great many pagan elements entered into Christian practice. Then Islam came to the Balkans. In those areas where conversion from Christianity was common, we see a fascinating application of layers: Christian peoples who still maintained pagan practices were converted to a Sufi folk Islam, which was itself brimming with the pagan, Christian, Zoroastrian-Persian and shamanistic elements that it picked up on its Turkic wanderings about the Middle East and central Asia. The stunning vibrancy of this religious culture cannot be understated. It is simply syncretism run wild. This Islam is native to Europe – it is a Slavic Islam, and a unique expression of a people bound to a land, place and time. Despite the recent wars in the former Yugoslavia where Serbian and Croatian Christians attempted to eradicate Muslim life and culture in Bosnia and Hercegovina, and the recent attempts of Wahhabi groups to eradicate folk Islam, this Slavic Islam survives to this day. It is an example of a syncretism that was created by circumstance, fostered by distant rulers, then ignored, and it prospered through benign neglect, until it was forced by its enemies to defend itself. Indeed it is still surviving. In a real and animated sense, Balkan Islam is supremely adapted for its environment.

Often syncretism can reside in a single person. Saints' cults are paradigmatic of this syncretism, and they combine the individual and the group in a fruitful tension that breeds a variety of practice and belief. Saints frequently become the repository of syncretistic practices, usually by preserving pagan religious practices. In the presence of an alien religion attempting to convert the inhabitants of a region, saint worship becomes a tidy way of allowing outwardly forbidden practices to enter into an orthodox faith through a back door. Saints' cults, as the veneration of single people, can be intricately bound up with mysticism, as we saw in the institutions of the Baktashiyya, who combined and blended aspects of Sufi worship from all corners of the Islamic, Christian and Shamanistic worlds. The Baktashiyya are what is referred to as a heterodox group: they failed to accept dominant belief. By pushing certain Shi'a notions about Ali to their logical, albeit unorthodox, extremes, they merely pursued one potential path of Shi'a Islam. In an area of loose religious control like the Balkans, such a form of Islam can thrive, for there are few orthodox rulers to enforce uniformity.

Mary veneration is related to saints' cults, but is bound up in a set of assumptions and practices that are more universal in scope. We traced in some detail the development of Mary from the simple woman of the Gospel accounts to the goddess of Roman Catholicism. The cult of Mary in official and unofficial Roman Catholicism is another example of syncretism unbound. Goddess worship had a widespread appeal in the Mediterranean region and beyond in the centuries before Christianity. Ancient Judaism had no greater foe than the veneration of the goddesses of its neighbours, and perhaps even a home-grown incarnation we could call a Hebrew goddess. Early Islam, as we saw in our introduction, contended with a robust Arabian polytheism which contained many goddesses. But Roman Christianity eventually enshrined Mary as a de facto goddess. Contemporary Roman Catholicism (through nineteenth- and twentieth-century popes) eventually saw the promulgation of the dogmas of Mary's immaculate conception and her assumption into heaven. The papacy's endorsement of such dogmas was an attempt to promote its own power by endorsing ideas about Mary that would be divisive in the Christian world. The two popes who promulgated the Immaculate Conception and the Assumption knew well enough the effects these pronouncements would have: they deliberately created wedges between Roman Catholicism and other Christian denominations, and so separated the Roman faith from its competitors in a radical way. This theory that such endorsements were an attempt to shore up papal power is made stronger by the fact that the immaculate conception was promulgated at the same time as the idea of the papal infallibility. By a clever turn, accepting the immaculate conception became tantamount to accepting the papal infallibility, and accepting the papal infallibility, in turn, makes the Immaculate Conception's veracity a foregone conclusion.[6] The Church's work with Mary has been by turns both conservative and liberal in its goals and impulses.

It has been conservative, maintaining the medieval hold of the papacy on the theological texture of the Church, while it has been liberal in allowing entry into normative Catholic doctrine to a set of ideas about the divine feminine that are radical in their implications. Like the ascent of a new god to a position of power in the old pantheon, Mary's climb has all the earmarks of an old fashioned *coup d'état*. By investing Mary with divine attributes, the Church has made her more than a woman. If she has not yet been made a goddess by these transformations, she has made important and irrevocable steps in that direction.

The Kabbala, Judaism's mystical branch, also allowed the feminine into the Jewish faith in ways the normative tradition would never allow. We saw the striking parallel between Mary and the *Shekinah-Matronit*, and looked at how, in the grand calliope of characterizations of God, which culminated in works as such as the *Zohar*, an unfettered Kabbalism reanimated a pagan world for its devotees. The inherent genius of the Kabbala is that it maintains the monotheistic standard of Judaism while cavorting in a kosher Olympus. We get, in a real sense, the best of both worlds: paganism nestled in the heartland of mainstream monotheism.

The much-maligned practical and magical arm of the Kabbala shows the fruits of this wedding of paganism and Judaism. The practical Kabbalist uses the powers of his/her abstract and esoteric art to harness the powers of nature in the same way as magicians the world over. The creation of life from lifeless matter, the transformation of people into animals or objects in the natural world and the control of the weather are all parts of the magician's set of skills. The Kabbalist, as a Jewish magician, moulds the ancient craft of sorcery into a Jewish matrix. The wonder-working rabbi who makes and animates a golem engages in an esoteric craft: he becomes a stand-in for God, using a power distressingly and tantalizingly similar to the Divine's to create a creature from base matter. The syncretism here is one of transference and slippage: the exclusive prerogatives of the Jewish God are adopted by people. Pagan power assumes a Jewish costume and polytheism, which often depicts people sharing in the effluence of divine power, gets a Hebrew expression.

We can very well place Akbar's syncretism in a class entirely on its own. It is in the same vein as saint worship, as a syncretism of one person, but Akbar's syncretism is not found in the context of a pre-existing religion. He tried to create an entirely new faith by combining elements of India's prolific religious scene into one encompassing creed. He accepted elements from Hinduism, Islam, Jainism, Zoroastrianism and even Christianity to create a unique concoction that was so idiosyncratic that it was doomed from its inception to die when its creator's heart stopped beating. The Divine Faith was a courtly religion that failed to find much favour even in the court where it had its nativity. We may find Akbar's attempts to end the religious rivalry in India crude, and there is an element of hubris in his project: one man, albeit a king who sees his rule as divinely sanctioned, cannot effectively steer his polity on a religious course by brute strength alone. But if his syncretism is lacking organic progression, it has a certain autochthonous element, and a beautiful internal harmony. If that harmony is so symmetrical that we run the risk of holding a boring artefact in our expectant hands, we can forgive Akbar. His project was huge and, like most colossal endeavours, doomed by its sheer magnitude to fall short of its mark.

His syncretism has the lasting mark of certain cultural and psychological trends. Akbar had a mind congenitally incapable of orthodox thinking. The men who surrounded him and attempted to convert him to their religions – the Jain, Sikh, Hindu, Christian, and Muslim scholars, priests and officials – were constantly confronted with this ineluctable fact: Akbar would never embrace a religious system wholeheartedly. He left many a theologian and missionary perplexed: after a warm and enthusiastic reception, where it appeared he was ready to convert to the faith being peddled before him, he hedged and dodged. In the end, he never embraced a particular religion. In the people who surrounded him, this left an unpleasant aftertaste – who was this great man, after all? In a land where religious definition was tantamount to personal identification, his lack of identity was baffling and even enraging.

Akbar was a man with absolute power over a part of India and was able, as few people have ever been in that charmed and disturbed land, to mould multiplicity into unity, even if it was a unity that met only with Akbar's satisfaction. The fact that the Divine Faith did not live much longer than Akbar's body is not a real statement about the feasibility of creating a viable syncretistic religion, but it may be a tale of the fruitlessness of fighting for a cause for which a time or place is simply not ready. Akbar pulled from the pincers of orthodoxy a tiny gem of tolerance and broad-mindedness in marked contrast to what came before and after him, but only the bald fact of his absolute power made the Divine Faith possible. A resurgent Hinduism, a robust Islam and a militant Sikhism would not have allowed a less powerful man to carve out his own religious niche, but would have squashed it because his religion was designed to seek self-definition by the inclusion of other people's beliefs.

In this way, Akbar's faith was presciently post-modern. He had an existential freedom to sample religions that other people would not receive until recently. Without the punitive muscle of orthodox religions forcing him into conformity, he was able to shave the very best from the religions he saw paraded in front of him, and discard those slivers that he found insipid, bland or monstrous. That he was imperfect in this quest is without question. But it is not the specific instantiation of the Divine Faith that holds appeal – it is the general impulse behind its creation. This was one person's syncretism, and as such it may be a case study for future journeys into this zone.

The fundamentalist agenda in religion: what it leaves in and what it leaves out

American religious life has been periodically visited by a renewal of orthodoxy that stems back to the Puritan predecessors and to certain trends in Protestantism from England and, to a lesser extent, the Continent;[7] the United States returns to the pattern of the Great Awakening of the early eighteenth century, when Protestant America first looked back with nostalgic yearning to a time period of Puritan harmony that probably never existed.

This fantastical Puritanism is supposed to be the American religious foundation, but there were, in fact, numerous religious traditions in Colonial America, many near contemporaries of Puritanism, and none with the sole right to claim itself the original forebear. The New England states were indeed home to the Puritan colonists. But even in New England, Rhode Island was a bastion for escapees from Puritan oppression, and it became an early example of a society that promoted religious diversity and tolerance. The New Netherlands was founded by the materialist Dutch, and early attempts at establishing religious uniformity there failed miserably. The quest for settlers and the drive toward money-making were always the paramount concerns of the citizens of the Dutch Colonies (and New Yorkers, indeed, seem to continue this inheritance). Pennsylvania was a haven for Quakers, while Maryland had a Catholic ruling elite that fought an unsuccessful struggle to maintain their power over the colonial government. In the southern colonies, especially Virginia, the uniformity of the Anglican Church was more established, but pesky dissenting groups continued to agitate for power and position. Many of the ruling elite in the colonies were not traditional Christians at all. Many of the key figures in the framing of the Declaration of Independence and the Constitution were under the sway of French philosophical trends, and adhered to a type of deism: the belief, based solely on reason, in a God who created the universe and then abandoned it to its own workings, exerting no influence on the natural world, including supernatural interventions like miracles. Such a system is completely at odds with traditional Protestant Christianity. The supposed American common and unitary religious heritage, which is supposed to be expressed in a certain American uniformity about religion, is actually far more complex than the myth purports. Early colonial America was far too large, its population too diffuse, and its citizenry too accustomed to self-reliance, to favour any designs of uniformity of religion. There was no shortage of attempts, but for all the effort, they failed, and a grudging acceptance of religious diversity was the lot of colonial America. This actual religious heritage is a far more complex image than American mythical history.[8]

The Puritans themselves were radical Protestants whose main pre-occupation was the purging of papal elements still lurking in the liturgy and practices of the Church of England. These mostly Mediterranean elements were the host of practices, doctrines, opinions and beliefs Christianity carried north as it fled the sea that was its manger, and reached cooler, more temperate lands. These papal elements are what much of this work has focused upon: Mary veneration and worship, the collection of official and unofficial saints, the use of images to facilitate prayer and church service, and even the burning of incense. These varied articles, of course, were used in the pagan religions of Christianity's birth region. So the attempt to purge the Church of England of these syncretistic elements seems to have been generalized in America to an impulse to pare down or otherwise suppress portions of American life that the religious right and Protestant fundamentalists viewed as 'pagan'. By pagan, of course, they meant *godless*, since they never recognized in pagan religiosity any quality other than a demonic one (or, more charitably, saw it as erroneous). Even today, the fights Americans see in the press over abortion, gay marriage and even pronouncing of the word 'God' in the Pledge of Allegiance, are not merely disputes about whether or not gay people can marry and receive the same rights and privileges as heterosexuals, or whether a zygote is allowed to mature into a baby. They are disputes that have a broader and simpler agenda: to Christianize (and here, specifically, Protestantize) America and Western Europe and keep it that way, to maintain those Christian elements that are in place, and to create wider and deeper inroads where they do not exist.

One of the legacies of the broad Judaeo-Christian tradition is the belief in the primacy of revealed religion, and by necessity, the falsehood of anything outside that revealed religion (and its set of established or endorsed interpretations). The lasting legacy of the traditions found in the Hebrew Bible, and imbibed deeply by rabbinical Judaism, Christianity and Islam, is quite simple: truth and falsity are simple and binary notions. A stated ethical simplicity is the great hallmark of the West's Abrahamic religions. The towering moral and ethical stature of the three Abrahamic faiths is both their greatest strength and, ironically, the source of their lasting failings. They allow so much into their towering structures that, indeed, it seems that all of human nature and the sweep of history can be rendered explicable. But what they leave out – the ethical variability that is our birthright and hallmark as human beings – leads, in profound ways, to the birth of their neglected and outcast children.

Fundamentalism, both of the Islamic and Christian variety, and of the violent and the non-violent variety, shares this inheritance. For the fundamentalist, it is not enough to live a religious life in a religious community of one's own choosing. Certain actions in the wider culture (abortion, gay marriage) must be fought and the moral grandeur of the monotheistic faith must be brought down upon the impurity or sin. Many fundamentalists seem content to let others live in perceived impurity, and the sin that such blindness generates. Hasidic Jewish groups, the Haredim, the Amish and others are content to live in insular communities and leave the wider world to its iniquity. But certain groups cannot let some issues be ignored, and it is these issues that become contentious battlegrounds. Al-Qaeda and some evangelical Christian churches share this impulse in common. They will leave others alone only if those others obey certain definitional borders. Unless non-fundamentalists rise to point out the inconsistencies of such an approach, the penalty we will incur is a restriction of our freedoms – or worse yet, the relinquishment of our minds and bodies to the people with this agenda.

The Graeco-Roman world: syncretism's golden age

A healthy culture is magnanimous enough to allow its citizens broad freedoms. An ill culture lacks suppleness. An unhealthy culture retreats from the neurosis that is the symptom of its disease, into the stereotyped responses that worked in the past. There is, in a real sense, a very stark and simple question: do we believe that religion does not change over time, that it is static and never receives transforming elements from human hands? Or do we believe that it is changeable, mutable and subject to transformation? Most fundamentalists say that we live in an age of degeneration, that the golden age of monotheism has passed, but that the blueprint of an infallible creed is still with us, so we just need to turn away from sin and error and embrace a doctrine without thought or compunction – that faith relieves us of the burdens of extreme reflection.

The fundamentalist versions of Judaism, Christianity and Islam have had their golden ages. But syncretism in the West had its great vibrant age as well. It was an age where marked flux and change, and continual mutation of religious movements and philosophies were the outstanding norm. It was an age that shared some of the basic strengths and weaknesses of our own. This era, the so-called Hellenistic Age, or the Graeco-Roman Age, is one we have touched upon throughout this book. Digging deeper into this area will now provide us with interesting parallels to our own time, and will offer a natural conclusion to the issues we have raised. Like most of the topics in this work, the religious atmosphere of Hellenism and the Graeco-Roman world is so vast it is a virtual sea, but we must handle some general points here. The syncretistic nature of Graeco-Roman religion has continually been remarked upon,[9] because

the negotiation of various cultural identities in the relatively close proximity of the Graeco-Roman world spawned a profusion of religions and
cults that borrowed heavily from each other.[10]

The substratum of the Hellenistic world was the Greek city state. Following the golden age of Athens, and the destructive civil war between
Athens and Sparta (431–404 BC), the political climate changed dramatically with the succession to power of Alexander of Macedonia (356–323
BC). His remarkable conquests laid the groundwork for what would be
the first world culture in the West, and a precursor of the Roman Empire.
A more flexible version of the Greek language, derived from Athenian
and called *koine*, was spoken as the *lingua franca* across a wide swathe
of this new empire. With increased travel, communication and this new
common tongue, Greek culture broke free of the restraints of the city
state and gathered world influences. Alexander's empire and its successor states stretched from North Africa to India, and along the way it met
nearly every possible cultural and religious permutation.[11]

Syncretism, in the sense of the divinities of various peoples being identified in common, and their cultic practices being combined, occurred
almost immediately in this matrix. The Greek armies that conquered
Egypt, the Middle East and India often viewed the local divinities as
merely local expressions of the gods and goddesses of the Greek world.
The Greek Zeus became Zeus-Ammon-Re in Egypt, Zeus Jupiter in Italy,
and Zeus-Hypsistor or Zeus-Baal-Shamayim in Syria. The Greek goddess
Artemis was identified with the old deity Diana of Aricia, Demeter was
identified with Ceres, and Hephaestus with Vulcan.[12] Perhaps because
of a strong racial and cultural affinity the identification of the Greek
and Roman gods and goddesses was so complete that in the popular
conception, they are identical and the syncretistic seam is all but invisible. In other areas of the Graeco-Roman world the fit was less hand in
glove, but no less vibrant. A process of accommodation coupled with
transformation carried gods and goddesses from one culture to another,
and they lost characteristics here and there but gained novel ones to replace them. For example, the old Persian *magus* became a far different
person in Western mythology than in his Persian cradle. And Mithras,
a lesser deity in the Zoroastrian pantheon, became a paramount god in
the Roman version, and his cult was one of the competitors of nascent
Christianity.[13]

However, we are most interested by some of the later developments
of Hellenistic syncretism. During the period after Rome took over the
hegemony of Alexander's former conquests following the three Punic
Wars (246–146 BC), cults of personal deities became popular, and from
this milieu, the burgeoning Christian movement received its most lasting
influences. The cult of Isis in Egypt was widely popular and was spread
along the byways of the Roman Empire, but Roman or Hellenistic Isis

had little in common with the brooding deity of the Egyptian pantheon. The transformed Isis was worshipped in an open shrine, in daily services, with lustrations of Nile water and plumes of incense, and her devotees periodically practised animal sacrifice. She took on many of the attributes of other gods and goddesses and claimed their titles and epitaphs, and eventually became, in essence, the Great Mother Goddess of the entire cosmos, with room remaining in her cosmic mansion only for Osiris, her consort, and Horus, her divine son. Even the older vegetative cults associated with the cycle of the seasons, always popular in the ancient world, were affected by this makeover. The great earth-based cults of antiquity – of Cybele, the Mother Goddess, Tammuz or Adonis (from the Semitic *Adon* or 'Lord'), Atargatis (or Derceto, the Syrian Goddess), Baal (or 'Bel', from the Semetic 'Master') – began to drift away from their strictly local, earth-based veneration, and achieve more cosmic proportions.[14]

The profusion of cults, the exchange of names and the identities and epitaphs of gods and goddesses led to a refinement of faith in gods rather than a degeneration (as we would imagine a profusion of gods might cause). Religious cults in the ancient world were nearly always tied to specific locations. Place was one of the hallmarks that gave a god or goddess a distinguishing mark. With the rise of a world culture, divinities needed to embrace wider identifying marks: they required a cosmic significance. Purely local gods and goddesses simply become world gods. As such, a growing tendency toward monotheism in pagan religions in this period is one of the more interesting manifestations of this type of Hellenism. As more gods and goddesses were equated with each other, certain people expressed an interest in seeing a harmony behind this profusion. This rise of monotheism was coupled with other interesting trends: the personal god cults of this period were practical, reflecting the philosophical systems of this time's obsession with ethical conduct. These were moral or ethical creeds, and their metaphysical elements were downplayed. There was a growing trend to view the world dualistically – as divided in two, between heaven and earth, or between good and evil, or light and dark. The personal god was invested with the ability to manoeuvre in both realms and to grant personal salvation to devotees. Usually, this god or goddess expressed his or her wishes through revelation, and expressed a divine will through grace. Many of these cults included aesthetic renunciation, in one form or another, as an ethical cornerstone. The theology of salvation expressed by Hellenistic religion(s) is, of course, an echo of trends that Christianity would adopt. Christianity was formed in the Hellenistic milieu, and evolved from its Jewish/Palestinian roots into a rigorous syncretistic religion that combined elements of its Jewish heritage with the Graeco-Roman world and its numerous religions and philosophies at large.

There was a tension in the Greek world between the conception of the

Greek gods and goddesses as separable entities, and conceptions of them as merely the individualized expressions of some greater, unified god. We can see in the works of Plato and Aristotle this tension playing out in its entirety. The god of Aristotle's *Metaphysics* has little in common with the cavorting Zeus of popular religion.[15] The god of the *Metaphysics* is the ordering principle of the universe. This god, called the Unmoved Mover in the Aristotelian tradition, performs a role much like a master of ceremonies of the universe. He keeps the cosmos moving. And he is certainly the only god. Aristotle created a type of philosophical monotheism that would be used by Christian, Muslim and Jewish theologians in the Middle Ages as the linchpins of their towering systems.

The emergence of monotheism in Hellenistic paganism: the example of the *Hymn to Zeus*

But it was not until the Hellenistic Age that this concept began to receive a clearer formulation. Early on, Cleanthes (*c*.300–200 BC) began the rehabilitation of the randy Zeus to a cosmic, bloodless deity. His *Hymn to Zeus* begins:

> Most glorious of immortals, Zeus
> The many-named, almighty ever more[16]

The use of the proper noun 'Zeus' is offset by what comes next: he is called by many names, but the purely local manifestations are not important. Cleanthes is interested in addressing the monotheistic harmony behind the bouquet of identities. This god is nature's great king and is not controlled by fate like the classical Zeus. He holds the reigns of the physical world in his hand:

> Hail to thee! On thee 'tis meet and right
> That mortals everywhere should call.
> From thee was our begetting; ours alone
> Of all that live and move upon the earth
> The lot to bear God's likeness[17]

Zeus is praised for his omnipotence and this god's new role as a universal deity is stressed. The next four lines contain the extraordinary likening of humanity to this god's children who bear his image. Certainly, the likening of the classical gods and humanity as parents to children is not a new occurrence. What is extraordinary is that the relationship is not viewed as genetic, but spiritual. Cleanthes is not relating this to the birth of demigods or the heroes of old, but to a more penetrating relationship.

We are told:

> For thee this whole vast cosmos, wheeling round
> The earth, obeys, and where thou leadest
> It follows, ruled willingly by thee.
> In thy unconquerable hands thou holdest fast,
> Ready prepared, that two-tined flaming blast
> Ever living thunderbolt:
> Nature's own stroke brings all things to their end.
> By it thou guides alright the sense instinct
> Which spreads through all things, mingled even
> With stars in heaven, the great and small
> Thou art King supreme for evermore[18]

Zeus' symbolic hand, which wields an equally symbolic two-edged sword, permeates the universe, and is the vehicle of 'the universal word' that controls, subsumes and literally pulses through the universe. Cleanthes is here engaged in some typical Stoic manoeuvres. As a Stoic, he was a pantheist and believed that god literally permeates the universe, and that god does not have a body or separable substance from the material world. But he offers some key differences from the common Stoic sentiments about god. Zeus has a generative quality that reminds us more of the God of the Jewish and Christian tradition than of typical Stoic cosmology. Cleanthes' god is a creator in a way that is quite similar to biblical sentiments.[19]

But that creative and proprietary power of god ends when, in 'their wicked work, in their strange madness', human beings, who have free will, decide to do evil. Again, this section bears a strong resemblance to the later Jewish and Christian traditions. For god, everything is in harmony and the good and evil that humans see is balanced:

> Yet even so thou knowest to make the crooked straight
> Prune all to excess, give order to the orderless;
> For unto thee the unloved still is lovely –
> And thus in one all things are harmonized
> The evil with the good, that so one Word
> Should be in all things everlasting[20]

We are then told how various people 'seeing see not' and 'neither hearing hear' god's universal law. These people engage in pursuits that keep them at arm's distance from happiness. They wander the earth, pointlessly, 'forever seeking good and finding ill.' Finally, Zeus takes an interest in his children:

> Who dwellest within the dark clouds, wielding still
> The flashing stroke of lightning, save, we parry,
> Thy children from this boundless misery[21]

This hymn has often been cited for its obvious parallels with Christian notions of God's providential powers. For a Stoic to speak of God in such reverently personal tones is unusual, but not unique; Marcus Aurelius, in his famous *Meditations*, often spoke of God or Zeus or the Divine Fire in pietistic language we would expect in devotion to a personal god.[22] What stands out in Cleanthes' *Hymn to Zeus* is the obvious connection with God's personal nature and oneness. We see here a departure from Stoic conceptions of God: God in the *Hymn* is both a force that permeates the universe and a father to a brood of human children. Again we have an obvious connection to the complex set of ideas that accompany the Judaeo-Christian God, in a divinity that is both personal and universal, and is a force that is also a being. Cleanthes' monotheism would have vast areas of connection with later Christian monotheism.

It is often said that the corruption of late paganism was the reason for its downfall and the success of Christianity. The old cults of pagan Graeco-Roman culture are said to have no longer answered the basic questions of existence, and the cosmic significance of Christ's resurrection filled the gap left by the pagan religion's basic iniquity. We can see the religious coloration of this explanation – it is the winner's excuse for eradicating the loser. Even if we accept the premise that the pagan religions of the late Graeco-Roman age were corrupt (And this is a tricky assumption. Did they have corrupt practices? Corrupt ideas? What is a good working definition of corruption?), we are still left with the important example of Apollonius of Tyana. We will examine him in some detail, since his life and career run counter to the idea that late paganism was in decline.

The hero of Graeco-Roman syncretism: Apollonius of Tyana

The story of Apollonius of Tyana was written by Flavius Philostratus, who was born in AD 172 in Lemnos, and studied philosophy and rhetoric in Athens and Rome. We know he was connected with the royal household because he tells us that Empress Julia Domna, the wife of Emperor Septimus Severus, put into his hands documents related to Apollonius that prompted him to write his memoir. Apollonius was probably born in AD 2 and died in AD 98. So he lived several generations before Philostratus wrote of his life. We also know of Apollonius from other sources, but it is Philostratus' account that we are most familiar with.

Philostratus' work details the life and career of Apollonius of Tyana, a Pythagorean philosopher whose reputation was sufficiently high to draw the ire of Eusebius, the great historian of the early Church. In fact, the author of the *History of the Church* took the time to write a rebuttal of Philostratus' work, which shows that Apollonius' life and career were sufficiently Christ-like that a special effort was necessary to rebut their parallels with Jesus Christ. So we have a unique pair of documents: a work of great length about a man whose parallels to Christ were noted, even by the Church itself, and a rebuttal by one of Christianity's great early chroniclers of this work and life.

The commissioning of the memoir of Apollonius by the wife of Emperor Septimus Severus is telling. It is reported that this emperor was of a severely syncretistic bent, worshipping at a private temple the statues of Alexander the Great, Orpheus, Apollonius of Tyana, Abraham and Christ.[23] The spirit of the age was inclusive, and a work about Apollonius of Tyana, as a representative of the late pagan spirit of reformation, was in keeping with this bold spiritual-entrepreneurial ethos.

Philostratus begins with Apollonius' birth, which was heralded by a vision: his mother was visited by Proteus, the god of transformation and omniscience. She was told that she would have a child. She asked who he would be and was told that he would be Proteus, the god himself. That a god of change should be Apollonius' spiritual father does not expose any instability in his character. Quite the contrary, it highlights certain assumptions about Apollonius as we follow his career and his wanderings around the Graeco-Roman world. He was a man ready to embrace nearly everything he saw, and incorporate a great variation of ideas into a foundation of religion that had a wide range.

At first we only glimpse this. Apollonius is a Pythagorean philosopher, and continues in the tradition of that ancient form of thought and practice. He is a vegetarian[24] who does not wear animal skins. He does not trim his beard or hair. He does not offer animal sacrifices to the gods, and he exercises sexual control.[25] He rejects wealth and privilege, and at his parent's death gives away his patrimony to relatives and siblings.[26] As a form of mental discipline, he remains silent for five years, only communicating by gestures. And he wanders about Asia Minor reforming practices in temples. He begins to gather disciples about him, drawn by his superior piety and discipline. The traditional role of Pythagorean philosophers as stationary sages seems unsuited for Apollonius, who plans a trip to India with some of his more ardent followers. He seeks to learn the lore of the Brahmins, who are rumoured to be superior to any sage for the breadth and depth of their wisdom. It is here that Apollonius begins a tour of the known world.

When he reaches the border with Mesopotamia, and the end of the Roman Empire, we begin to see a pattern that will develop as he travels further afield: reminders of Greek culture's wide sway greet him. Only a few days' journey into Mesopotamia, he comes across the settlement of the Eretrians – Greeks who were captured by the Persians and taken into captivity. There they continued to write in Greek and exhibit Greek customs despite their exile and isolation. Apollonius and Damis, his chief disciple, reconsecrate their tombs and temples, and pour out libations to the gods.

After this stop, he visits the famous Magi, and although he is impressed by their wisdom, he explains to his disciples that they are not wise in all respects.[27] He explains Pythagorean principles to the king of Babylon, who is impressed enough by Apollonius to send him to India under royal auspices. When the party reaches India, he finds the unabashed syncretism continues. There the party encounters a statue and shrine to the Indian Dionysus. They find a sign that reads: 'Dionysus, the son of Semele and of Zeus, from the men of India to the Apollo of Delphi.' They continue to run across the tracks of Greek culture, especially the trail of Alexander the Great. They even encounter an elephant that was alive in the time of Alexander, which has gold rings around its tusks and horns, and an inscription on its harness: 'Alexander the son of Zeus dedicates Ajax to the Sun.'[28] Eventually, Apollonius mixes with the natives, and encounters an Indian king whose education and training bear a marked resemblance to Greek ideals:

> 'Our customs' said the King, 'are dictated by moderation, and I am still more moderate in carrying them out; and though I have more than other men, yet I want little, for I regard most things as belonging to my own friends . . . I share even my wealth with my enemies . . .'[29]

The Indian king's life of moderation echoes Greek values. Later the king goes on to explain how young men are trained in philosophy as children. Yet the king does not approach the Brahmins in the life of virtue, and when Apollonius encounters them, it is obvious that the Brahmins are the high water mark for a philosophical life. Apollonius learns little from the Magi, but he has nothing but untiring respect for the Brahmins, whose bodily control and mental discipline is without peers in the world. The head Brahmin knows Apollonius' life story before Apollonius even utters a word.[30] Their self-knowledge is so complete that they call themselves gods,[31] and like Apollonius, they believe in reincarnation – and they have an intimate knowledge of the various incarnations of themselves, Apollonius and any visitors. They can expound on a vast array of topics: they discuss with Apollonius the physical composition of the cosmos[32] and the bisexual nature of the universe.[33]

These philosophical discussions are interspersed with picturesque and exotic details about this imaginative Indian countryside. We read about pepper trees that are guarded and cultivated by apes,[34] a woman who is half-black and half-white,[35] and dragons and unicorns. These are some of the specific details that Eusebus seeks to deride in his essay about Philostratus' work, but these scenes are in keeping with Graeco-Roman modes of story telling, which we can see in examples of Graeco-Roman novels, where outlandish stories are told for their salacious content alone and are mixed with philosophizing, historical discussion and the recounting of ancient legend.[36]

Every so often in Philostratus' tale, we are reminded that beneath the veil of Indian exoticism, a very explicable Greek world is present: we encounter a river dedicated to Aphrodite,[37] the area where the Brahmins live is called an acropolis,[38] and the Brahmins speak an excellent, Attic Greek.[39] The lesson Philostratus seeks to teach (through Apollonius) is both clear and cloudy, both apparent and concealed: the gods and goddesses of the Indians are really the gods and goddesses of the Greeks. The apparent differences between the spiritual realms of both cultures are just that: merely apparent. The idea of an all-embracing, world religious culture continues to float to the surface in Philostratus' *Life of Apollonius*. Of course, there are tensions between the Greek and Indian worlds, but these tensions are always mitigated by a sense that these two worlds can communicate with each other. The explanation of this fabulous congress is not simply to do with Alexander's conquest of parts of India. It has as much to do with the idea that syncretism is at work all over the known world: that men of superior religious gifts reach identical conclusions about divine matters because divine matters are fixed and stable across cultural boundaries, despite the shifting contexts.

When Apollonius returns to Greece from India, he hits his stride. His visit to India has increased his stature as a sage. He travels to Ionia and reforms the cultic practices in the various cities of Asia Minor. In keeping with the theme of classical Greek culture revisited, Apollonius tours the historical ruins of Troy, and at Achilles' tomb he is visited by Achilles' ghost, who allows Apollonius to question him.[40] He begins in earnest his career as a healer, exorcist and reformer of Graeco-Roman religion. He casts a devil out of a young man,[41] he denounces the senseless cruelty of the gladiatorial contests,[42] and he continues to reform practices in shrines and temples. A famous (in antiquity) scene unfolds where one of Apollonius' disciples is to marry a beautiful woman. The sage quickly discovers that the woman is not human, but a vampire who, once married, consumes her spouses. Through Apollonius' intercession, his friend is saved.[43] He also helps the Spartans, whose reputation for manly forbearance has suffered considerably in recent times because of their loss of martial prowess, to throw off the yoke of effeminate practices.[44]

At about this time, the political realm enters into Philostratus' tale. We are told that Nero has outlawed philosophers from entering the city of Rome. Nero's dissolute activities are outlined in some detail.[45] But the warnings about entering the imperial city are not heeded by Apollonius, and when he does enter the city, fanfare awaits him. His first deed, which is rather conspicuous for a man who is not even supposed to be within the walls of Rome, is to raise a girl from the dead.[46] Philostratus downplays the event somewhat, claiming the girl may very well not have been dead, but merely under the influence of some spell.[47] (This utterance is pounced upon by Eusebius, who sees in it all sorts of subterfuges about the real source of Apollonius' power.)

The force of his personality, and some distractions in Nero's court prevent Apollonius from being jailed and killed. Following his sojourn in Rome, Apollonius turns to the western regions of the known world, near the Pillar of Hercules (Gibraltar). He also travels to Gadeira, another land known for its philosophical sagacity: the people of this region are so tuned to the philosophical virtues that they have an altar to old age and death. We get descriptions of this exotic land that we have come to expect from Philostratus' narrative, which always has an eye turned toward the classical world: we see the altars of Hercules, and exotic trees known as the 'trees of Geryon', which drip blood from their bark.

Apollonius' journey in Gadeira ends with a long discussion about Nero, and with harbingers of his eventual downfall. The political element of the story gathers steam as he meets with Titus, just back from his sacking of Jerusalem and the quelling of the Jewish revolt, and Apollonius extols his virtues and predicts his rise to power. Then he travels back to Greece and eventually goes to Egypt, the furthest extreme of the known world in the south, and the border area of Egypt and Ethiopia where the naked philosophers dwell.

The overlap of locations and sacred sites continues in Egypt. Philostratus explains that the Nile and the Indus act in much the same way, providing the lands of Egypt and India with a congenial climate conducive to the contemplative life. The gods and goddesses of Egypt and India also overlap on essential points, so much so that the pan-Hellenic syncretism that we saw in India seems also present in Egypt, even down to the names of the gods and goddesses and their functions in the cosmic pantheon. Later we learn that this is no coincidence. For although the naked sages are held in less esteem by Apollonius than the Brahmins, the naked sages and Apollonius agree that their settlements in Ethiopia are an extension of the Indian settlements, and that they are merely separated by vast periods of time and great distances. Here we see another world of Hellenic overlap, and again we are given picturesque and exotic details that we would expect in a Graeco-Roman novel, as Apollonius and his followers search for the source of the Nile.[48]

In the interim, Titus becomes the emperor and showers favour on Apollonius. He is not destined to reign for long, however, and upon his death he is succeeded by Domitian, who does not have the same favourable disposition to philosophy and its practitioners.[49] Like Nero, he outlaws the discipline, and makes it a crime for philosophy to be practised in the city of Rome or for its devotees to enter its walls. He trumps up charges against Apollonius, the gravest of which is that the sage had set himself up as a god, and then sacrificed a small boy for the purposes of augury.

Apollonius goes to Rome to face the charges, despite knowing it will mean his certain death.[50] Once the sage enters the city, he is promptly arrested, and Domitian has his hair shorn and puts him in chains.[51] (But as Apollonius prepares for his defence, he shows us that he is capable of taking off the fetters at will.[52]) When his trial occurs, he is questioned about his role in various miracles, and when they reach his rescue of Ephesus from a plague, the emperor grows wary, believing the sage will report the emperor's incestuous marriage and 'his other misdemeanours' as the potential source of the pandemic. So he orders the proceedings to end and deems Apollonius innocent of all the charges.

Apollonius then declares to the emperor following his ruling that: '. . . my soul, you cannot take, Nay you cannot take even my body, "For thou shalt not slay me, since I tell thee I am not mortal"' (from the *Iliad* 22.13).

The sage vanishes, and we later learn that he has joined some of his disciples at a prearranged meeting place. Apollonius lives for a few more years and then dies, or appears to die. Philostratus tells us that there are many stories regarding his 'death'. The most plausible for Philostratus was that the sage was assumed into heaven, for never in Philostratus' wide travels, he tells us, has he heard of or seen a tomb for the man of Tyana, Apollonius.

Eusebius on the 'similarities' between Apollonius and Christ

Though the two are by no means completely similar, the parallels between the life of Jesus and that of Apollonius are close, and there were enough comparisons made in antiquity between the two figures that Eusebius wrote a short treatise to combat these specious claims. This short essay, from the great historian of Christianity, is a disappointment. We would expect a full frontal assault on Apollonius, but instead Eusebius displays an uncharacteristic timidity. He spends most of the essay attacking small issues, like supposed inconsistencies in Philostratus' statements about the sage. For example, he points out that Philostratus asserts that Apollonius knew all languages from birth, even though the sage repeatedly requires interpreters to communicate with non-Greeks. Eusebius is also appalled at Philostratus' claims that Apollonius is omniscient, and feels compelled to give numerous examples of his failure to know future events.

Eusebius is also guilty of the oldest trick in philosophical debate: he never attacks the powerful sage directly, but instead attacks the followers and the compilers of his legacy. Eusebius believes that Philostratus is distorting Apollonius' record for his own nefarious purposes. He constantly calls Philostratus 'the lover of truth', to show him a liar, taking advantage of the pun on his name. But perhaps the greatest shortcoming of Eusebius' essay is that he accuses Apollonius of the same faults of which Jesus' enemies accuse him. He claims that Apollonius uses demons to cast out demons, a charge the Pharisees make against Jesus.[53] Additionally, Philostratus asserts that the girl who Apollonius raises from the dead was perhaps not really dead. Eusebius pounces on this, forgetting or ignoring that Jesus says the same thing when he raises a girl from the dead.[54] And Eusebius repeatedly scolds Apollonius' disciples for being slow to see Apollonius' divine nature, and informs us this is a sure proof that he was merely a man. Once more Eusebius, an excellent student of the Gospels and Christian history, seems uncharacteristically forgetful about his scripture: one of the favourite themes of all the Gospels is how slow-witted Jesus' disciples were in discovering their master's true nature. Part of the charm of the Gospel narratives is that most readers are aware of the narrative truth of Jesus, while those around him are not.

It should not surprise us that Eusebius was unwilling or incapable of a strong attack against *The Life of Apollonius of Tyana*. The issues involved were so foundational that even a man like Eusebius had trouble with any real or sustained effort to lay them out, let alone combat them. Very simply, we are dealing with two kinds of truth. The Christian truth believes in the veracity of the Christian message and the fundamental falsehood and perversion of all others. (How else can we explain Eusebius' reliance on the arguments of the Pharisees to prove Apollonius a fraud?) But the truth of Apollonius is one that accumulates detail as it progresses; it is cosmopolitan and expansive, incorporating elements as it moves along the well-travelled roads of antiquity. Apollonius is not a preacher from rural Galilee never destined to leave Roman Palestine. His religion is syncretistic, and as such is not bashful about taking its message on the road, even during its formative stages. The faiths of Judaism, Islam and Christianity developed from fixed points by founders who did little in the way of extensive travel. So their religions were already static in the mythological imagination by the time they reached the stage of conquest and missionary endeavours. But Apollonius moved in a world that yielded to his notions of religion because it was already connected by bonds of kinship, commonality and shared presupposition. This involved compromise, which is frightening for Abrahamic monotheism, since compromise is often viewed as hand-in-glove with corrosion. But Apollonius' compromise did not sacrifice any lofty morality. Although a pagan, Apollonius was a monotheist, and believed in a type of universal morality that was explicitly applicable to all. The boundary between the Pythagorean philosopher and his faith and beliefs was not set against a hard world: the membrane was permeable, and ideas and actions floated across it in a constant current.

The vibrancy of late Hellenistic paganism

The end of Hellenistic paganism was more than just an end to a host of religions and philosophies. It was the end, really, of a certain set of assumptions about the divine world. In the face of a rising fundamentalism, there has been a counter-rise in nostalgic longing for the tolerance of polytheism in recent years.[55] And if we wish to see those assumptions at work again, in our world, we may turn to the host of neo-pagan religions that may or may not reflect their predecessors. Or we might think of the death of paganism as not a death at all. We can see examples of paganism enriching Christianity in its formative years and beyond, and also paganism being enriched by Christianity.[56] In this view, paganism did not die as much as it simply folded into Christianity. Christians drank deeply from the pagan well on all levels of culture, from the popular to the erudite. The shared Greek language of the Christian and Hellenic traditions allowed communication unfettered by translation. Christians in the east of the former Roman Empire were Greek-speakers and could read pagan books unhindered. In fact, most intellectuals in the Latin West could adequately read Greek.

But there is still, for many, the old pull of grief for a true paganism. If paganism survived in syncretistic holdovers or revivals in the Abrahamic religions, it is comforting but hardly exhilarating. Some yearn, perhaps, for the multi-storey world of gods and goddesses. Some would like to think that Christianity, Judaism and Islam did not win because they were superior to their predecessors, but because they played unfairly. The idea of a dead or dying paganism as a corrupt faith that deserved its death is certainly a victor's tale. We also get glimpses in the historical record of a late paganism that was not as sick as its opponents supposed or hoped it was.

In the mid nineteenth century, a manuscript obtained from a monastery in the Wadi Natrun in Egypt was found to be by John of Ephesus, a bishop in that city in the sixth century already known as the writer of a Church history.[57] John was a vigorous proselytizer of Christianity and travelled widely in that capacity. It was already known that he travelled to Lydia, Phrygia and Caria in Asia Minor, in AD 542, to convert the locals. When the new manuscript was found, the nineteenth-century scholars who examined it found its claims difficult to believe. John explains in vibrant detail the rigorous Greek paganism he found in the Maeander Valley in central Asia Minor, three centuries after Constantine's conversion to Christ. This area had extensive Greek settlements for 1,000 years. John reported that he found thousands of pagans in the towns high in these mountains and a famous temple that had jurisdiction over some 1,500 other sacred sites in the region.[58] An old man whom John met in this region explained that the shrine was a meeting place for priestly representatives from all over the mountains; they came yearly to expound on the law and receive instruction about how to carry out priestly duties. John's descriptions of this pagan region have led to a general reassessment of paganism's supposed demise. This description, by the pen of a confirmed Christian, adds to the veracity of the idea that paganism did not die of corruption. It paints, rather inadvertently, a negative image of Christian expansion and conquest, as if the new faith simply rolled over a warm body.

Yet, for all its seeming loss, paganism lives. It has only been altered. The three Abrahamic faiths have borrowed and blended elements from the pagan faiths that surrounded them. In significant ways, Western monotheism is permeated with pagan holdovers and revivals. We need not travel back to a mythical mountainous interior region in Asia Minor to discover holdovers of paganism. There are no more lost worlds of paganism awaiting discovery, where centuries'-old cults to the gods and goddesses thrive in a rich pantheon. To connect with the eternal pagan, we simply need look up at our local Green Man.

Chapter summary

Paganism continues to exist today. As we saw in the example of the Church of Lukumi Babalu Aye, pagan groups often face social and legal discrimination, even in political cultures that are supposed to ensure religious freedom. Much of this discrimination points to a deep ambivalence toward paganism, and a fundamental lack of understanding of the debt that the Abrahamic religions owe to paganism, both in antiquity and modern times.

In a similar vein, late Paganism in antiquity was not moribund. On the contrary, it was incredibly vibrant when Christianity was a little-known phenomenon during the first three generations after the death of Jesus. In fact, the first Roman author known to comment on the new sect did so nearly 80 years after Jesus' crucifixion.[59] The influx of cults from the east, like Mithraism and the Orphic mysteries, invigorated late Roman paganism, in which we find an expression of ideas that eventually find their way into or, at the least, are shared by Christianity: the idea of a personal saviour whose death atones for the sins of the community, and the equally forceful assertion of transcendent monotheism despite this personal saviour, to name only two.[60] Paganism invigorated Christianity during its formative years by challenging it to become a faith that answered the needs of the various peoples of the scattered Roman world. The answers that pagan groups like those of Mithras and Orpheus provided for life's complexities provided Christianity with a model for success in its evangelical ventures. This was seen in the life of Apollonius of Tyana, who, although a Pythagorean philosopher, was widely eclectic in his religious tastes. He travelled extensively through the Roman world and beyond it, seeking the wisdom of the Brahmins, the naked sages of Ethiopia, and the mysterious residents of Gadeira, where philosophy reigned to the extent that the people built a temple dedicated to death. Apollonius ran afoul of Roman emperors and officials. He dealt with treacherous and backbiting disciples, he healed the sick and raised the dead to life, and he preached at and reconsecrated pagan temples. No one was ever able to find his tomb – leading to speculation that he was subsumed into heaven. Apollonius was such a threat to the early Church that Eusebius wrote a short treatise refuting the Sage of Tyana's work. In the writing, he ironically wound up drawing more parallels to the life and workings of Christ, which obviously was not his stated goal. This shows us the close interpenetration between paganism in late antiquity and the early Christian movement. Both trends informed each other to offer a fine example of religious syncretism. The border between 'Christian' and 'Pagan' in Rome in the first two or three centuries of the spread Christianity (as well as later outside the boundaries of Rome) is far from clear. What is clear is that the dividing lines between the religions was far from fixed.[61]

Draw your own conclusions

How did syncretism play a role in creating unity in the Graeco-Roman world?

What accounts for the emergence of monotheistic tendencies in late Roman paganism?

The *Hymn* of Cleanthes expresses ideas about God that are monotheistic, but is this a monotheism similar to the Christian type, or more like the Stoic conception of God? In other words, is this God a personal being, or a principle?

Apollonius sees Greek influence everywhere. Is Apollonius' religion really a form of syncretism, or is it a kind of arch-Hellenism?

What, if anything, did Christianity 'learn' from Graeco-Roman paganism?

Further reading

For a history of colonial American religious pluralism:
Patricia U. Bonomi (2003), *Under the Cope of Heaven: Religion, Society, and Politics in Colonial America*, Oxford: Oxford University Press.

For readings in late paganism:

Polymnia Athanassiadi and Michael Frede (eds) (1999), *Pagan Monotheism in Late Antiquity*, Oxford: Clarendon Press.

Frederick C. Grant (ed.) (1953), *Hellenistic Religions: The Age of Syncretism*, New York: The Liberal Arts Press.

Flavius Philostratus (1912), *The Life of Apollonius of Tyana*, F. C. Conybearne (trans.), Cambridge, MA: Harvard University Press.

For Roman pagan views of Christianity:

Robert L. Wilken (1984), *The Christians as the Romans Saw Them*, New Haven, CT: Yale Unversity Press.

For an extended treatment of the problems of conversion from paganism:

Richard Fletcher (1997), *The Barbarian Conversion*, New York: Henry Holt.

For examples of Graeco-Roman novels:

B. P. Reardon (ed.) (1989), *Collected Ancient Greek Novels*, Berkeley, CA: University of California Press.

For an excellent example of late Roman Stoic literature:

Marcus Aurelius (1964), *The Meditations*, Maxwell Staniforth (trans.), London: Penguin Classics.

Notes

1 Migene Gonzalez-Wippler (1989), *Santeria: The Religion: A Legacy of Faith, Rites and Magic*, New York: Harmony Books, pp. 2–3.

2 Laure Goering, 'Catholicism Stirs Cultural Challenge in Africa', *Chicago Tribune*, 15 April 2005.

3 Gonzalez-Wippler, *Santeria*, p. 73.

4 US Supreme Court Case *Church of Babalu Aye v City of Hialeah*, 508 US 520 (1993).

5 Charles Steward and Rosalind Shaw (eds) (1994), *Syncretism/Anti-Syncretism: The Politics of Religious Synthesis*, London and New York: Routledge, p. 208.

6 George H. Tavard (1996), *The Thousand Faces of the Virgin Mary*, Collegeville, MN: Liturgical Press, pp. 192–201.

7 For a summary of the Puritans, see Bonomi, *Under the Cope of Heaven*, 'The New Heaven and the New Earth', pp. 17–21.

8 For a treatment of the Great Awakening, see Bonomi, *Under the Cope of Heaven*, 'The Great Awakening in America', pp. 131–60. For diversity in early American religion, the early chapters of *Under the Cope of Heaven* are indispensable. Bonomi shows how the peculiar circumstances of American life, both geographically and socially, made tolerance all but inevitable. For the Great Awakening's connection to Protestant fundamentalism, see Karen Armstrong (2000), *The Battle for God*, New York: Alfred A. Knopf, pp. 78–81, and pp. 87–92.

9 Grant, *Hellenistic Religions*, p. xiii.

10 Steward and Shaw, *Syncretism/Anti-Syncretism*, p. 4.

11 W. H. McNeil (1963), *The Rise of the West: A History of the Human Community*, New York: New American Library, pp. 278–321.

12 Grant, *Hellenistic Religions*, pp. xiii.

13 This was explored on pages 76–7.

14 Grant, *Hellenistic Religions*, pp. xxxvi–vii.

15 For a general discussion of the development of monotheism in late pagan religions, see M. L. West, 'Towards Monotheism', in Athanassiadi and Frede, *Pagan Monotheism in Late Antiquity*, pp. 21–40. Here, West speculates that polytheistic religions moved from polytheistic roots where gods and goddesses had specific functions and cults with little overlap, to councils of gods and goddesses who acted under the influence of one dominant god. From this developed a uniformity of divine will that developed into a form of monotheism in the late Greek world. See Frede, 'Monotheism and Pagan Philosophy in later antiquity', pp. 41–68 in the same book for a treatment of the philosophical monotheism of Aristotle (and the Peripatetics), Plato (and the Platonists), and the Stoics and their connections to Christian monotheism. In this article Frede throws into crisis the whole notion that there is a fundamental difference between Greek and Christian philosophical notions about God.

16 Grant, *Hellenistic Religions*, p. 152.

17 Grant, *Hellenistic Religions*, p. 152.

18 Grant, *Hellenistic Religions*, p. 153.

19 Grant, *Hellenistic Religions*, p. 153.

20 Grant, *Hellenistic Religions*, p. 153.

21 Grant, *Hellenistic Religions*, see pp. 152–4 for the entire poem.

22 Aurelius, *The Meditations* is replete with pietistic language. See 5.27, p. 87, 6.7, p. 91 and particularly see 7.9, p. 106, where he combines piety to one god with pantheism: 'All things are interwoven with one another; a sacred bond unites them . . . Every thing is coordinated; everything works together in giving one form to the universe. The world-order is a unity made up of multiplicity. God is one, pervading all things; all being is one, all law is one . . .'

23 Philostratus, *The Life of Apollonius of Tyana*, Introduction, pp. xiv–xv.

24 Philostratus, *The Life of Apollonius*, vol. 1, pp. 19–21.

25 Philostratus, *The Life of Apollonius*, vol. 1, p. 35.

26 Philostratus, *The Life of Apollonius*, vol. 1, pp. 31–3.

27 Philostratus, *The Life of Apollonius*, vol. 1, p. 79.

28 Philostratus, *The Life of Apollonius,* vol. 1, p. 147.

29 Philostratus, *The Life of Apollonius*, vol. 1, p. 183.

30 Philostratus, *The Life of Apollonius*, vol. 1, p. 267.

31 Philostratus, *The Life of Apollonius*, vol. 1, p. 269.

32 Philostratus, *The Life of Apollonius*, vol. 1, p. 307.

33 Philostratus, *The Life of Apollonius*, vol. 1, p. 309.

34 Philostratus, *The Life of Apollonius*, vol. 1 p. 239.

35 Philostratus, *The Life of Apollonius*, vol. 1, p. 237.

36 Reardon, *Collected Ancient Greek Novels*, for examples. Particularly see the novels *Chaereas and Callirhoe*, pp. 17–124, *Leucippe and Clitophon*, pp. 170–288 and *Daphnis and Chloe*, pp. 288–348. These works show how marvellously eclectic was the ancient novel.

37 Philostratus, *The Life of Apollonius*, vol. 1, p. 233.

38 Philostratus, *The Life of Apollonius*, vol. 1, p. 253.

39 Philostratus, *The Life of Apollonius*, vol. 1, p. 251.

40 Philostratus, *The Life of Apollonius*. vol. 1, p. 377.

41 Philostratus, *The Life of Apollonius*, vol. 1, p. 391.

42 Philostratus, *The Life of Apollonius*, vol. 1, p. 397.

43 Philostratus, *The Life of Apollonius*, vol. 1, pp. 405–7.

44 Philostratus, *The Life of Apollonius*, vol. 1, p. 411.

45 Philostratus, *The Life of Apollonius*, vol. 1, p. 445.

46 Philostratus, *The Life of Apollonius*, vol. 1, pp. 457–9.

47 Philostratus, *The Life of Apollonius*, vol. 1, p. 459.

48 Philostratus, *The Life of Apollonius*, vol. 2, p. 101.

49 Nor does Domitian to Christians, as Eusebius explains the cranky emperor's persecutions in his (1981) *History of the Church*, G. A. Williamson (trans.), New York: Penguin Classics, Book 3, pp. 125–7.

50 Philostratus, *The Life of Apollonius*, vol. 2, p. 173.

51 Philostratus, *The Life of Apollonius*, vol. 2, p. 245.

52 Philostratus, *The Life of Apollonius*, vol. 2, p. 257.

53 *NJB* Matthew 12.24, Mark 3.22.

54 *NJB* Mark 5.39, Luke 8.52.

55 G. W. Bowersock (1990), *Hellenism in Late Antiquity*, Ann Arbor, MI: University of Michigan Press, p. 6, and Fletcher, *The Barbarian Conversion*, pp. 62–4.

56 Bowersock, *Hellenism in Late Antiquity*, p. 52.

57 Bowersock, *Hellenism in Late Antiquity*, p. 2.

58 Bowersock, *Hellenism in Late Antiquity*, p. 2.

59 Wilken, *The Christians as the Romans Saw Them*, p. xii.

60 Kurt Rudoph (1987), *Gnosis: The Nature and History of Gnosticism*, San Francisco: Harper, pp. 286–7.

61 In the *Barbarian Conversion*, Richard Fletcher sums up the difficulty of distinguishing a dividing line between paganism and Christianity in the first five centuries of their coexistence. On page 53 he quotes Martin of Braga d. 580 discussing the difficulties of keeping newly minted Christians along the orthodox path. They continue to 'mutter spells over herbs' and 'invoke the names of demons in incantations.' Fletcher concludes: '[Martin's] castigation makes very plain the difficulty, not indeed for him but for the modern historian, of drawing hard and fast boundaries between Christianity and pagan, religion and superstition, piety and magic, the acceptable and the forbidden.' Elsewhere, as Fletcher discusses the work of missionaries in Northern Europe in the same period (the 500s), he points out the 'competitive' element between Christian missionaries and pagan priests and priestesses. Often, this occurred in the arena of competing miracles. Fletcher aptly says that alongside Christianity '[t]here existed an alternate network to the one presented by Christian teachers. There were other persons about, easily resorted to, claiming access to means of explaining misfortune, curing sickness, stimulating love, wreaking vengeance, foretelling the future, advising when to undertake a journey, interpreting the flight of birds or the patterns on the shoulder-blades of sheep' (p. 64). These practices persisted well into modern times. Fletcher explores this in some detail in the final chapter of *The Barbarian Conversion*, 'Slouching Toward Bethlehem', pp. 508–24.

Select Bibliography

1 The Exalted Cranes: the Question of Purity and Impurity

R. Abraham, J. Elrich and Avner Tomaschorf (trans.) *Pirkei Avot*, A Kaplan Kusick Foundation Project.

Karen Armstrong (2000), *The Battle for God*, New York: Alfred A. Knopf.

Ian Bradley (2003), *The Celtic Way*, London: Darton, Longman & Todd.

John Corrigan, Frederick M. Denny, Martin Jaffee, Carlos M. N. Eire (1998), *Jews, Christians and Muslims: A Comparative Introduction to the Monotheistic Religions*, Upper Saddle River, NJ: Prentice Hall.

N. J. Dawood (trans.) (1997), *The Koran*, New York: Penguin.

Caroline Ebertshäuser, Herbert Haag, Joe H. Kirchberger, Dorothee Sölle, Peter Hienegg (trans.) (1998), *Mary: Art, Culture and Religion through the Ages*, New York: A Crossroad Herder Book.

Bard Ehrman (2003), *Lost Christianities: The Battles for Scripture and the Faiths We Never Knew*, Oxford: Oxford University Press.

Martin Ewens (2002), *Afghanistan: A Short History of Its People and Politcs*, New York: HarperCollins.

Richard Fletcher (1997), *The Barbarian Conversion*, New York: Henry Holt.

Sir James George Fraser (1993), *The Golden Bough: A Study in Magic and Religion*, New York: Wordsworth Reference.

G. R. Hawting and Abdul-Kader A. Shareef (trans.) (1993), *Approaches to the Qur'an*, London and New York: Routledge.

Albert Hourani (1991), *The History of the Arab Peoples*, Cambridge, MA: The Belknap Press of Harvard University Press.

W. H. McNeil (1963), *The Rise of the West: A History of the Human Community*, New York: New American Library.

Donald Meek (2000), *The Quest for Celtic Christianity*, Edinburgh: Handsel Press.

Maria Rosa Menocal (2002), *The Ornament of the World: How Jews, Muslims and Christians Created a Culture of Tolerance in Medieval Spain*, Boston: Little, Brown & Co.

George W. E. Nickelsburg (2003), *Ancient Judaism and Christian Origins: Diversity, Continuity and Transformations*, Minneapolis: Fortress Press.

Elaine Pagels (2003), *Beyond Belief: The Secret Gospel of Thomas*, New York: Random House.

Rafael Patai (1990), *The Hebrew Goddess*, Detroit, MI: Wayne State University Press.

Daniel Pipes (1990), *The Rushdie Affair*, New York: Birch Lane Press.

Michael Pollack (1980), *Jews, Mandarins and Missionaries*, Philadelphia: Jewish Publication Society.

Kurt Rudolph (1987), *Gnosis: The Nature and History of Gnosticism*, San Francisco: Harper.

Salman Rushdie (2000), *The Satanic Verses*, New York: Picador Press.

Malise Ruthven (2004), *Fundamentalism: A Search for Meaning*, Oxford: Oxford University Press.

Peter F. Sugar (1997), *South-eastern Europe under Ottoman Rule, 1354-1804*, Seattle and London: University of Washington Press.

George H. Tavard (1996), *The Thousand Faces of the Virgin Mary*, Collegeville, MN: Liturgical Press.

2 Family Resemblances: the Crypto-Jews of Spain and Portugal Become the Syncretistic Marranos

Pierre-Antoine Bernheim (1996), *James, Brother of Jesus*, John Bowden (trans.), Paris: Noesis.

T. Carmi (trans. and ed.) (1981), *The Penguin Book of Hebrew Verse*, Hebrew and English edition, New York: Penguin.

J. Corrigan, F. Denny, M. Jaffee, C. Eire (1998), *Jews, Christians and Muslims: A Comparative Introduction to the Monotheistic Religions*, Upper Saddle River, NJ: Prentice Hall.

Richard Fletcher (1990), *The Quest for the Cid*, New York: Alfred Knopf.

David M. Gitlitz (1996), *Secrecy and Deceit: The Religion of the Crypto-Jews*, Philadelphia and Jerusalem: The Jewish Publication Society.

David Gitlitz and Linda Kay Davidson (1999), *A Drizzle of Honey: The Lives and Recipes of Spain's Secret Jews*, New York: St Martin's Press.

Rita Hamilton and Janet Perry (trans.) (1984), *The Poem of the Cid*, London: Penguin Classics.

Albert Hourani (1991), *The History of Arab Peoples*, Cambridge, MA: The Belknap Press of Harvard University Press.

Jonathan Irvine Israel (2002), *Diasporas Within a Diaspora: Jews, Crypto-Jews, and the World of Maritime Empires 1540–1740*, Leiden, The Netherlands: Brill.

Francine Klagsburn (1996), *Jewish Days*, illustrated by Mark Podwol, New York: Farrar, Strauss & Giroux.

Hyam Maccoby (1981), *Revolution in Judea: Jesus and the Jewish Resistance*, New York: Taplinger.

Moses Maimonides (1989), *Mishneh Torah, Hilchot Yesodei Hatorah (Laws of the Foundation of the Torah)*, Rabbi Eliyahu Touger (trans.), Jerusalem and New York: Moznaim Publishing.

Maria Rose Menocal (2002), *The Ornament of the World: How Jews, Muslims and Christians Created a Culture of Tolerance in Medieval Spain*, Boston, Little, Brown & Co.

James T. Monroe (1974), *Hispano-Arabic Poetry: A Student Anthology*, Berkeley, CA: University of California Press.

George W. E. Nickelsburg (2003), *Ancient Judaism and Christian Origins: Diversity, Continuity and Transformations*, Minneapolis: Fortress Press.

Michael Pollack (1980), *Jews, Mandarins and Missionaries*, Philadelphia: Jewish Publication Society.

Joachim Prinz (1973), *The Secret Jews*, New York: Random House.

Andrew Rippin (1993), 'Interpreting the Bible through the Qur'an', in G. R. Hawting and Abdul Kader A. Shareet (eds), *Approaches to the Qur'an*, London: Routledge.

Neal Robinson (1996), *Discovering the Qur'an*, London: SCM Press.

Dan Ross (1984), *Acts of Faith: A Journey to the Fringes of Jewish Identity*, New York: Schocken Books.

Cecil Roth (1947), *A History of The Marranos*, Philadelphia: The Jewish Publication Society.

Joselit Weissman (1994), *The Wonders of America: Reinventing Jewish Culture, 1880–1950*, New York: Hill and Wang.

3 The House of War: Islam for the Shady Grove

Henrik Birnbaum and Speros Vryonis, Jr (eds) (1972), *Aspects of the Balkans: Continuity and Change,* The Hague and Paris: Mountain Press.

G. W. Bowersock (1990), *Hellenism in Late Antiquity,* Ann Arbor, MI: University of Michigan Press.

John Corrigan, Frederick M. Denny, Martin Jaffee, Carlos M. N. Eire (1998), *Jews, Christians and Muslims: A Comparative Introduction to the Monotheistic Faiths*, Upper Saddle River, NJ: Prentice Hall.

Robert Elsie (2001), *A Dictionary of Albanian Religion, Mythology and Folk Culture*, New York: New York University Press.

Richard Fletcher (1997), *The Barbarian Conversion*, New York: Henry Holt.

David Fromkin (1989), *A Peace to End All Peace,* New York: Avon Books.

Michael Gilsenan (1973), *Saint and Sufi in Egypt: An Essay in the Sociology of Religion*, Oxford: Clarendon Press.

Albert Hourani (1991), *The History of Arab Peoples,* Cambridge, MA: The Belknap Press of Harvard University Press.

Alex Metcalfe (2003), *Muslims and Christians in Norman Sicily: Arabic Speakers and the End of Islam*, London and New York: Routledge Curzon.

William Morris (ed.) (1994), *Webster's New World Dictionary*, Boston: Houghton Mifflin.

Sabrina Petra Ramet (1992), *Balkan Babel: Politics, Culture and Religion in Yugoslavia*, Boulder, CO: Westview Press.

James Charles Roy (1999), *The Vanished Kingdom: Travels through the History of Prussia,* Boulder, CO: Westview Press.

Stanford Shaw (1976), *History of the Ottoman Empire and Modern Turkey: Volume I: Empire of the Gazis: The Rise and Decline of the Ottoman Empire, 1280–1808*, Cambridge: Cambridge University Press.

Peter F. Sugar (1977), *South-eastern Europe under Ottoman Rule, 1354–1804,* Seattle and London: University of Washington Press.

S. Vryonis Jr (1972), 'Religious Changes and Patterns in the Balkans, 14th–16th Centuries', in Birnbaum and Vryonis (eds) *Aspects of the Balkans*, pp. 151–76.

Dame Rebecca West (1994), *Black Lamb and Gray Falcon: A Journey Through*

Yugoslavia, New York: Penguin Books.

Robert L. Wilken (1984), *The Christians as the Romans Saw Them*, New Haven, CT: Yale University Press.

4 Mysticism and Saints' Cults in the Abrahamic Religions

Issachar Ben-Ami (1998), *Saint Veneration among the Jews of Morocco*, Detroit, MI: Wayne State University Press.

Vladimir Bobrovnikov (1991), 'Post-Socialist Forms of Islam: Caucasian Whhabis', in ISIM Newsletter, March 2001, p. 29.

John Corrigan, Frederick M. Denny, Martin Jaffee, Carlos M. N. Eire (1997), *Jews, Christians and Muslims: A Comparative Introduction to the Monotheistic Faiths*, Upper Saddle River, NJ: Prentice Hall.

John B. Dunlop (1998), *Russia Confronts Chechnya: Roots of a Separatist Conflict*, Cambridge: Cambridge University Press.

Lawrence Durrell (1961), *Clea,* New York: Dutton Paperbacks.

Caroline Ebertshäuser, Herbert Haag, Joe H. Kirchberger, Dorothee Sölle, Peter Hienegg (trans.) (1998), *Mary: Art, Culture and Religion through the Ages*, New York: A Crossroad Herder Book.

Encyclopaedia of Islam (1991), Moscow: Nauka Press.

W. H. C. Frend (1976), *Religion, Popular and Unpopular in the Early Christian Church*, London: Variorum Reprints.

David Fromkin (1989), *A Peace to End All Peace*, New York: Avon Books.

Marc Gaborieau (1983), 'The Cults of Saints in Nepal and Northern India', in Stephen Wilson (ed.), *Saints and their Cults*, Cambridge: Cambridge University Press.

Rivka Gonen (2003), *Contested Holiness: Jewish, Christian and Muslim Perspectives on the Temple Mount in Jerusalem*, Jersey City: Ktav Publishing House.

Keneath Hart Green (1993), *Jew and Philosopher: The Return to Maimonides in the Jewish Thought of Leo Strauss*, Albany, NY: SUNY Press.

Robert Hertz (1983), 'St Besse: a study in an alpine cult', in Stephen Wilson (ed.), *Saints and their Cults*, Cambridge: Cambridge University Press.

Albert Hourani (1991), *The History of Arab Peoples*, Cambridge, MA: The Belknap Press of Harvard University Press.

Alexander Knysh (2000), *Islamic Mysticism: A Short History*, Boston: Brill.

Ralph Lerner (1972), *Medieval Political Philosophy*, Ithaca, NY: Cornell University Press.

V. S. Naipaul (1981), *Among the Believers*, New York: Vintage Books.

V. S. Naipaul (1998), *Beyond Belief,* New York: Vintage Books.

H. T. Norris (1993), *Islam in the Balkans*, Columbia, SC: University of South Carolina Press.

Elaine Pagels (1992), *The Gnostic Paul: Gnostic Exegesis of the Pauline Letters*, Harrisburg, PA: Trinity Press International.

Rafael Patai (1983), *On Jewish Folklore*, Detroit, MI: Wayne State University Press.

Ivana Della Portella (1999), *Subterranean Rome*, Venice: Konemann Press.

Leo Strauss (1980), *Persecution and the Art of Writing*, Chicago: University of Chicago Press.

5 The Eternal Feminine: Mary, the Christian Goddess

Janice Capel Anderson and Stephen D. Moore (eds) (1992), *Mark and Method: New Approaches in Biblical Studies*, Minneapolis: Fortress Press.

Athanasius (1980), *The Life of Antony and the Letter to Marcellinus*, Robert C. Gregg (trans.) New York: The Paulist Press.

Max Bax (1995), *Medjugorje: Religion, Politics, and Violence in Rural Bosnia*, Amsterdam: VU Uitgeverij.

David Bakan (1991), *Maimonides on Prophecy: A Commentary on Selected Chapters of The Guide of the Perplexed*, Northvale, NJ, London: Jason Aronson, Inc.

Stephen Benko (1993), *The Virgin Goddess: Studies in the Pagan and Christian Roots of Mariology*, New York: E. J. Brill.

G. W. Bowersock (1990), *Hellenism in Late Antiquity*, Ann Arbor, MI: University of Michigan Press.

Frank Moore Cross (1973), *Canaanite Myth and Hebrew Epic: Essays in The History of the Religion of Israel*, Cambridge, MA: Harvard University Press.

Caroline Ebertshäuser, Herbert Haag, Joe H. Kirchberger, Dorothee Sölle, Peter Hienegg (trans.) (1998), *Mary: Art, Culture and Religion through the Ages*, New York: A Crossroad Herder Book.

Jamal Elias (1988), 'Female and Feminine in Islamic Mysticism', in *The Muslim World*, 78, Hartford, CT: Duncan Black MacDonald Center.

J. K. Elliot (trans.) (1993), *The Apocryphal New Testament: A Collection of Apocryphal Christian Literature in an English Translation*, Oxford: Clarendon Press.

Epiphanius (1995), *The Panarion of St Epiphanius, Bishop of Salamis, Selected Passages*, Philip R. Amidan (trans.), New York: Oxford University Press.

Eusebius (1981), *The History of the Church*, G. A. Williamson (trans.), New York: Penguin.

Richard Fletcher (1997), *The Barbarian Conversion*, New York: Henry Holt.

Paul Johnson (1988), *The History of the Jews*, New York: Perennial Library, Harper & Row.

The Koran (2000), N. J. Dawood (trans.), New York: Penguin Classics.

Harry J. Leon (1995), *The Jews of Ancient Rome*, Peabody, MA: Hendrickson Publishing.

George W. E. Nickelsburg (2003), *Ancient Judaism and Christian Origins: Diversity, Continuity and Transformations*, Minneapolis: Fortress Press.

Elaine Pagels (1988), *Adam, Eve and the Serpent*, New York: Random House.

Rafael Patai (1990), *The Hebrew Goddess*, Detroit, MI: Wayne State University Press.

Philo of Alexandria (1995), *Philo's Collected Works*, C. D. Yonge (trans.), Peabody, MA: Hendrickson Publishing.

Michael Pollack (1980), *Jews, Mandarins and Missionaries*, Philadelphia: Jewish Publication Society.

Ivana Della Portella (1999), *Subterranean Rome*, Venice: Konemann Press.

Alexander Roberts and James Donaldson (eds) (1951), *The Ante-Nicene Fathers: Translations of the Writings of the Fathers down to A.D. 325*, Grand Rapids, MI: Eerdmans Publishing Company.

Charlene Spretnak (2004), *Missing Mary: The Queen of Heaven and Her Re-emergence in the Modern Church*, New York: Palgrave Macmillan.

George H. Tavard (1996), *The Thousand Faces of the Virgin Mary*, Collegeville, MN: Liturgical Press.

Robert L. Wilken (1984), *The Christians as the Romans Saw Them*, New Haven, CT: Yale University Press.

6 The Practical Kabbala: How to Build a Golem

Karen Armstrong (2000), *The Battle for God*, New York: Alfred A. Knopf.

David Bakan (1991), *Maimonides on Prophecy: A Commentary on Selected Chapters of The Guide of the Perplexed*, Northvale, New Jersey, London: Jason Aronson Inc.

Erich Bischoff (1985), *The Kabbala: An Introduction to Jewish Mysticism and its Secret Doctrines*, York Beach, ME: Samuel Weisner, Inc.

Sir Lancelot C. L. Breton (1992), *The Septuagint with Apocrypha*, Peabody, MA: Hendrickson Publishing.

Harold Bloom (ed.) (1987), *Gershom Scholem: Modern Critical Views*, New York, New Haven and Philadelphia: Chelsea House Publisher.

F. Brown, S. Driver and C. Briggs (2004), *The Brown-Driver-Briggs Hebrew and English Lexicon*, Peabody, MA: Hendrickson Publishing.

Frank Moore Cross (1973), *Canaanite Myth and Hebrew Epic: Essays in The History of the Religion of Israel*, Cambridge, MA: Harvard University Press.

Howard Eilberg-Schwartz (1994), *God's Phallus and Other Problems for Men and Monotheism*, Boston: Beacon Press.

Paul Johnson (1988), *The History of the Jews*, New York: Perennial Library, Harper & Row.

Paul Johnson (1997), *The Quest for God: A Personal Pilgrimage*, New York: Harper.

Aryeh Kaplan (trans.) (1989), *The Bahir*, York Beach, ME: Samuel Weisner, Inc.

Aryeh Kaplan (trans.) (1997), *Sepher Yetzirah: The Book of Creation in Theory and Practice*, York Beach, ME: Samuel Weisner, Inc.

Dovid Katz (2004), *Words on Fire: The Unfinished Story of Yiddish*, New York: Basic Books.

Eduard Yechezkel Kutscher (1982), *A History of the Hebrew Language*, Jerusalem: The Magus Press, Hebrew University.

Moses Maimonides, Shlomo Pines (trans.) (1963), *The Guide of the Perplexed*, Volumes 1, 2 and 3, Chicago: University of Chicago Press.

Daniel C. Matt (1996), *God and the Big Bang: Discovering the Harmony between Science and Spirituality*, Woodstock, VT: Jewish Lights Publishing.

George W. E. Nickelsburg (2003), *Ancient Judaism and Christian Origins: Diversity, Continuity and Transformations*, Minneapolis: Fortress Press.

Simo Parpola (1993), 'The Assyrian Tree of Life: Tracing the Origins of Jewish Mysticism and Greek Philosophy', in *Journal of Near Eastern Studies*, Vol. 52, 3 (July 1993), pp. 161–208.

Rafael Patai (1990), *The Hebrew Goddess*, Detroit, MI: Wayne State University Press.

Jane Prentence and Nigel Pennick (1995), *A History of Pagan Europe*, London: Routledge.

Howard Schwartz (1988), *Lilith's Cave*, illustrated by Uri Shulevitz, New York: Harper & Row.

Gershom Scholem (1973), *Sabbatai Sevi: The Mystical Messiah, 1626–1676*, Gershom Scholem and R. J. Zwi Werblowsky (trans.), Princeton, NJ: Princeton University Press.

Gershom Scholem (1987), *The Origins of the Kabbalah*, Philadelphia: Jewish Publication Society.

Gershom Scholem (1991), *On the Mystical Shape of the Godhead*, New York: Schocken Books.

Gershom Scholem (1996), *On the Kabbalah and Its Symbolism,* New York: Schocken Books.

Tanakh (2003), Hebrew and English, Philadelphia: Jewish Publication Society.

Joshua Trachtenberg (1961), *Jewish Magic and Superstition: A Study in Folk Religion*, Philadelphia: Jewish Publication Society.

Herbert Weiner (1992), *9½ Mystics: The Kabbala Today*, New York: Collier Books.

Raymond L. Weiss and Charles Butterworth (eds) (1975), *The Ethical Writings of Maimonides*, New York: New York University Press.

7 Akbar: One Man's Syncretism

S. R. Bakshi and S. K. Sharma (1999), *The Great Moguls: Akbar*, Vol. 3, New Delhi, India: Deep and Deep Publications.

Valerie Berinstain (1997), *India and the Mughal Dynasty*, New York: Discoveries Harry N. Abrams Publishers.

Irfan Habib (ed.) (1997), *Akbar and His India*, Delhi, India: Oxford University Press.

Albert Hourani (1991), *The History of Arab Peoples,* Cambridge, MA: The Belknap Press of Harvard University Press.

R. Krishnamurti (1961), *Akbar: The Religious Aspect*, Baroda, India: Baroda Press.

W. H. McNeil (1963), *The Rise of the West: A History of the Human Community,* New York: New American Library.

Malise Ruthven (2004), *Fundamentalism: A Search for Meaning*, Oxford: Oxford University Press.

8 Living with Religious Complexity: Syncretism in its Golden Age

Karen Armstrong (2000), *The Battle for God*, New York: Alfred A. Knopf.

Polymnia Athanassiadi and Michael Frede (eds) (1999), *Pagan Monotheism in Late Antiquity*, Oxford: Clarendon Press.

Marcus Aurelius (1964), *The Meditations*, Maxwell Staniforth (trans.), London: Penguin.

Patricia U. Bonomi (2003), *Under the Cope of Heaven: Religion, Society and Politics in Colonial America*, Oxford: Oxford University Press.

Eusebius (1981), *The History of the Church*, G. A. Williamson (trans.), New York: Penguin.

Richard Fletcher (1997), *The Barbarian Conversion,* New York: Henry Holt.

Migene Gonzalez-Wippler (1989), *Santeria: The Religion: A Legacy of Faith, Rites and Magic*, New York: Harmony Books.

Frederick C. Grant (ed.) (1953), *Hellenistic Religions: The Age of Syncretism,* New York: The Liberal Arts Press.

W. H. McNeil (1963), *The Rise of the West: A History of the Human Community,* New York: New American Library.

Flavius Philostratus (1912), *The Life of Apollonius of Tyana*, F. C. Conybeare (trans.), Cambridge, MA: Harvard University Press.

B. P. Reardon (ed.) (1989), *Collected Ancient Greek Novels*, Berkeley, CA: University of California Press.

Kurt Rudolph (1987), *Gnosis: The Nature and History of Gnosticism*, San Francisco: Harper.

Malise Ruthven (2004), *Fundamentalism*, Oxford: Oxford University Press.

Charles Steward and Rosalind Shaw (eds) (1994), *Syncretism/Anti-Syncretism: The Politics of Religious Synthesis,* London and New York: Routledge.

James Tatum (ed.) (1994), *The Search for the Ancient Novel*, Baltimore, MD: Johns Hopkins University Press.

George H. Tavard (1996), *The Thousand Faces of the Virgin Mary*, Collegeville, MN: Liturgical Press.

Robert L. Wilken (1984), *The Christians as the Romans Saw Them*, New Haven, CT: Yale University Press.

Index of Names and Subjects